exploring

InDesign CS

exploring

InDesign CS

Terry Rydberg

THOMSON

DELMAR LEARNING

Australia Canada Mexico Singapore Spain United Kingdom United

THOMSON

DELMAR LEARNING

Exploring InDesign CS
Terry Rydberg

Vice President, Technology and Trades SBU:
Alar Elken

Editorial Director:
Sandy Clark

Senior Acquisitions Editor:
James Gish

Development Editor:
Jaimie Wetzel

Marketing Director:
Dave Garza

Channel Manager:
Bill Lawrensen

Marketing Coordinator:
Mark Pierro

Production Director:
Mary Ellen Black

Production Manager:
Larry Main

Production Editor:
Dawn Jacobson

Art and Design:
Thomas Stover

Technology Project Manager:
Kevin Smith

Technology Project Specialist:
Linda Verde

Editorial Assistant:
Marissa Maiella

Cover Design:
Steven Brower

Cover Image:
Closed On Sunday, Oil on Canvas,
© David Arsenault

Library of Congress Cataloging-in-Publication Data:
Card Number:

ISBN: 1401873901

NOTICE TO THE READER

Publisher does not warrant or guarantee any of the products described herein or perform any independent analysis in connection with any of the product information contained herein. Publisher does not assume, and expressly disclaims, any obligation to obtain and include information other than that provided to it by the manufacturer.

The reader is expressly warned to consider and adopt all safety precautions that might be indicated by the activities herein and to avoid all potential hazards. By following the instructions contained herein, the reader willingly assumes all risks in connection with such instructions.

The publisher makes no representation or warranties of any kind, including but not limited to, the warranties of fitness for particular purpose or merchantability, nor are any such representations implied with respect to the material set forth herein, and the publisher takes no responsibility with respect to such material. The publisher shall not be liable for any special, consequential, or exemplary damages resulting, in whole or in part, from the readers' use of, or reliance upon, this material.

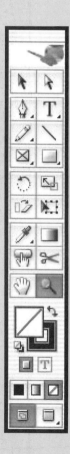

| contents |

contents

CONTENTS

8 Type Continuity: Applying Styles 196

9 Page Continuity: Master Pages 220

ADVENTURES IN DESIGN: HIGH-IMPACT DESIGN ON A LOW BUDGET 236

10 Business Forms 240

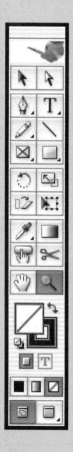

| preface |

preface

INTENDED AUDIENCE

You are about to launch into the new horizons of Adobe InDesign CS. You are part of a new generation of typesetters and designers, working with a new standard in digital page production. InDesign is the rising star in page layout programs, and whether you are an educator, a graphics student, or a professional, these pages will be a clear and concise guide to the world of electronic page production.

Unlike books that focus exclusively on software, *Exploring InDesign CS* integrates typographic principles with software proficiency. Just as plunking out a few keys on a Steinway piano doesn't make you a concert pianist, simply using great software doesn't make you a skilled typesetter. To excel, you must understand the characteristics of type and know how those characteristics become a major design element in your document. Many designers use powerful page layout software, but their typesetting looks crude and unprofessional. This book will not just teach you how to use software; it will introduce you to the principles of typesetting necessary to create successful and appealing pages.

Adobe InDesign CS is the most powerful tool for manipulating text and graphics on the market today. In 15 years as a graphic designer and educator, I have never seen a new program emerge as rapidly and decisively as the one you are about to explore. First introduced in 2000, InDesign is now setting the pace for worldwide leadership in digital page layout and taking over graphics production departments.

BACKGROUND OF THIS TEXT

I have worked with hundreds of students in classroom and industry settings and have made the following observations regarding software textbooks:

- Books that teach software without teaching typography create technicians, not typesetters. Typesetting is an art, and typography is emphasized throughout *Exploring InDesign CS*. The power of Adobe InDesign CS, when combined with the knowledge of typography, will give you the ability to create documents with impact.

- A textbook with a step-by-step approach must also provide opportunities for independent problem solving and application. *Exploring InDesign CS* does contain exercises, with step-by-step instructions, the first time a feature or technique is introduced. Then it provides you the opportunity to apply what you have just learned by offering an array of projects at the end of the chapter. These projects include directions to give you just enough guidance to accomplish the project, but without the step-by-step instruction found in the textbook exercises.

- Skills must be learned in sequence and applied in context. *Exploring InDesign CS* should be completed from the beginning to the end. Each skill creates a foundation that forms the base for the exercises and projects presented in the next lesson. Techniques are introduced and then applied in the context of an industry-level project. This project-based approach uses previously introduced skills over and over again—which increases mastery.

Exploring InDesign CS is designed to be used in either a classroom or personal setting. It was written for those who have keyboarding skills and already know computer basics—launching programs, using a mouse, saving, and printing.

TEXTBOOK ORGANIZATION

The textbook is organized sequentially and skills are added layer upon layer.

Chapter 1: The InDesign Workspace

Introduces the basic tools and functions of the program. If you are already familiar with Photoshop and Illustrator this chapter will be a great review.

Chapter 2: Type, Tools and Terms

Creates a knowledge base essential for setting type. You will create text frames, use the Character and Paragraph formatting modes in the Control palette, modify attributes of type and text frames, and distinguish between serif and sans serif typefaces.

Chapter 3: The Fine Art of Setting Type

Teaches how to identify the anatomical parts of letters, read mark-up, format paragraphs, and use hyphens and dashes correctly.

Chapter 4: Combining Type and Images

Shows you how to create linked and multi-column text frames, place, scale and crop images, use optical and manual kerning, and apply the coordinates and measurement system for precise sizing and placement.

Chapter 5: Tabs and Tables

Discusses the difference between left, right, center, decimal, and aligning tabs. Then you will learn to set tab leaders and create tables from "scratch" and from text.

Chapter 6: Grids, Guides and Aligning Objects

Will increase your productivity by introducing the following essential production techniques: creating publication grids, aligning and distributing objects, managing object layers, and copying and pasting.

Chapter 7: Managing Elements: Text Wrap and Layers

Will bring order to your documents through the power of layers and text wrap. Design effects including feathering and transparency will be introduced.

Chapter 8: Type Continuity: Applying Styles

Focuses on speed and efficiency in preparing text-heavy documents. You will learn how to use the Pages palette and a document library, and create character and paragraph styles.

Chapter 9: Page Continuity: Master Pages

Covers page continuity through the use of master pages. You will learn how to setup automatic page numbering and create continuation and jump lines. You'll also use the Pages palette to add and delete pages.

Chapter 10: Business Forms

Shows you how to create a corporate identity for a new business. You will focus on design, typographic, and production considerations as you put together business forms and collateral material.

Chapter 11: Designing With Type

Introduces special type techniques including text on a path, creating outlines and gradient blends, using the Pathfinder tool, and creating inline graphics.

Chapter 12: Production Essentials

Discusses how to define and create color as well as preflighting and packaging your document upon completion.

Chapter 13: Basic Graphic Elements

Explores InDesign's drawing functions. You will learn how to create basic shapes, use the Pen tool, and integrate drawn elements with text. Adobe Illustrator users will find this chapter a great review.

FEATURES

The following list describes some of the salient features of the text:

- Learning goals are clearly stated at the beginning of each chapter.

- The book has been written to meet the needs of design students and professionals for a visually oriented introduction to basic design principles and the functions and tools of InDesign CS.

- Exercises and projects utilize tools and techniques that a designer might encounter on the job to complete "real life" projects.

- In Review sections are provided at the end of each chapter to quiz a reader's understanding and retention of the material covered.

- Exploring on Your Own sections offer suggestions and sample projects for further study of the content covered in each chapter.

- Full-color section provides stunning examples of projects included in the textbook.

- The accompanying CD-ROM contains directions and necessary components for completing additional projects that correspond to each chapter's learning goals.

HOW TO USE THIS TEXT

The following features can be found throughout the book.

✦ Charting Your Course and Goals

An introduction and chapter objectives start off each chapter. They describe the competencies that the reader should achieve upon understanding the chapter material.

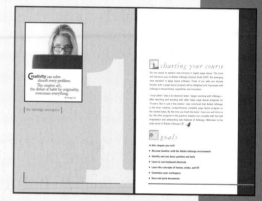

✦ Don't Go There

These boxes appear throughout the text, highlighting common pitfalls and explaining ways to avoid them.

DON'T GO THERE

Tabs, indents, and insets can be confusing. Sometimes when the first column of text is left aligned you may want to use a left indent instead of a tab. That method works perfectly. However, don't use a left inset instead of a left indent because the inset will affect all the text in the frame—which may not be what you want at all!

✦ Try This

Boxed sections entitled *Try This* present tasks for the reader to experiment with. Following along with these will give the reader hands-on experience with InDesign CS.

TRY THIS

Tabs are pretty simple once you understand them. Creating the three tables in Figure 5–14 will solidify your tab skills. Mark up each project first, and create each project in its own text frame.

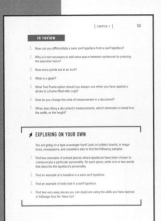

In Review and Exploring on Your Own

Review Questions are located at the end of each chapter and allow readers to assess their understanding of the chapter. The section Exploring on Your Own contains exercises that reinforce chapter material through practical application.

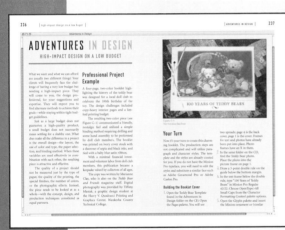

Adventures in Design

These spreads contain examples that show readers how to approach a design project using the tools and design concepts taught in the book.

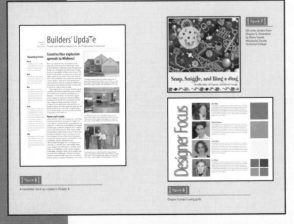

Color Insert

The color insert showcases the work that other designers have created using Adobe InDesign CS. Many of the images show the completed exercises and projects contained in the book and accompanying CD ROM.

THE LEARNING PACKAGE

E.Resource

This electronic manual was developed to assist instructors in planning and implementing their instructional programs. It includes a detailed lesson plan for each chapter. This lesson plan summarizes the concepts, keyboard shortcuts, and projects covered in classroom demonstrations. Lesson plans are designed to be printed and saved in a three-ring binder. The complete instructor's guide enhances institutional consistency in instruction among faculty members with diverse backgrounds and skill levels.

ISBN: 1-4018-7391-X

ABOUT THE AUTHOR

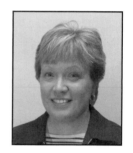

Terry Rydberg is an instructor at the Harry V. Quadracci Printing and Graphics Center at Waukesha County Technical College, and has extensive experience working in the graphics industry as a page layout professional and a corporate trainer.

Her educational background includes AAS degrees in graphic design and printing and publishing; a BS in Vocational, Technical, and Adult Education; and an MA in Education. Her career parallels the industry's evolution from phototypesetting and paste-up to digital production methods. Rydberg teaches advertising design, graphic design, typography, portfolio development, digital page layout, advanced digital page layout, and color theory. She is an annual presenter at the Ladd Marek Teachers' Institute, a professional development conference for high school graphics instructors. She developed *Graphic Design for Educators*, a masters-level course designed to assist instructors with portfolio development and the visual component of curriculum design.

A committed educator, Rydberg has served as school board chair, graphics advisory board member, new instructor mentor, curriculum writer, and student advisor. In 2003 she received the *Distinguished Alumni Award* from Western Wisconsin Technical College in La Crosse.

ACKNOWLEDGMENTS

It has been an honor to be a Delmar Learning author. I would like to acknowledge James Gish, acquisitions editor; Jaimie Wetzel, developmental editor; Dawn Jacobson, production editor; Tom Stover, art and design; and Marissa Maiella, editorial assistant. Their expertise, combined with Delmar's great marketing team, made this project a reality.

A huge debt of gratitude goes to my husband Mark, who shares my passion for type. His eye for detail combined with wonderful editing skills were a lifesaver. Thank you, my friend.

I owe much to my college instructors who modeled great teaching: Bob Andraschko, Jerrilyn Brewer, Rich Westpfahl, and Phil Brochhausen. My associate dean, Dean Flowers, encouraged me to write this book, and the talented students at the Harry V. Quadracci Printing and Graphics Center generously provided artwork.

And most of all, thanks to my children and to my parents, Paul and Shirley Tollefson, and my father-in-law, Mel Rydberg, whose love and encouragement are a continual source of strength and inspiration.

Delmar Learning and the author would also like to thank the following reviewers for their valuable suggestions and technical expertise:

ALAN LAYNE
Chair, Communication
    Graphics Department
Modesto Junior College
Modesto, California

SAM GRANT
School of Entertainment
    and Design
Miami-Dade College
Miami, Florida

PHILIP BROCHHAUSEN
Chair, Graphic Design/Visual
    Communications
Western Wisconsin Technical
    College
La Crosse, Wisconsin

CLAUDIA MCCUE
Owner, Practicalia, LLC:
    Training Company
Lawrenceville, Georgia

JOHN SHANLEY
Owner, Phoenix Creative
    Graphics
Hillsborough, New Jersey

This textboox was produced in InDesign CS by Phoenix Creative Graphics, Hillsborough, NJ.

QUESTIONS AND FEEDBACK

Delmar Learning and the author welcome your questions and feedback. If you have suggestions that you think others would benefit from, please let us know and we will try to include them in the next edition.

To send us your questions and/or feedback, you can contact the publisher at:

Delmar Learning
Executive Woods
5 Maxwell Drive
Clifton Park, NY 12065
Attn: Graphic Arts Team
800-998-7498

Or the author at:

Harry V. Quadracci Printing and Graphics Center
Waukesha County Technical College
800 Main Street
Pewaukee, Wisconsin 53072
trydberg@wctc.edu

Creativity can solve
almost every problem.
The creative act,
the defeat of habit by originality,
overcomes everything.

ᴓ George Lois

the InDesign workspace

1

charting your course

You are about to explore new horizons in digital page layout. This book will introduce you to Adobe InDesign Creative Suite (CS)©, the emerging new standard in page layout software. Those of you who are already familiar with a page layout program will be delighted and impressed with InDesign's extraordinary capabilities and innovation.

I must admit I was a bit skeptical when I began working with InDesign—after teaching and working with other major page layout programs for 15 years. But in just a few weeks I was convinced that Adobe InDesign is the most creative, comprehensive, complete page layout program on the market today. By the time you finish this book I hope you will think so too. No other program in the graphics industry can compete with the bold imagination and astounding new features of InDesign. Welcome to the wide world of Adobe InDesign CS!

 goals

In this chapter you will:

- **Become familiar with the Adobe InDesign environment**
- **Identify and use basic palettes and tools**
- **Learn to use keyboard shortcuts**
- **Learn the concepts of frames, stroke, and fill**
- **Customize your workspace**
- **Save and print documents**

GETTING STARTED

Before you begin this book you should be familiar with a computer keyboard and have a basic understanding of how to operate a mouse. You should know how to launch applications, make choices from menus, click with a mouse to select objects, and drag to highlight text. If you are already familiar with Adobe Photoshop or Adobe Illustrator, this chapter will be a quick review.

figure | 1–1 |

Look for this icon to launch Adobe InDesign CS©.

Launch InDesign by double-clicking on the icon shown in Figure 1–1 on the Desktop (Mac) or selecting Adobe InDesign CS from the Start menu (Windows).

Figure 1–2 shows you the Adobe InDesign CS interface. The InDesign document sits in the middle of a work area called the pasteboard.

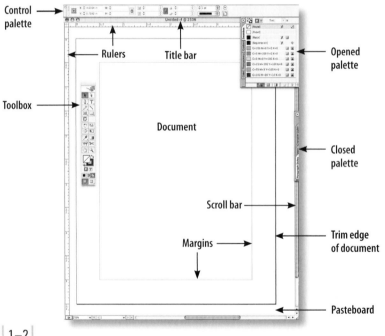

figure | 1–2 |

The InDesign CS workspace.

Palettes, Palettes, and More Palettes

InDesign uses a palette system for managing text, graphics, frames—any element you have in your document. When you first launch InDesign you see the menu bar at the very top of your screen with the Control palette directly below the menu bar, a Toolbox and lots of vertical tabs at the right. These tabs display the names of InDesign's many palettes, and one or two of these palettes may be open on your desktop. Let's get familiar with these features one at a time.

Your One-Two Palette Punch

Among the several dozen palettes in the InDesign arsenal, there are two that you will want to have open all the time as you work—the Control palette and the Toolbox.

figure | 1–3 |

The Control palette.

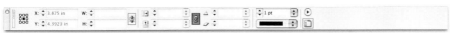

The Control palette looks like this when the document is empty or nothing is selected.

The Control palette looks like this when it is in Character formatting mode.

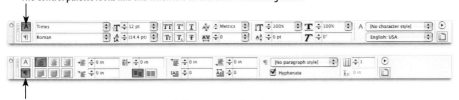

Here's the Control palette with Paragraph formatting mode active.

The Control palette offers quick and convenient ways to do much of what you need to do in your documents. The fields and options in the Control palette are like a chameleon, changing from Character formatting mode to Paragraph formatting mode or to any number of other modes depending on what you are doing. At times the Control palette will duplicate the options and settings of other InDesign palettes that are displayed on your screen. If the Control palette does not appear on your desktop, press Option+Command+6 (Mac) or Alt+Control+6 (Windows) to toggle the Control palette on and off.

You will also want to keep the Toolbox open all the time. You can access the Toolbox by choosing Window>Tools. If you have worked with other Adobe software programs, the Toolbox will look familiar.

The upper left tool (black arrow) is the Selection tool. Use it when you want to select, resize, or move an entire item (frame, line, text path, etc). The upper right tool (white arrow) is the Direct Selection tool. Use it when you want to select just part of an item, the points

figure | 1–4 |

The Toolbox—your
production arsenal.

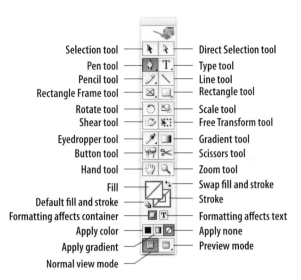

Selection tool — Direct Selection tool
Pen tool — Type tool
Pencil tool — Line tool
Rectangle Frame tool — Rectangle tool
Rotate tool — Scale tool
Shear tool — Free Transform tool
Eyedropper tool — Gradient tool
Button tool — Scissors tool
Hand tool — Zoom tool
Fill — Swap fill and stroke
Default fill and stroke — Stroke
Formatting affects container — Formatting affects text
Apply color — Apply none
Apply gradient — Preview mode
Normal view mode

on an item's path, the content inside the item, or to modify its shape. (If you are familiar with QuarkXPress, the Selection tool is similar to the Item tool and the Direct Selection tool is similar to the Content tool.)

Directly below the Direct Selection tool is the Type tool (capital T). You will probably spend a lot of your time using the Type tool—typing, editing, or working with tables. Because you'll be using it so much, you'll learn to use keys on your keyboard to switch from the Type tool to other tools, without going over to the Toolbox. This will make you very efficient.

figure | 1–5 |

A small arrow in the
lower right corner
of a tool indicates
that more tools are
hidden underneath.

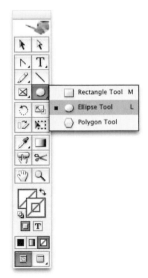

Rectangle Tool   M
Ellipse Tool   L
Polygon Tool

Two rows below the Type tool is the Rectangle tool. Notice the little arrow in the lower right corner. This means that other tools are "hidden" underneath the tool that is showing. Click and hold down the tool button to reveal a menu showing the hidden tools: the Ellipse and Polygon tools. Look for the little arrow in the lower right corner of other InDesign tools; there are more tools to be discovered below the surface. We will use several of these basic tools as we begin working with text frames in a few moments.

Palettes for Every Occasion

You can access all of InDesign's other palettes from the Window menu. Some may be visible at the right edge of your screen—neatly tucked away in vertical alignment. Click on the name of one of these palettes. It will pop out, perhaps grouped with other palettes. Click on the palette name again and it will snap back to the edge of the screen.

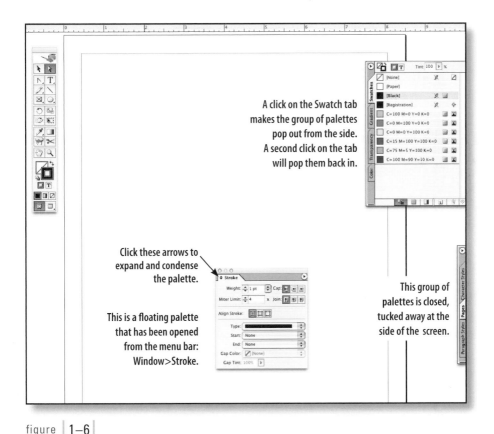

A click on the Swatch tab makes the group of palettes pop out from the side. A second click on the tab will pop them back in.

Click these arrows to expand and condense the palette.

This is a floating palette that has been opened from the menu bar: Window>Stroke.

This group of palettes is closed, tucked away at the side of the screen.

figure | 1–6 |

Palettes can be nested together in groups. The Stroke palette is shown as a floating palette.

Click on another palette to pop it out from the edge. Click on the name of the palette and drag it away from the edge of the screen. When you release the mouse button you will have a "standalone" or floating palette. The name of the palette is now horizontal. On most floating palettes you will see two small up and down arrows next to the palette name. Click on the arrows several times to expand or condense the amount of information you can see in the palette. Put the palette back by clicking on the name again and dragging it back onto the palette bar at the edge of your screen.

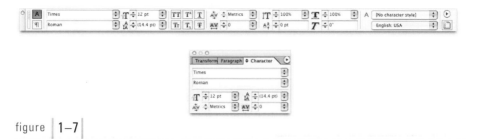

figure 1–7

The lower palette was accessed from Window>Type & Tables>Character. All the functions in this palette are duplicated in the Control palette, shown above.

InDesign allows you to customize the combination of palettes to fit your preferences and the jobs you do. You can work in a palette while it is still grouped with other palettes in vertical formation, or you can drag it out on the desktop area so the palette name is horizontal, whichever is more convenient for you. If you want, you can even attach the palettes to the left edge of your screen.

Using Your Tools

Let's make a document to get familiar with basic InDesign tools.

1. Choose File>New>Document and the New Document dialog box will appear on your screen. Press the Tab key to jump to each field in the New Document dialog box (or any dialog box in InDesign). When the field is highlighted, simply type your new information over the old information in the field. It is not necessary to re-select a field that is already highlighted!

figure 1–8

The New Document dialog box.

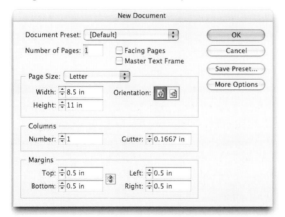

2. Enter these values:
   Number of Pages: 1
   Page Size: letter (8.5 × 11)
   Orientation:
      Portrait (first icon)
   Columns: 1
   Margins: 0.5 (for all four).

Be sure that the Facing Pages and Master Text Frame options are not selected. Click OK. You will see your document outlined in black, on the pasteboard of the window, with colored guides designating the one-half inch margin on all sides.

Portrait orientation means that the height of your document is greater than the width. Landscape orientation means that your document is wider than it is high.

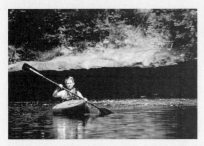

Landscape
Orientation

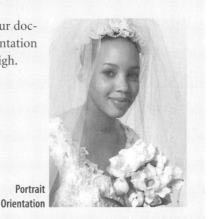

Portrait
Orientation

3. In the Toolbox, click on the Rectangle tool. Your cursor will turn into little crosshairs with a dot in the middle. Go back to your document, click your mouse button somewhere on the left side of your document, and make a rectangle by dragging your mouse down and to the right. Release the mouse.

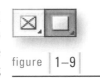

figure | 1–9

The Rectangle tool.

4. Let's take a look at the rectangle you have just drawn. The eight small hollow boxes at the corners and at each side of the rectangle are called selection handles. When the selection handles are visible the item is considered "active." Click somewhere else on your document. The selection handles disappear, meaning the item is not active. An item must be selected in order to work with it. In addition to selection handles, shapes have bounding boxes. Bounding boxes indicate the outermost points of a shape. The bounding box for the rectangle you have just drawn is the same dimension as the rectangle. Look at the odd-looking shape in Figure 1–10. The rectangle that delineates its outer edges is the bounding box. A bounding box always has four straight sides, no matter what shape you have drawn. If the circle, shown in the Figure 1–10, was activated with the Selection tool, the bounding box would be displayed as a square.

figure | 1–10 |

Two of these three shapes are active. The circle is not active.

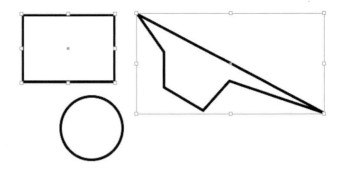

5. Go back to the Toolbox and click on the Selection tool. Your cursor should now look like a black arrow. Click on your document outside the rectangle. You have just deselected the rectangle. Notice how the bounding box has disappeared. Slowly move the Selection tool toward the edge of the rectangle (do not click the mouse button). When the arrow touches the edge, a small square appears next to the tail of the arrow. This means you can now select the rectangle again. Click when the small box appears by the tail of the arrow and you will see your frame handles again. Your rectangle is now selected. (Notice that when your rectangle is selected and you move your cursor over the edge of the rectangle [without clicking the button], the arrow icon loses its "tail.")

figure | 1–11 |

Recognize these selection icons:
A. the Selection tool is over the document.
B. the Selection tool is ready to select an object.
C. the Selection tool is ready to move the item.

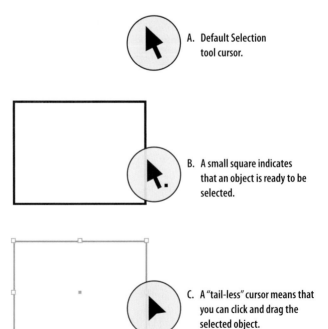

A. Default Selection tool cursor.

B. A small square indicates that an object is ready to be selected.

C. A "tail-less" cursor means that you can click and drag the selected object.

6. With your rectangle selected, you can move it to a different place or change its size. To move it, click on the edge of the rectangle and drag it. Release the mouse button to "drop" the rectangle in the new location.

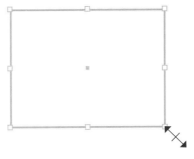

figure | 1–12 |

When the Selection arrow is over a frame handle it changes shape. The double-ended arrow means that you can drag the handle to change the dimensions of the object.

To resize the rectangle, move the cursor over one of the frame handles. The icon turns into small opposing arrows, with a line in between. Drag the frame handle to change the shape of the rectangle. You can drag the frame handles in, out, or diagonally to change the size and shape.

Keyboard Shortcuts

When you made your new document, you may have noticed that on the right side of the menu, across from the word Document, there is a Command (Mac) or Control symbol (Windows), followed by the letter N. This is called a keyboard shortcut. If you hold down the Command key (Mac) or the Control key (Windows) on the keyboard and then press the letter N, the New Document dialog box will appear on your screen. By using the keyboard shortcut, you did not need to use the menu choices to make a new document.

figure | 1–13 |

The symbols on the right side of a menu show keyboard shortcuts you can use.

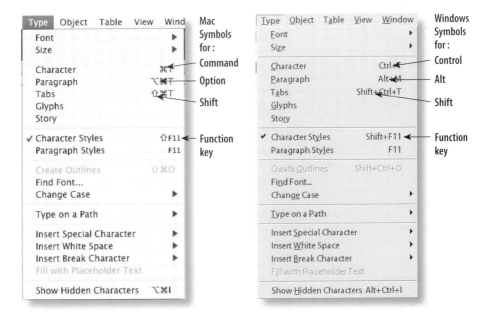

You may have also noticed that when you move your cursor over a tool on the Toolbox and pause for a moment before you click on the tool, a label appears with the name of the tool and a letter in parentheses. This letter is the keyboard shortcut to select the tool.

Keyboard shortcuts are indispensable for the designer who wants to be fast, efficient, and the first candidate in line for a raise. Keyboard shortcuts will save you oodles of time because you don't have to move your mouse all the way up to the menu bar or over to a palette to do your editing. Using keyboard shortcuts is your key to productivity—use them whenever you can!

figure | 1–14 |

Tooltips show the name and shortcut key for each tool in the Toolbox.

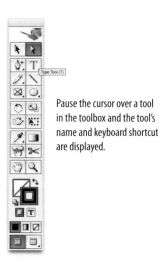

Pause the cursor over a tool in the toolbox and the tool's name and keyboard shortcut are displayed.

In the following exercise you will use shortcuts to make a new document and create a rectangle.

1. Close, but don't save, the document you just made by pressing Command+W (Mac) or Control+W (Windows). Make a new document by using keyboard shortcuts: Command+N (Mac) or Control+N (Windows). You get the same New Document dialog box as you did when you made your first document using the menu bar. Make the same size document: 8.5 × 11 with 0.5 margins.

2. Next, you will draw a rectangle, but instead of going over to the Toolbox, press the letter M. This will instantly select the Rectangle tool. Draw a rectangle and then press the letter A. You have now selected the Direct Selection tool. The Direct Selection tool differs from the Selection tool because you can modify just part of an object—one side or one or more anchor points—instead of the whole item.

3. Play with your rectangle using the Direct Selection tool by selecting and dragging the sides and anchor points. Your rectangle will quickly lose its rigid 90-degree angles.

4. With your shape selected bring the Direct Selection arrow slowly to the tiny box in the center of the object. Notice that the white arrow becomes a black arrow. Click and move the object around.

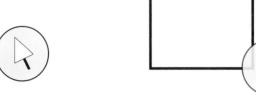

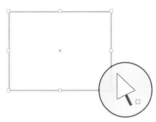

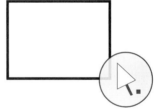

A. Default Direct Selection tool cursor.

B. The Direct Selection tool is ready to select the side of the frame.

C. The Direct Selection tool is ready to select an anchor point on a frame.

D. The Direct Selection tool is ready to move the whole object.

figure | 1–15

The Direct Selection tool uses many of the same visual cues as the Selection tool, shown earlier. Notice that the solid tiny square means that the whole frame can be moved.

NOTE: To avoid unpleasant surprises, always deselect an object when you are finished working on it. You can deselect an object by clicking off it, or by using the keyboard shortcut: Shift+Command+A (Mac) or Shift+Control+A (Windows).

Getting Text into Your Frame

You will appreciate good typing and keyboard skills as you begin to spend more time working with text. In the next exercise you will learn how to enter text and draw some basic shapes.

1. Close your document without saving it and make another (remember to use your keyboard shortcut). This time, make your document 7 inches wide and 6 inches high (leave the 0.50 margins). Press the Tab key to highlight the Height field, enter

6 and click OK or press Return. (Whenever an InDesign button is pulsating in OSX, you can press the Return key instead of moving your mouse and clicking OK. In Windows, you press the Enter key when the OK button has the "focus".)

2. Notice that your document is wider than it is high. This is Landscape format. Press M to get the Rectangle tool and draw a rectangle. Now press T. Your cursor changes into a vertical bar with a small crosshair near the bottom and dotted lines around it. Click inside the rectangle. Your cursor now becomes a blinking cursor in the upper left corner of the rectangle, your rectangle has become a text frame, and you are ready to type in it.

figure | 1–16 |

The Type tool cursor changes depending on how it is used.

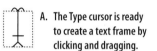

A. The Type cursor is ready to create a text frame by clicking and dragging.

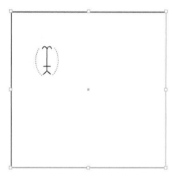

B. The Type cursor positioned over a selected frame.

Enis nulla corero consed duis at eros- to odo dolorperosto et aute dip enibh er aliquisi er adigna ali- quat, volestrud etumsan dignit ipis duisci exero odolor sumsandre feu facinis elesto odoloreet er sis accummy nis alissi bla consequ

C. The Type cursor positioned over a frame already containing text.

NOTE: You can also create a text frame by dragging with the Text tool cursor. When the cursor is blinking inside the frame, you are ready to type.

3. Type a sentence or two about yourself, your dog, your week-end—anything you want.

4. Highlight all your text with Command+A (Mac) or Control+A (Windows). There are other methods of selecting your text. For instance, you can drag and highlight text with your mouse, or choose Select All from the Edit menu, but those methods are slower. Keyboard shortcuts are always the way to go!

5. Increase the size of your text with Shift+Option+Command+> (Mac) or Shift+Alt+Control+> (Windows) Use the shortcut 6

or 7 times and watch the size of your type get larger. Again, you could do this in the Control palette, but to beat the drum one more time—keyboard shortcuts are tricks of the trade for a good typesetter!

Stroke and Fill

Near the bottom of the Toolbox are two squares—one overlapping the other (see Figure 1–17). The square on the right is the Stroke box; to the left is the Fill box. Click back and forth on these squares a few times. Whichever icon you click overlaps the other to indicate that it is active. You cannot have both Stroke and Fill modes selected at the same time.

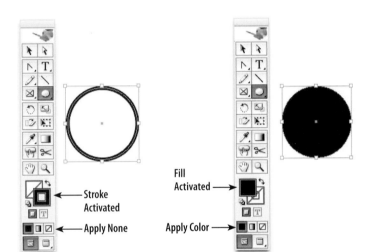

Stroke Activated
Apply None
Fill Activated
Apply Color

figure | 1–17 |

The square on the top is the active one. The shape on the left is stroked—notice which icon is in the active mode. In the right example the shape is filled—again, notice the Fill icon is on the top.

Now let's go back to the document we were working on in the last series of steps and see what we can do with stroke and fill:

1. With the text cursor inside the frame, select all of the type and click the Fill box. There is a "T" in the box indicating that the Fill will be applied to your type. Near the bottom of the Toolbox is a row of three icons. Click on the small square with the red diagonal line. A diagonal red line replaces the "T" in the Fill box and it looks like your text has disappeared! It hasn't. All you have done is removed the "fill" of your text by using the Apply None button. Now, select all the invisible text again using Command+A (Mac) or Control+A (Windows).

2. Select the Stroke icon and click on the small black square on the right side of the row containing the Apply None button.

You have used the Apply Color button to outline your text with a stroke. Make the Stroke box active and click the Apply Color button.

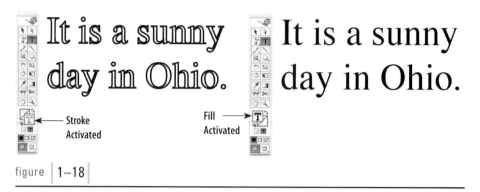

figure | 1–18 |

The text on the left has a stroke; the text on the right has a fill.

TRY THIS

Before moving on, play with the stroke and fill of your text to get used to how these tools work.

3. Click and hold the Rectangle tool until the menu appears, and select the Ellipse tool (the shortcut key is "L"). Draw a perfect circle by holding the Shift key while you drag the Ellipse tool. When you release the mouse button, a stroke is automatically applied because the Stroke mode was active when you drew the object.

NOTE: You can press X to toggle between the Stroke and Fill icons. Pressing Shift+X swaps the Stroke and Fill color.

4. Press M to activate the Rectangle tool. Draw a perfect square by holding down the Shift key as you drag the frame. Again, a stroke is automatically applied.
5. Select the Line tool (the shortcut is "\"). With the Stroke tool still active and Apply Color on, click and drag to draw several diagonal lines on your document. Switch to the Selection tool and select any line, notice the shape of the bounding box. Now, select the Line tool again, hold down the Shift key, and draw perfectly horizontal and vertical lines.

6. Hold down the Shift key and draw one more line, but do not release the mouse button. Instead, move the mouse to rotate the free end of the line in a circle, like hands on a clock. Notice how the line snaps to 45-degree increments. The Shift key constrains lines to horizontal, vertical or 45-degree increments. Close this document without saving it.

NOTE: Holding down the Shift key constrains rectangles to perfect squares, ellipses to perfect circles, and lines to horizontal, vertical, or 45-degree increments.

Two Types of Frames

InDesign includes two tools for making rectangle boxes called "frames." One frame has an X in it, one doesn't. Both frames can hold either pictures or text—there's really no difference between a "picture" frame and a "text" frame. When you click inside any frame with the Type tool, you will get a blinking cursor for typing.

1. Make a new document using the default settings.
2. Use the Rectangle tool to draw a rectangle that covers about half your document.
3. Now choose the Rectangle Frame tool—the box with the X inside it—to the left of the Rectangle tool. Click and drag a second rectangle on the other half of your document; there will be an X inside the new rectangle.

figure | 1–19

On the left is a frame made with the Rectangle Frame tool. The frame on the right was made with the Rectangle tool. Both can hold text or graphics.

So, why are there two frame tools? For convenience. If you were laying out a 16-page newsletter you could use frames made with the Rectangle tool to indicate where the type should be placed and frames made with the Rectangle Frame tool, with the X, to indicate where photos should be placed. This would be particularly helpful if another person was going to work with you on part of your project.

Navigating

Let's do a little navigating around your document with the two frames. Your document sits in the middle of an area called the pasteboard. At the right and bottom of the pasteboard are scroll bars. You slide the scroll bars up and down, or right and left to reposition your document inside the InDesign window. You can also click on the triangles to move your document around. If you are working in Windows, these triangles will be at either end of the scroll bars. If you are working on a Mac, the triangles will be in the lower right corner.

figure │ 1–20│

Scroll bars and arrows help you position your document.

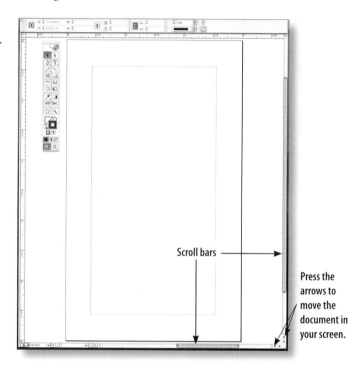

Scroll bars

Press the arrows to move the document in your screen.

figure │ 1–21│

Hold down the spacebar and click to make the Hand tool turn into the grabber hand. If you are using the Type tool, access the grabber hand by pressing the Option (Mac) or Alt (Windows) key.

Borem ing eros dolutpat, quat autem ing exerit aut am, veliquat, consectet nissisim eugiamet in etue dolore delis duis

Borem ing eros dolutpat, quat autem ing exerit aut am, veliquat, consectet nissisim eugiamet in etue dolore delis duis

Another way to move your document around is to use the Hand tool. Whenever the Type tool is not active, you can hold down the spacebar to temporarily switch to the Hand tool. You will see a little fist appear on the screen. Click and drag with your mouse and the fist will grab on to your document and move it wherever you like.

To access the Hand tool while you are using the Type tool in an active frame, you press the Option (Mac) or Alt (Windows) key. (If you press the spacebar to access the grabber hand while using the Text tool, you will simply add spaces to the text you are working on.)

NOTE: If the Type tool is active, but you are not typing in an active frame, you must use Option+Spacebar (Mac) or Alt+Spacebar (Windows) to access the Hand tool.

You can also select the Hand tool in the Toolbox or by using the "H" shortcut key, but using the Spacebar (or Option/Alt) and mouse is probably faster and more convenient.

Changing Your View

In the lower left corner of your document window is the Zoom text field. This field shows the size at which InDesign is displaying your document on the screen. When you are seeing your document at its actual size, the view percentage is 100. Anything larger than 100% is said to be larger than life, and less than 100% is smaller than actual size. You can access the Zoom preset list by clicking on the downward-pointing triangle to the right of the Zoom text field. Notice that you

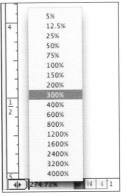

figure | 1–22

The Zoom preset list is in the lower left corner of the screen. If none of the preset percentages suit you, type a new percentage in the Zoom text field.

can view your document from 5% all the way to 4000%! If none of those view percentages are just right, you can type any percentage in the Zoom text field, press Return or Enter, and your document view will immediately change.

> **TRY THIS**
>
> Go ahead and change your view to some obscure percentage using the Zoom field and preset list.

Another way to change your view—and often the fastest way—is to use keyboard shortcuts. To quickly view the document at actual size, press Command+1 (Mac) or Control+1 (Windows). This method is quick and efficient, and after using it a while it becomes automatic. Other keyboard shortcuts for viewing options are shown in Table 1–1. Try each of them and you will see how fast they are.

Table 1–1 Keyboard shortcuts for changing view percentage

Function	Mac	Windows
View at 100%	Cmd+1	Ctrl+1
View at 200%	Cmd+2	Ctrl+2
View at 400%	Cmd+4	Ctrl+4
View at 50%	Cmd+5	Ctrl+5
Fit page in window	Cmd+0 (zero)	Ctrl+0 (zero)

The Zoom tool in the Toolbox is accessed by pressing Z. Select the Zoom tool and click on your document to magnify the view. As you click, hold the Zoom tool directly over the place in your document you want magnified and that place will come to the center of your screen. Hold down the Option (Mac) or Alt (Windows) key and click to reduce the view percentage.

Get in the habit of zooming in and zooming out quickly and frequently. Too many beginning designers work with very small text at 100% view—or less! Give your eyes a break. Zoom into your document so you can comfortably see punctuation marks, where your cursor is, how many characters you have highlighted—all the small details of your document. After you have finished working up close, zoom out using the appropriate keyboard shortcut.

Customizing Your Workspace

Designers have their individual preferences for how things should be arranged and organized on the desktop. This is easy to do in InDesign—even when more than one person works on the same machine.

Dock the Control Palette

You can dock the Control palette at the top or bottom of your screen, or you can have it float—meaning you can drag it around

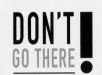

As you learn to work with InDesign you will be surprised at how many hours you will spend sitting in front of a computer. When setting up your workstation, finding a good chair should be top priority. Try out several until you find the one that is correct for you and for your computer table. When working at the computer it is important to maintain good posture, keep a forearm position that is approximately parallel with the keyboard, and place your feet on the floor. Get up and stretch several times every hour.

Most of all, adjust the view in InDesign so that you are not craning your neck, squinting your eyes, or keeping your nose a few inches from the screen to view your work. Years of sitting like a pretzel will ultimately take their toll.

and position it anywhere you want to. Click on the round button with the small arrow, at the extreme right of the Control palette and select your preferred position from the menu. If you choose Dock at Top or Dock at Bottom, the Control palette will immediately jump to that position. When you choose Float, the palette will jump to the center of the screen. Click on the gripper bar at the left side of the palette and drag it where you want it.

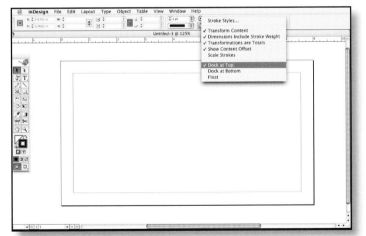

figure | 1–23

The Control palette can be docked at the top or bottom of the screen or float wherever you move it.

Arranging Your Palettes

Arrange the palettes on your desktop where you want them to be—by putting the Toolbox where it is most convenient for you. At this point you may not have a preference for other palette configurations, but pull a couple palettes out onto the desktop just for fun and note their names and placement. Choose Window>Workspace>Save Workspace. In the Save Workspace dialog, type **Workspace 1** and press Return or Enter.

Now rearrange your desktop with a different dock for the Control palette, different palettes, and Tools placement. Choose Window>Workspace>Save Workspace and name it "Workspace 2." Toggle between the two workspaces by selecting their names from the Windows>Workspace menu. See how you can customize your desktop to just about any configuration you want? Very neat. Very organized. Very friendly for your co-workers.

Saving Your Work

There is one—and only one—advantage your old typewriter had over word processing: once you typed a word on your typewriter, it was there to stay. Not so with electronic page layout programs. You need to save your work and save it often.

To save your document, press Command+S (Mac) or Control+S (Windows) or select File>Save. The dialog box will ask you first of all what you want to name your document. The Save As field will be highlighted when the dialog box is displayed, so just begin typing the name you want for the document.

figure | 1–24

The Save As dialog box on a Macintosh.

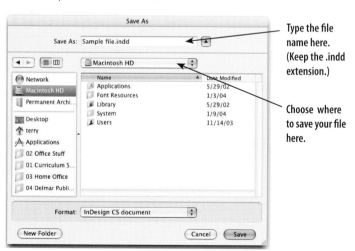

Type the file name here. (Keep the .indd extension.)

Choose where to save your file here.

Next tell your computer where you want it saved: on the desktop? on your hard drive? on a server? in a folder? which folder? Be sure to remember where you save your document because you will have to find it later.

NOTE: If you lose a document but know you saved it somewhere, you can do a Find or Search (if you remember the name of the file) and your computer will locate it for you.

Save and Save As

After you have saved a project the first time, pressing Command+S (Mac) or Control+S (Windows) automatically saves your document with the edits you have made, in the same location and with the same name as your previous Save. Save As also saves your work, but the Save As dialog is displayed to allow you to rename and relocate your document.

For instance, say you have been working on a Valentine's Day ad for South Side Grocery. You complete the ad, save and print the document, and get the customer's approval. The customer loves your layout and decides you should make a version for three other stores in the city. And all the other versions need to be done by 5:00 today!

This is a great time to use Save As. Open the original file, named "South Side Grocery." Immediately use Save As (Shift+Command+S [Mac] or Shift+Control+S [Windows]) and name the new file "North Side Grocery." The South Side Grocery file remains unchanged, and you are now working on a different file—the North Side Grocery ad. When this ad is done you save it, print it, and again use Save As to name the next file "West Side Grocery". The previous file, North Side Grocery, stays just as you left it while you move on to complete the West Side Grocery ad, and so on. You can also use Save As to rename your document such as North Side Grocery-Backup and then save the backup version to a jump drive or a file server.

Save a Copy

Save a Copy (Option+Command+S [Mac] or Alt+Control+S [Windows]) is a little different than Save As. Suppose you want to keep a visual record of each production step in a project. You begin the project and perform the first step. Use Save a Copy and name the file "Step 1." Your original file is still on the screen and you continue on to the next step. When you finish this step, use Save a Copy and name this file "Step 2". You will continue building your document, saving and naming incremental versions. Unlike Save As, the Save a Copy option allows you to continue working on the original file while the copy goes wherever you tell it to go.

Save a Copy to the Rescue

Let's say it's 10:15 and you are busy getting the Zaza Toys layout ready for a client meeting at 10:30. All of a sudden you get a huge brainstorm that will radically change the look of the layout. The client has already approved the layout you are just finishing and since it's due in 15 minutes you don't want to take the chance of messing it up. So you use the Save a Copy option and name the copy "Client_Approved." Client_Approved, completed at 10:15, is now saved somewhere on your desktop, but the original Zaza Toys file is still open. You make all kinds of changes. You go wild.

Your creative director walks by to see if you are ready for the meeting that will begin in just a few minutes. She looks at your screen and gently, but firmly, suggests you change the document back to the way it was about 10 minutes ago. In a few clicks you have Client_Approved opened and printed. You arrive at the client meeting on time and unruffled.

Printing Your Document

When you are ready to print your document, press Command+P (Mac) or Control+P (Windows) or choose File>Print. There are literally dozens of options in the Print dialog box, but for now all you need to do is select the printer you want to use on the General options page of the dialog. Select the Setup options page (in the list on the left side of the dialog box), set Paper Size to Letter, and make sure Orientation is Portrait. If your document is smaller than 8.5 × 11, your finished piece will look better if you set Page Position to Centered.

figure | 1–25 |

The General options in the Print dialog box allow you to select how many copies and which pages of your document to print.

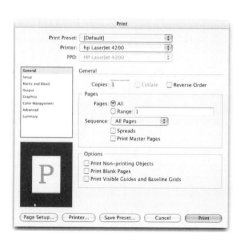

In the lower left corner is a shaded box with a white rectangle and the letter "P." This is a preview of how the printer is set to print your document. The white area is the size of your paper. The "P" is the size of your document and is represented with a slight shade of blue. If you change Paper Size to something other than letter, this preview will give you an idea of how your document will print in relation to the size of the paper it will be printed on.

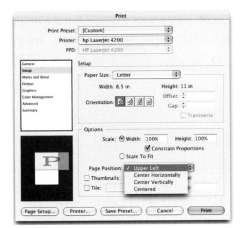

figure | 1–26

The preview in the lower left corner is showing that the document is not positioned properly on the paper because the Page Position field is not set properly. Always check these two fields before printing your document.

SUMMARY

If you are already familiar with Adobe Photoshop or Adobe Illustrator, this chapter was an easy review. If learning Adobe InDesign is your first adventure into the world of digital page layout this chapter covered a lot of new territory. Finding your way around the InDesign workspace was the focus of this chapter. The next chapter will build on these concepts. Like practicing the piano, using InDesign for at least 30 minutes each day will help solidify these basics and help pave the way for a continual increase in your skill level.

in review

1. Which icon is the InDesign icon?

2. What is the difference between the Selection tool and the Direct Selection tool?

3. What are the keyboard shortcuts for accessing a) the Selection tool, and b) the Direct Selection tool?

4. Tiny squares that show the outermost dimensions of a shape are called _____ _____.

5. How are the Rectangle Frame and Rectangle tools different?

6. What are two methods of deselecting an object?

7. What is a stroke? What is a fill?

8. What is the difference between Save and Save a Copy?

9. What is the keyboard shortcut for increasing the size of type?

10. Why should you focus on good posture when working at your computer?

11. What is the keyboard shortcut for New Document?

12. What is the keyboard shortcut for View at 100%?

13. What is the keyboard shortcut for toggling between Stroke and Fill?

14. What is the keyboard shortcut for the Rectangle tool?

15. What is the keyboard shortcut for the Rectangle Frame tool?

↗ EXPLORING ON YOUR OWN

Two quick projects will review most of the skills you learned in this chapter. The CD that accompanies this book contains a folder for each chapter. Inside that folder are various resources, including a student handout that contains directions for each chapter's projects. Open the CD and find the Chapter 01 folder. Inside that folder is a file called 01 Student Handout.pdf that you can refer to when creating the Chapter 1 projects shown below. As you are working, concentrate on using keyboard shortcuts to adjust your view so that you are not straining to see your work.

01A Snowman and Robot

01B Basic Shapes

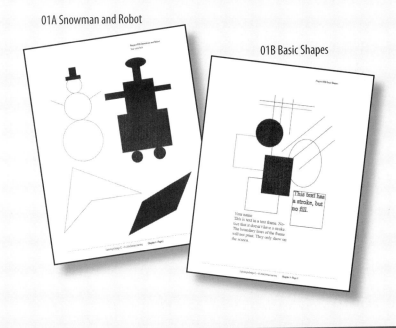

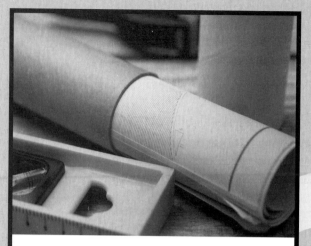

Every **great ability**
        develops and reveals itself
increasingly
        with every new assignment.

℞ Baltasar Gracian

type, tools and terms

charting your course

You are dreaming a designer's worst nightmare. A weary vacationer has just come home and his mailbox is overflowing. He plops the stack of mail onto the kitchen counter and begins the sorting process. "Keep, throw, keep, keep, throw, throw…oh, this one looks interesting, maybe I'll look at it later…" until the whole stack of mail has been separated. He picks up the stack of rejects and moves slowly to a designer's nemesis—the circular file. You helplessly call out in your sleep, "Hey, don't throw that stuff! I spent *days* designing those direct response mailers!" You watch your pieces fall into the dark abyss of the garbage can and you shudder as the lid closes, sealing the fate of all your hard work.

This "nightmare" is actually reality for many designers who do not know how to set type. It doesn't take the average reader more than a glance to decide whether or not to read a printed piece. If a design doesn't pass the "once-over" test, out it goes. That's the bad news. The *good* news is that by picking up this book, you have taken the first step in learning how to use type as a powerful communication tool. And by the time you complete *Exploring InDesign* you will know how to correctly set good type. In Chapter 1 you learned how to find your way around the InDesign workspace. This chapter will introduce you to basic and concepts. Knowing both InDesign *and* typography will give you a competitive edge in the marketplace—and save your printed pieces from the garbage can!

 goals

- **Distinguish between serif and sans serif typefaces**
- **Read and interpret project markup**
- **Differentiate between a text frame and a rectangle frame**
- **Define type family, typeface, font, point size, and leading**
- **Define picas**
- **Use the Character and Paragraph formatting modes of the Control palette**
- **Modify the attributes of text frames**
- **Insert glyphs**

AN EYE-Q TEST...

Figure 2-1 shows some examples of type. Which example in each pair would you most likely read?

A   B

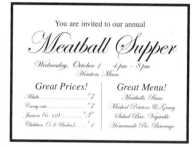

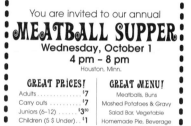

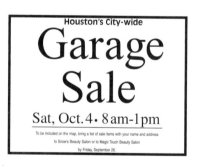

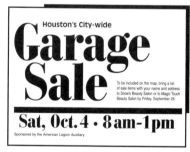

figure | 2–1

Use of type is the main variable in each pair of designs.

If you selected "B" for each pair, you have just proven the power of good typesetting. Typesetting should enhance readability and strengthen the message. The type on a page should attract the reader's attention and create a visual path for the eye to follow. Type use can make or break a layout!

FIRST THINGS FIRST

When a client gives you a rough layout, how exactly do you get started?

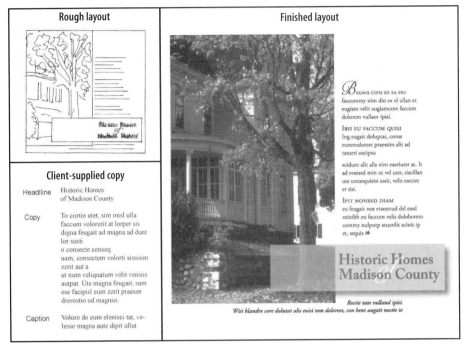

First, you must read the text and understand the purpose of the piece you are going to design. Determine which information is most important. Take responsibility for ensuring the document's accuracy and ultimate success. Never assume that the copy provided to you is totally accurate.

figure | 2–2

The upper left example is a rough layout. Client-provided copy (lower left) indicates headline and text. The finished piece is on the right.

- Proofread phone numbers and zip codes. Go online and test web addresses.

- Ask if product names require a ™ or ® symbol.

- Check that names are spelled correctly throughout the document.

- Consult a calendar to verify days and dates. Check that day, date, and time information is consistent throughout the document.

- Proofread headings and subheads (they are often overlooked in the proofing process).

If the client gives you actual finished samples of the printed pieces to re-create, look for ways the pieces could be improved and discuss those changes with the client. Do not duplicate poor typesetting! Because you are the professional, the client is coming to you for your insight and expertise. Make your client look good, and he will regard you as a valuable resource.

Finally, ask how the job will be printed and finished. Will it be drilled (three-hole punched)? Will it be stitched (spine stapled)? Will it be mailed? Will there be photos and colors? Find out as much information as possible because those specifics will determine how you build the InDesign document.

Select a Great Typeface

Once you understand the purpose and the specifications of the project, you must put some thought into the personality you want the piece to express. The blend of typeface, image, layout, and color will create a distinct personality in each piece you design. Personalities can range from formal and powerful to wacky and whimsical. The typeface selection will play a big part in communicating that personality.

Let's say you just inherited a huge amount of money and can now have the cosmetic surgery you always dreamed of. You look in the yellow pages to choose a cosmetic surgeon. Which surgeon will you choose from the list shown in Figure 2–3?

Choose Your Cosmetic Surgeon

John Davis, M.D.   John Davis, M.D.
JOHN DAVIS, M.D.   John Davis, M.D.
John Davis, M.D.   JOHN DAVIS, M.D.
JOHN DAVIS, M.D.   John Davis, M.D.
John Davis, M.D.   JOHN DAVIS, M.D.

figure | 2–3 |

The selection of appropriate typefaces is one of the most critical steps in any design job.

Selecting Typeface and Point Size

Launch InDesign. Follow these steps in making a sample document.

1. Create a document by pressing Command+N (Mac) or Control+N (Windows). The New Document dialog box will open. Your settings should be:

    Document Preset: [Default]
    Number of Pages: 1
    Facing Pages: Off ("Facing pages" is another way of saying two-page spreads, similar to the left- and right-hand pages of a book. We're not going to use facing pages…yet.)
    Master Text Frame: Off
    Page Size: Letter
    Width: 8.5 in.
    Height: 11 in.
    Orientation: Portrait
    Number of columns: 1 (ignore the Gutter field for now),
    Margins: 0.5 in. (top, bottom, left, right).

2. Press the Return or Enter key. Remember, it's easier and faster to press the Return key rather than to click OK with your mouse.

3. Your document will appear in a window with two rulers—one at the top and the other along the left side of your window. The upper left corner of your document should be at zero on the horizontal ruler, and the upper right corner should be at 8.5. Along the vertical ruler, the upper left corner of your document should be at zero and the lower left corner should be at 11. Your document should look like Figure 2–4. You will also notice a colored line around the inside of your document. This

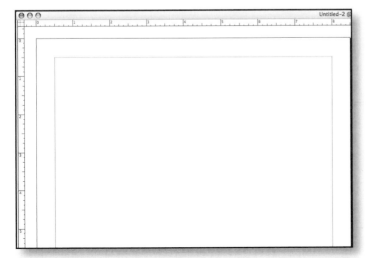

figure | 2–4

The upper half of your newly created document. Note the upper left corner positioned at 0,0.

is the half-inch margin you set in the New Document dialog box. (If InDesign has been set to use a different measurement system such as points and picas, the units of measure on the rulers won't make much sense. We will cover changing the ruler units of measure in the next chapter, so don't worry about them for now.)

Here's how to change the pesky "Facing Pages" default that pops up each time you create a document. With InDesign launched and with no file open, press Command+Option+P (Mac) or Control+Alt+P (Windows). This brings up the Document Setup dialog box. Deselect Facing Pages and if Master Text Frame has a checkmark, deselect that also. Press Return. This procedure modi-

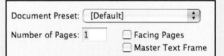

fies your document default preferences so that future documents will reflect those settings. (InDesign has dozens of built-in, or default, settings. Changing these default settings is a way of customizing the software to fit your work and will be introduced throughout the book.) Once you have created this new basic document setup, you can begin a new file by simply pressing Command+Option+N (Mac) or Control+Alt+N (Windows). A new document will be created—without facing pages.

Using Text

Use the keyboard shortcut T to select the Type tool from the Toolbox. Put your cursor inside the upper left margin of your document, and then click and drag a rectangular frame down and across the page. Wherever you stop will be the size of your frame. If your frame is too small or you don't like the shape of it, hold down Command (Mac) or Control (Windows) and press the letter Z. This is one of the best shortcuts to know—Undo. (InDesign allows you unlimited undos. Don't you wish your life had unlimited undos?) Now draw a new frame.

Make sure a blinking cursor is in your frame and type three or four sentences. If you don't see a blinking cursor, check to see that you have the Type tool selected and click inside the box. Type a few paragraphs about the fondest memories you have of elementary school.

One of the first rules you may have learned in junior high typing class was to put two spaces between sentences by pressing the spacebar twice after each period. This is the first habit you will have to break when using InDesign. The practice of using two spaces between sentences began in the days of typewriters. Type on old-fashioned typewriters was monospaced, which means that each character was allotted the same amount of space in the text line whether it was an "i" or an "m." The extra space was inserted to visually separate sentences.

With electronic publishing, most of the fonts used are proportional, which means that each character has been allocated just the right amount of space.

Rule #1: Don't press the spacebar twice at the end of sentences when using proportional type.

After typing three or four sentences, press the Return key once and type three or four more sentences about something else. Pressing the Return key more than once is the second habit you will have to break. With the old typewriter (and with some low-end software programs), you press the Return key twice to separate paragraphs.

Rule #2: Only one Return after each paragraph.

We will learn how to add extra spacing between paragraphs in a later chapter, but start getting into the habit of one return after each paragraph now.

If your text frame is too small to contain all your text, you can make it bigger. (If you see a small red square, with a plus sign in the lower right corner of your box, it means the text is overset. The frame is not big enough to contain all the information you want to put in.) To make the frame larger, hold down the Command (Mac OS) or Control (Windows) key, and you will see the text frame handles. Drag on any handle to resize the frame. A text frame looks different than a non-text frame (see Figure 2–5). The extra boxes are the in port and out port indicators and will be introduced in a future chapter.

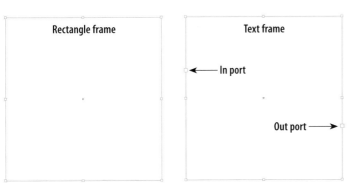

figure | 2–5 |

You can recognize a text frame by the extra little boxes, the in port and out port indicators. Clicking in any frame with the Type tool will convert it to a text frame.

Changing Typefaces

You had a brief introduction to the Control palette in Chapter 1, and after this chapter you will be best friends. You already know that the functions in the Control palette are duplicated in the "official" palettes that you can open by choosing them from the Window menu. Although the Control palette is mighty powerful, it doesn't have all the capabilities available in the other palettes. It is also worth mentioning that your document must contain a text frame for the Control palette to display either of the two text mode controls. This chapter will focus on the Character formatting mode of the Control palette.

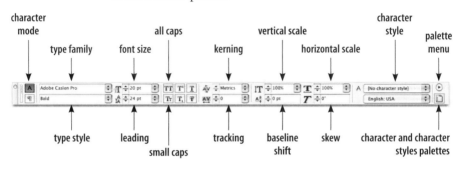

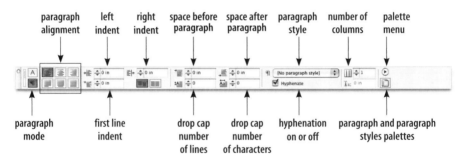

figure | 2–6 |

The top figure shows some of the controls available for Character formatting. On the bottom, the controls available in the Paragraph formatting mode are shown.

In Figure 2–6, at the far left are two icons, one on top of each other. The top icon with the letter "A" inside tells you that the Character formatting mode is active. To the right of that icon is the name of the default font used in your text frame, probably Times New Roman.

In the early days of printing, type was set by hand, letter by letter. A printer needed an actual piece of metal type for each letter and symbol in every size of any given typeface. The set of all the characters of a particular typeface in a specific point size was called a font. Our modern typefaces are not metal but digital, and you don't purchase a new font for each point size you plan to use. Today, the terms *font* and *typeface* are often used interchangeably, as in the case of this textbook. The font shown in Figure 2–7 is Americana.

	!	"	#	$	%	&	'	(	)	*	+	,	-	.	/	0	1	2	3	4
5	6	7	8	9	:	;	<	=	>	?	@	A	B	C	D	E	F	G	H	I
J	K	L	M	N	O	P	Q	R	S	T	U	V	W	X	Y	Z	[	\	]	^
_	'	a	b	c	d	e	f	g	h	i	j	k	l	m	n	o	p	q	r	s
t	u	v	w	x	y	z	{	|	}	~	¡	¢	£	⁄	¥	ƒ	§	¤	'	"
«	‹	›	fi	fl	–	†	‡	·	¶	•	,	„	"	»	…	‰	¿	`	´	ˆ
~	¯	˘	˙	¨	˚	¸	˝	˛	ˇ	—	Æ	ª	L	Ø	Œ	º	æ	ı	ł	ø
œ	ß	¹	–	°	ó	Ö	ö	Ê	û	¼	¬	Ë	½	Õ	ú	é	í	Ð	î	®
¦	þ	Ā	ý	Á	Ç	ñ	ð	Å	µ	Ù	È	Š	õ	Ñ	Ú	Â	ô	ÿ	É	Ò
â	×	÷	ç	²	ù	À	Û	ž	Ÿ	Ä	Î	ï	Ó	å	Ý	™	³	Ž	¾	€
ò	ü	ë	±	á	Ï	ì	Í	©	ä	à	š	ì	Ô	Þ	è	ã	Ü	ê		

figure 2–7

A font includes all the characters, numbers, symbols and punctuation of a particular typeface in a particular point size.

Notice the little strokes at the end of the letters. Those are called serifs. Now drag the cursor across a few lines of type, and when the type is highlighted (or selected), release the mouse. Click on the arrow to the right of the font name and scroll to find the font named Helvetica. Select the font and watch your highlighted type change to Helvetica.

Helvetica is a sans serif font. The French word "sans" means "without." A sans serif typeface does not have little finishing strokes. Compare the lines of text on your screen that are in Times and those that are in Helvetica. Can you tell the difference between the typefaces? Fonts are categorized into two main categories: serif and sans serif. Figure 2–8 shows some examples.

Times	**Helvetica**
Garamond	Futura
Americana	Myriad
Minion	Tekton
Bernhard Modern	**Vag Rounded**
University	Gill
TRAJAN	**Techno**

figure 2–8

Serif (right) and sans serif (left) typefaces come in all shapes!

Select all the text in your box by using the keyboard shortcut Command+A (Mac) or Control+A (Windows). The selected text should be displayed in two fonts: Times and Helvetica. Now when you look in the Type family field in the Control palette you will see that it's blank. When a field is blank, it means there are two or more different values for that field in your selected text—in this case, Times and Helvetica. With all the text still selected, change the font back to Times by selecting the font name from the Type family list.

NOTE: A field is any place in a dialog box or palette where you can enter a name or numerical value. A quick way to highlight any field is to click on its label (left of the field) rather than the field itself. If the field has an arrow(s) on the right, click it to access a menu of presets. When the field has up and down arrows on the left, you click them to change the value in the field. Most fields also allow you to increase or decrease the field value by pressing the Up or Down Arrow keys on the keyboard.

figure | 2–9 |

The choices on the Type Style list.

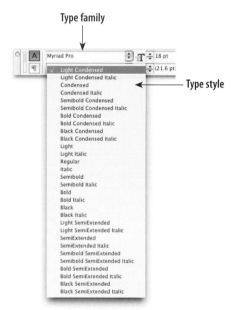

There are several ways to select a typeface in the Control palette. The most common method is to click the menu control to the right of the Type Family field and move up or down the list to the name of the font you desire. This method works great unless you are lucky enough to have hundreds of fonts! With a long list of fonts, scrolling through typeface names beginning with A to get to those beginning with Z may take forever. (Actually, it will only take a few seconds but it seems like an eternity and it's not very efficient.) A more direct way to select a typeface is to type the name (or the first several letters) of the typeface in the Type Family field on the

Control palette. And finally, a "quick and dirty" method to jump to a typeface is to open the Type Family menu and type just the first letter of the typeface. The list will automatically jump to the first typeface beginning with that letter. For instance, if you type a T for Times, the list would jump to the first typeface beginning with "T", making it much easier to find the font name Times.

Changing the Size of Type

To the right of the Type Family is the Font size field (the default is set at 12 points). Type specifications are measured in points and picas. Twelve points equal one pica. In terms of inches, there are 72 points in an inch, so there are 6 picas in an inch.

figure | 2–10 |

As type size increases, the point size also increases.

You can change the point size by selecting the text, highlighting the Font size in the Control palette, entering a new value, and pressing Return. But when working in a page layout program, you want to do things as quickly and efficiently as possible. The quick way to increase point size is to highlight the text and press Command+Shift+> (Mac) or Control+Shift+> (Windows). To decrease the point size, press Command+Shift+< (Mac) or Control+Shift+< (Windows). These shortcuts will increase or decrease the type size by a specific amount set in the Units and Increments Preferences (the default is 2 points). If you also hold down the Option (Mac) or Alt (Windows) key, the point size will change in increments of five times the preference setting (5 × 2 points [default setting] = 10 points).

figure | 2–11 |

The Font Size field.

click these arrows to change point size in 1-point increments. font size click the menu control to select a preset size from the menu.

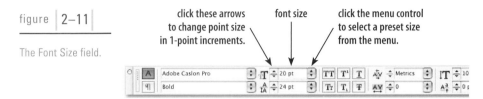

Changing the Type Style

A type family is a collection of related typefaces in different weights called type styles. You find the Type Style field underneath the Font Family field in the Control palette. When selecting type, you must know what the different type styles mean.

Light
Light Italic
Light Narrow
Light Narrow Italic
Light Condensed
Light Condensed Italic

Book
Book Italic
Book Narrow
Book Narrow Italic
Book Condensed
Book Condensed Italic

Bold
Bold Condensed Italic
Ultra
Ultra Italic
Ultra Condensed
Ultra Condensed Italic

figure | 2–12 |

Just like the members of your own family, these related typefaces from the ITC Garamond family come in all shapes and weights.

Changing Leading

Leading (rhymes with "sledding") is the vertical space between the baselines of text. The baseline is the imaginary line the type sits on. Like type, leading is measured in points, from baseline to baseline. There are two types of leading: auto leading and absolute leading. Auto leading is just what the name implies: determined automatically by the computer. The point size of the text is multiplied by 120% to get the leading value. (The default setting for auto leading is 120%, but you can change the percentage in the Justification dialog box.) For example, if point size is 12, leading will be 14.4 points (12 × 120% = 14.4). If point size is 10, leading will be 12 points (10 × 120% = 12). The Leading field is below the Font Size field on the Control palette (see Figure 2–6).

Leading is measured
from baseline to baseline.

figure | 2–13 |

The baseline is the
imaginary line a line
of type sits on.

Absolute leading means that you, the designer, set the leading value. You can do this in the Control palette or (because you are quick and efficient) select the text, hold down the Option (Mac) or Alt (Windows) key, and click the Up or Down Arrow keys. The leading value will change in increments determined by your preferences (the default setting is 2 points).

Leading can be positive (when the leading value is greater than the point size), negative (when the leading value is less than point size), or set solid (when the leading and point size values are equal). You will usually use positive leading in body copy, and negative or solid leading with large type (called display type).

When the leading is **greater** than the point size of type, it is *positive* leading.

Times Roman "18 point type/25 point leading"

figure | 2–14 |

Most of the time, you will want to use an absolute leading value. Auto leading usually looks a bit too wide. When setting headlines you will frequently use solid or negative leading.

When the leading is **less** than the point size of type, it is *negative* leading.

Times Roman "18 point type/15 point leading"

When the leading is **the same** as the point size of type, it is *set solid*.

Times Roman "18 point type/18 point leading"

Marked-up Copy

Markup is a universal system of coding that provides direction to people who work with type. Basic typographic markup consists of three measurements: size of type measured in points is listed first, as the numerator. Leading is the denominator, also measured in points. Line length or "measure," follows the "×" and is usually measured in picas. If you are given a marked-up document you immediately know what to enter in the various fields in the Control palette. Markup will be used in projects throughout this book.

figure | 2–15 |

The original copy (top) has been set according to the typographic markup specifications: set in Times Roman, 10 pt. font size, 11.75 point leading, line length 20 picas.

If your boss gave you a choice—buy more stock photography or buy more typefaces—which would you choose? If you're like me, the answer to this question is easy. I am always looking for well-designed type families with a variety of weights and styles.

Original copy

↓

set in: Times Roman 10/11.75 x 20

↓

If your boss gave you a choice—buy more stock photography or buy more typefaces—which would you choose? If you're like me, the answer to this question is easy. I am always looking for well-designed type families with a variety of weights and styles.

The pica-point measurement system is useful for working in small units of measure. Six picas equal one inch. Twelve points equal one pica. An inch is broken down into 72 tiny point-sized increments. It is easier to visualize how 5 points will look than how 0.069444 inches will look.

One helpful tool for getting a visual "feel" for the pica-point system and for measuring type and line measure is an E-gauge, which is available at most art supply stores. The E-gauge comes with a pica

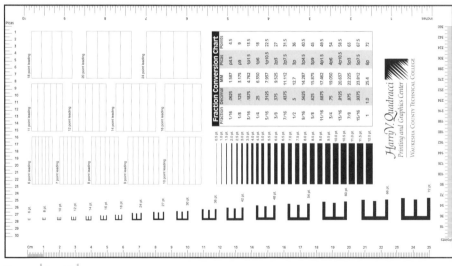

figure | 2–16 |

An E-gauge is an inexpensive, tool for measuring type. Graphics students at the Harry V. Quadracci Printing and Graphics Center in Pewaukee, Wisconsin use the sample shown here in miniature.

and point scale and a series of Es that descend in size. You can esti-mate the type size by matching a capital letter with the correspond-ing E on the E-gauge.

The image file (.eps) for the E-gauge shown in Figure 2–16 is included in the Chapter 02 folder on the accompanying CD. You can make one by printing the file on transparency film. *Caution: Do not run any film through a printer unless the film is designed for use in your specific printer!*

Putting It All Together

Let's use the Control palette as we put together a few simple proj-ects. In this first project you will make a custom-size document and create an information card. When you are setting type it is most efficient to do all the typing first. Then change all the type to the most frequently used typeface, point size, and leading. Finally, fine-tune individual words and passages of type.

figure | 2–17

Name: *(Your first and last name)*
Address: *(Where you are living while you attend school)*
City, State, Zip
Email: *(The email address you check most frequently)*
Phone: *(Type your local phone)*
Emergency: *(Number of a friend who could contact you in an emergency)*

The document size for the information card is 5 × 3 inches.

In the world of graphic design, the width is the first measure-ment given. In the document that you create in the following steps, the orientation will be landscape, since the width is greater than the height.

1. Create a new 5 × 3 inch document with 0.5-inch margins.
2. Select the Type tool by pressing T. Begin by lining up the lower horizontal line of the Type tool cursor to the upper left corner margins. Click and drag a text frame diagonally down to the lower right corner. Release the mouse. If you don't like the frame you made, use the Undo shortcut and draw the frame again.

figure | 2–18 |

The location of
the upper corner
of your text frame
will be determined
by the position of
the vertical and
horizontal crosshairs
on the lower part of
the I-beam.

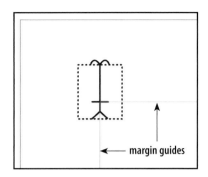

margin guides

3. Type **Name:** and then type your first and last name. Press Return.
4. Type **Address:** and then type your local address.
5. Type your city, state, and zip code.
6. Type **Email:** and complete the information.
7. Complete the rest of the form in a similar manner. Be sure to include the area code with your local phone number.
8. Press Command+A (Mac) or Control+A (Windows) to select all the type. Change the font and leading to Minion Pro 15 (point size) /19 (leading). If you don't have Minion Pro, select a similar typeface.
9. Print your document. Press Command+P (Mac) or Control+P (Windows). When the Print dialog box opens, look in the Printer field and make sure your printer is selected.
10. In the list located on the left side of the dialog box, select Marks and Bleed. When that option page is displayed, turn on the Crop Marks option and press Return (see Figure 2–19).

figure | 2–19 |

When you click on
each item in the
list, a new page of
options is displayed.

click here

turn on
crop marks

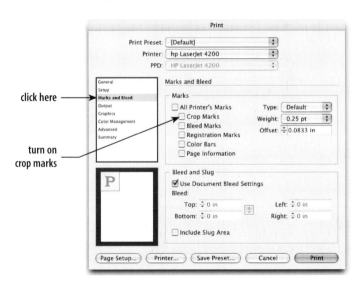

Your document will print with L-shaped lines at each corner that indicate the 5 × 3 size of the document printed on the letter-sized paper.

In the next project you will make a reference chart to keep with your InDesign materials. (The typeface used in this project is Minion Pro. If you don't have Minion Pro, select a similar typeface.)

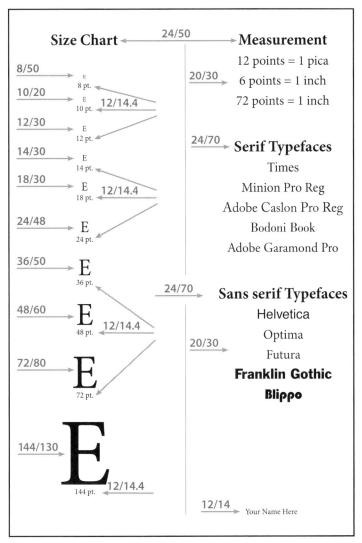

figure | 2–20

Use the markup shown in gray to format the chart.

Follow the markup to format the chart that you create in the following steps. Remember that point size is represented in the numerator (the first number), leading in the denominator (the second number).

1. Create a new 8.5 × 11 document. Margins 0.5 inch Columns: 2, Gutter Width: 1.0 inch

2. Using the Type tool, draw a text box from the upper left margin to the lower right margin of the left column.

3. Type all copy in the left column in Minion Pro Regular 12/14.4. Remember—Type first, format second. Type the copy first and then go back to change the point sizes and the leading.

4. Select the words *Size Chart* by triple-clicking with your mouse. Change the typeface to Minion Pro Bold, 24/50 pt.

5. Triple-click to select the first letter E. Change the point size to 8 points and the leading to 50 points. Notice that leading is measured from the imaginary line the E sits on (its baseline) to the bottom of the line above it.

6. Do not change the point size or leading of any of the size descriptions, 12 pt, 14 pt, 18 pt, and so on. They are already the correct size and leading, 12/14.4.

7. Use the example shown in Figure 2-20 to set the point and leading parameters for each E. Center each line of type by highlighting it and pressing Shift+Command+C (Mac) or Shift+Control+C (Windows).

8. Save your document. Type **E Chart** in the Save As field. Save the document to your desktop.

9. Use the Type tool to draw a text box from the upper left margin to the lower right margin of the right column.

10. Type the measurement portion. Set the top line, "Measurement," in Minion Pro Bold 24/50. Set the next three lines in Minion Pro Regular, 20/30. Center the type.

11. Set the line "Serif Typefaces" in Minion Pro Bold, 24/70. Center the type.

12. Find four or five serif-style typefaces available on your computer. If you aren't familiar with your font collection, this may be a hit-or-miss process. Type the names of your choices into your document. Each font name should be centered on each line, 20/30. Remember to press the Return key only once between lines of type.

13. Type **Sans serif Typefaces** in Minion Pro Bold 24/70, centered

14. Select four or five sans serif typefaces from your font collection and type the name of each different typeface on a separate line, 20/30. Center all the text.

15. Use the Frame tool to draw a text frame at the bottom of the page. Select the Type tool and type your name in Minion Pro Regular 12/14.

16. Select the Line tool from the Toolbox. While holding down the Shift key, draw a straight line between the two columns from top to bottom. Add a stroke if necessary.

17. Save and print your project.

More on Measuring...

Measuring and placement will be covered in detail in Chapter 4. But now is a good time to explain how units of measure work in combination with the palette fields. When your document is set to measure in inches and you want to set a value in points, simply replace the number and suffix (1 in) with the new unit of measure. In the case of points, enter 6 points by typing a "p" before the number as in "p6." For picas, the p follows the number; so 8 picas would be 8 p. If the document preference is set to points or picas and you want to enter a unit of measurement in inches, you will need to type the number plus the suffix "in" or the quotation mark (").

Changing the Units of Measure

Let's change the document's units of measurement preferences. Hold down the Control key, and click on the horizontal ruler (Mac), or right-click on the horizontal ruler (Windows). Choose a different unit of measurement. Do the same with the vertical ruler. That's how easy it is to change the measurement system used in any document. Using this method, you can switch back and forth between measurement systems whenever you want.

Using Palettes to Add, Subtract, Multiply, and Divide

When you are using the Selection tool (black arrow) and select an object, you will notice that the Control palette changes to display X, Y, W, and H fields. The W and H fields stand for the width and height of the selected object. Palettes allow you to add, subtract, multiply, and divide right in the field.

the width will be
divided by 3

figure | 2–21 |

You can add, subtract, multiply and divide in the palette fields by entering the correct symbol. Here, the width of the object will be divided by 3.

For instance, let's say your document's measurement system is set to inches and you have a 4-inch rectangle, but want to add 5 points to the width. With the rectangle selected, in the W field type **+p5** (5 points) after the 4 in and press Return. Five points will be added to the dimension and the resulting number in the W field will be converted to inches (4.0694 in). Use the hyphen (-) to subtract, the asterisk (*) to multiply, and the slash (/) to divide.

Indesign converts the dimension typed in a Control palette field to the current unit of measurement. For instance, if you are working in picas and type in **1"**, the value in the Control palette will read 6 picas when you press Return or Tab. When you are working in one measurement system and input a value in a different measurement system you must add that measurement's symbol. In this example the inch marks would need to be added because the unit of measurements is picas. If you are working in inches you must add a "p" after the number to indicate picas or before the number to indicate points.

Working with Text in a Frame

By now you know that you can click and drag with the Type tool to create a frame for text. As soon as you release the mouse a blinking cursor is wagging its tail at you, eager for you to begin typing. In the next project you will learn how to incorporate text frame options to create a stylish bookmark.

In Figure 2–22, notice how the text of the bookmark has plenty of room inside the bordered text frame. You will learn how to do this and other neat functions in the last section of this chapter.

Body copy: Caflisch
Script Pro Regular

40/30 ——→ *Wisdom*

27/30 ——→ *outweighs*

27/30 ——→ *any wealth.*
Add 0.5" space
after paragraph

Adobe Caslon Pro ——→
100/100

27/30 ——→ *Sophocles*

figure | 2–22 |

Notice how the
text has plenty of
"breathing" space
inside the border.

1. Create a new document, 8.5 × 11 in. Accept the default settings.
2. Select the Rectangle Frame tool and draw a small box somewhere near the upper middle part of your document.
3. Look at the Control palette to check what units of measurement you are using. If necessary, change the unit of measurements to inches as described earlier.
4. With the frame selected, change the W field to 2 in. and the H field to 7 in.
5. Add a border around the bookmark. You will do this by adding a stroke to the frame. Strokes can be various widths and styles. Click the text frame with the Selection tool (black arrow). Click the Stroke control at the bottom of the Toolbox so that it is on top. This makes the Stroke mode active. Make sure the border on the top square is black. If it is not, click the Apply Color button shown in Figure 2–23.

With the Selection tool still active, look at the right side of the Control palette. There are two fields that allow you to choose the weight and type of a stroke. Experiment a little bit by choosing different line weights and stroke styles from the preset lists. The bookmark project uses a 1-point solid stroke.

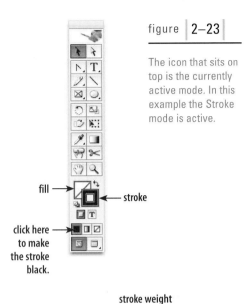

figure | 2–23 |

The icon that sits on top is the currently active mode. In this example the Stroke mode is active.

6. Now select the Type tool and click the frame. Press Command+B (Mac) or Control+B (Windows). The Text Frame Options dialog box opens. Enter .25" in the Top, Bottom, Left, and Right fields of the Inset Spacing area. Press Return.

fill →

stroke ←

click here → to make the stroke black.

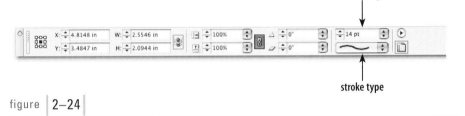

stroke weight

stroke type

figure | 2–24 |

The top field creates the stroke width; the bottom field selects a stroke type.

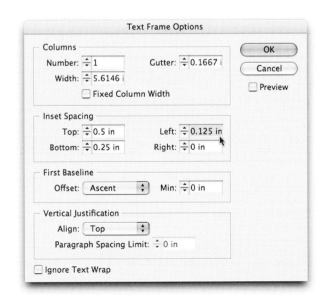

figure | 2–25 |

The Inset Spacing option in the Text Frame Options dialog box allows you to determine the amount of white space inside the edges of a text frame

Don't choke type by allowing it to bump into a frame's border. Always use a text inset when using bordered text frames! In the example shown in Figure 2–26, the left example is wrong and the right example is correct.

figure | 2–26 |

A text inset keeps the type away from the edges of a text frame.

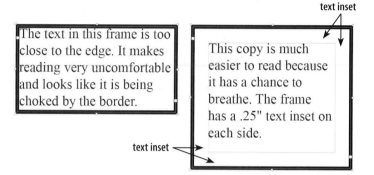

7. Make sure you are still using the Type tool. Now when you click on the text frame, notice that the cursor is .25" inches away from the edge of the frame.

8. Type the copy as shown earlier in Figure 2–22. Remember, "Type first, format second." Press a Return after the word, "wealth." Then type "Sophocles." Now look at the type specs for the project found on Figure 2–22. Follow the markup carefully. If you don't have Caflisch Pro, use a similar typeface.

9. Select all of your text. With all the type selected, click the Paragraph tool on the Control palette. Center the type horizontally by selecting it and pressing Shift+Command+C (Mac) or Shift+Control+C (Windows).

10. Add a decorative ornament. The decorative shape on the bookmark is called a glyph. Glyphs are characters, numerals, punctuation, ornaments or anything else included with a type family. Choose Type>Glyphs, the Glyphs palette will open displaying the entire list of characters and ornaments designed for this specific font. Look in the lower left corner of the Glyph window to see what font you are looking at. Click on the arrow to the right of the font names. Your whole font collection should show up—go ahead, show the glyphs from several other fonts. You can enlarge your view by clicking the large mountain icon in the lower right corner. Experiment by looking at Carta or Wingdings or Adobe Caslon Pro. To insert a glyph in your document, make sure your cursor is blinking

where you want the glyph to be placed. Double-click any glyph from the Glyph palette and that symbol will be placed at the cursor insertion point.

11. Double-click the glyph you inserted if it is not still highlighted. On the Control palette, click the Character formatting button to switch the Control palette back to character formatting mode. Now increase the point size and leading. The glyph shown in the project example is Adobe Caslon Pro 100/100.

figure | 2–27 |

Not all typefaces have such a huge array of glyphs. This chart is from Adobe Caslon Pro.

One Last Glance

Before you save and print your document, give it a final proof. Is everything spelled correctly? Is the size of the bookmark 2 × 7 inches? Is the combination of the typeface and selected glyph pleasing to the eye? Does the stroke have the same feel as the rest of the bookmark? Always give your projects an additional "once-over" before going to print. You will also want to look carefully at your project after it is printed. You will see things on the hard copy that you may miss on the computer screen. Make your edits and print again.

SUMMARY

We covered a lot of ground in this chapter. You were introduced to basic typesetting terminology: typeface, typestyle, font, serif and sans serif typefaces, leading, markup, picas, and points. Three important typesetting practices were covered: one space between sentences, one return after paragraphs, and type first, format second. You learned to use a text frame inset with type in a stroked box. You changed the units of measurement, drew containers for text using both the Frame and Type tools, modified the dimensions of a text box using the Control palette, and added a stroke of varying widths and styles. You learned typesetting techniques such as changing typefaces, point size, and leading, inserting glyphs, and centering type. You honed your production skills by memorizing and using shortcut keys. Now you are ready to begin the fine art of setting type.

1. How can you differentiate a sans serif typeface from a serif typeface?

2. Why is it not necessary to add extra space between sentences by pressing the spacebar twice?

3. How many points are in an inch?

4. What is a glyph?

5. What Text Frame option should you always use when you have applied a stroke to a frame filled with copy?

6. How do you change the units of measurement in a document?

7. When describing a document's measurements, which dimension is listed first: the width, or the height?

↗ EXPLORING ON YOUR OWN

You are going on a type scavenger hunt! Look on bulletin boards, in magazines, newspapers, and anywhere else to find the following samples.

1. Find two examples of printed pieces where typefaces have been chosen to communicate a particular personality. On each piece, write one or two words that describe the typeface's personality.

2. Find an example of a headline in a sans serif typeface.

3. Find an example of body text in a serif typeface.

4. Find two very easy pieces you can duplicate using the skills you have learned in InDesign thus far. Have fun!

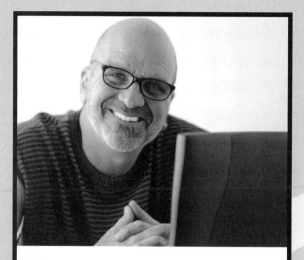

Experience
is that marvelous thing
that enables you to recognize
a mistake when you make it again.

℞ Franklin P. Jones

the fine art of setting type

3

charting your course

Sometimes it's tempting to cut corners. When working on that design job for your aunt, or doing a "freebie" for a volunteer ogranization, you may be tempted to throw typographic principles to the wind and just slam out the job. You may be able to get away with poor typesetting—occasionally. But sooner or later, your boss, creative director, or prepress technician will open your electronic files and be appalled at your unprofessional and unorthodox production skills. You don't want to gain a reputation for excellent design capabilities, but horrible production and typography skills. That's why it's so important to develop good production habits right from the start.

Design projects can range from pizza coupons to annual reports. You should incorporate basic typesetting standards in all the projects you do. High-end jobs go beyond the basics and require more time and effort to incorporate precise specifications, styles, baseline grids, and so on. You will learn to match the level of typesetting with the level of the project—but only after you thoroughly understand the basics of production and typography.

Putting type on a page without incorporating typographic principles is merely word processing. Creating text that enhances communication while incorporating correct typography is an art. Welcome to the fine art of setting type.

 goals

- **Identify the anatomical parts of letters**

- **Interpret "hidden" characters to identify hard and soft returns, spaces, and other hidden characters**

- **Use paragraph formatting features and punctuation: space before and after, drop and raised caps, hyphenation, optical margin alignment, ragged lines, justification, quotation marks, and prime marks**

- **Differentiate between hyphens and dashes, and use each correctly**

- **Calculate ideal line measure**

- **Interpret proofreading marks**

THE ANATOMY OF TYPE

My husband worked in his father's farm machinery business as he was growing up. While most of us can correctly identify a slow moving machine we pass on the road as a tractor, my husband can still identify the make, model, and era of almost any tractor he sees. Because he was surrounded by machinery on a daily basis, he learned how to identify specific features and differentiate between models.

The process of identifying typefaces works the same way. First, you learn to classify type as sans serif or serif. Then, you begin to recognize that different typefaces have different personalities (remember the example of choosing your cosmetic surgeon in Chapter 2?). But before we get any further with type identification and selection, you will need to recognize the anatomical parts that make up letters. It is difficult to discuss typeface selection with a person who says, "I need a letter g that has a wide line and a curved thing-a-ma-bob." Because choosing a typeface is a critical step in any project, we begin this chapter by discussing the anatomical parts of a letter.

You know from the last chapter that the baseline is the imaginary line type rests on. Figure 3–1 shows other terms you should become familiar with.

- **x-height**—the distance from the baseline to the top of a lower-case *x*
- **mean line**—a horizontal line drawn from along the x-height parallel to the baseline
- **cap height**—the space from the baseline to the top of a capital letter
- **ascender**—parts of a letter that extend above the mean line
- **descender**—letter parts that extend below the baseline
- **descent**—the distance from the baseline to the bottom of the longest descender
- **ascent**—the distance from the baseline to the top of the highest ascender
- **point size**— determined by adding the ascent and descent

figure | 3–1 |

Terms used to describe how type is measured.

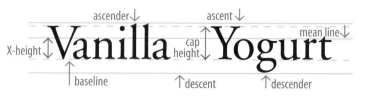

Point size is calculated by adding the ascent and descent. Variations in all of these measurements from typeface to typeface, make a 36-point font in one typeface look much different than a 36-point font in another typeface, as shown in Figure 3–2.

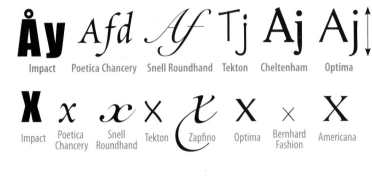

36 points from the tallest ascender to the lowest descender.

Impact   Poetica Chancery   Snell Roundhand   Tekton   Cheltenham   Optima

Impact   Poetica Chancery   Snell Roundhand   Tekton   Zapfino   Optima   Bernhard Fashion   Americana

figure | 3–2|

Notice the variation in the appearance of capital letters of these fonts——even though all are specified as 36-point. Different typefaces also have varying x-heights.

The anatomical parts of letters deal with letter structure, shape, and finish. Although some anatomical parts are specific to one or two letters, most parts appear in many letters.

Structure-related anatomy

Figure | 3–3|

Structural letter parts are the foundational components of a letter.

Apex	the pointed intersection where two strokes meet at the top of a letter	A M N
Arm	a horizontal or diagonal stroke having one end unattached	Y K Z E F L Z
Ascender	the part of a lower case letter that extends above the mean	b d f h k l t _meanline_
Bar	a horizontal stroke that connects two sides of a letter	e e H A
Bowl	the curve that forms a closed space in a letter	B b D d P p q
Crossbar	a horizontal stroke that crosses another	f t T
Descender	the part of a lettter that extends below the baseline	J g j p q y _baseline_
Hairline	very thin letter stroke or serif	A F H K M N
Leg	refers to the tail in upper and lowercase *K*	K k
Link	the curved stroke that joins the top to bottom of lower case 2-story *g*	g g g g g
Loop	the curved stroke of the lower case *g*	g g g g
Shoulder	a curved stroke that isn't closed	m n
Spine	the main curve of the upper and lower case *s*	s s s s

Structure-related anatomy (continued)

Stem	a vertical stroke within an upper or lower case letter	B d E F t l k l N
Stress	strokes go from thick to thin as in calligraphy. Connect thin areas to determine direction of stress	b b O O Q Q R R
Stroke	basic letter component representing one curved or straight pen stroke	A D H b l n Y
Tail	downward slanted stroke— one end attached to letter body	K k Q R X x y
Vertex	the point on the bottom of the letter where two strokes meet	N V W w v

Shape and finishing anatomy

Aperture	the amount of space between open ends of letters	C c S s G e a
Ball	a style of terminal shaped like a dot	f a c j r y
Beak	a style of terminal with a pointed end	f a c j r y
Bracket	a curved shape that joins a serif to the stem	P d f h H I
Counter	the closed or partially closed shape within a letter	e g B b a m
Crotch	the angled space formed when diagonal strokes meet	w v W y
Ear	the small part on top of a lower case *g*	g g g g g g g
Finial	a tapering end of letter	j c e t y
Serif	a cross, finishing stroke at the end of a letter. Can be wedge, square (slab) , hairline, or cupped	H H H H H
Slab serif	a serif wth a block shape	E H E H E
Spur	the lower extension on some upper case **G**s	G G G G G G
Square serif	See slab serif	
Swash	a decorative alternate letter that includes a flourish	K M N Q R W
Teardrop	a terminal shaped like a teardrop	a c f j r s
2-story A	has an upper and lower part as contrasted with a one-story A: a	a a a a a a a a a a
2-story G	lower case g with a loop connected with a link as contrasted with a one-story: g	g g g g g
Ligature	two or three letters connected into a single unit	fl fj ffi ffl st ft Th

Understanding Hidden Characters

There are right ways and wrong ways to create any document. You can have two documents whose printouts look identical—but upon closer examination, one is built with precision while the other is a patchwork of hodge-podge workarounds. One document will be easier to print and edit. The other will be a nightmare.

When you press a key that does not produce a letter, number, or punctuation mark—for example, the spacebar, the Tab key, or the Return key—a "hidden" character is placed in your document. By default, hidden characters are not visible. You can make the hidden characters in your document visible by pressing Command+Option+I (Mac) or Control+Alt+I (Windows). This keyboard shortcut is a toggle shortcut, which means you use the same key sequence to turn hidden characters on or off. Different hidden characters are represented on the screen by different symbols. When hidden characters are turned on, you can see these symbols on your screen, but they don't print. Your computer thinks a space between letters or a return at the end of a line is a character, just like a letter or number or punctuation mark, and treats it as such. Thanks to hidden characters, you can see your document as your computer sees it.

Your Portfolio¶

Don't underestimate the power of your portfolio. It must convince future employers that you can:¶

» • communicate visually¶
» • work within project specifications¶
» • understand and apply typographic principles¶
• understand a design objective and articulate your creative rationale¶
• find relationships between seemingly unrelated items¶
• prepare artwork correctly for final output: offset, flexo, web, screen printing, etc.¶
• use color effectively¶
» • create campaigns according to strategic marketing plans¶
• use software appropriately for specific projects¶

Without a portfolio, you have no evidence to support the claims that are made in an interview. #

figure | **3–5**

Hidden characters can be seen on your monitor, but do not print. Use the key in Figure 3–6 to identify what the hidden characters in this text block represent.

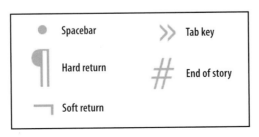

figure | **3–6**

Memorize what each of these symbols means.

NOTE: Hidden characters show the details of how your document was constructed—and tell even more about your typesetting abilities. Your supervisor or co-workers can take one look at the hidden characters in your document and have a pretty good idea of your software proficiency.

Understanding Paragraphs

Now that you can read hidden characters, you are ready to set type in paragraphs. One thing you will never want to forget is this: A paragraph is defined by pressing the Return key (Mac) or the Enter key (Windows). You create a new paragraph every time you press the Return key, whether you have typed a whole page or just one letter. From memorizing the hidden character symbols in Figure 3–6, you already know that a paragraph symbol looks like this: ¶. Every time you press Return, this symbol will show (if you have hidden characters turned on) and you will have created a new paragraph. (I work with hidden characters turned on most of the time. I want to see my document as the computer sees it!)

figure | 3–7

In text frame A, the Return key was pressed at the end of each line. In frame B, InDesign automatically wrapped the text from one line to the next.

A

Choosing Portfolio Pieces¶

It goes without saying that all the pieces in your¶
book should be strong. Ten to twelve pieces that¶
demonstrate your range of abilities is a good¶
starting number. Your first piece should knock¶
their socks off! And the last piece should also¶
leave a great impression. ¶

Choose pieces that are excellent examples of¶
design, use of color and type, and technique.¶
Do not include a poorly designed piece because¶
of its sentimental value. For instance, don't
include a weak pencil sketch done in *Drawing
101*, even if you received a grade of A. Poor pieces
dilute the impact of an otherwise strong book. #

B

Choosing Portfolio Pieces¶

It goes without saying that all the pieces in your
book should be strong. Ten to twelve pieces that
demonstrate your range of abilities is a good
starting number. Your first piece should knock
their socks off! And the last piece should also
leave a great impression. ¶

Choose pieces that are excellent examples of
design, use of color and type, and technique.
Do not include a poorly designed piece because
of its sentimental value. For instance, don't
include a weak pencil sketch done in *Drawing
101*, even if you received a grade of A. Poor pieces
dilute the impact of an otherwise strong book. #

Look at the two passages in Figure 3–7. How many paragraphs are in frame A? How many are in frame B? Even though the copy in frame A looks identical to the copy in frame B, it is actually 14 paragraphs, while column B is only two paragraphs. Each ¶ symbol represents a paragraph. The Return or Enter key was pressed at the end of each line in frame A, creating many more paragraphs than necessary. This is called *setting line for line*. The majority of the time, you will want to use the Return key only at the end of a whole paragraph so that the software will manage the line endings.

However, occasionally you will need to break a line manually within a paragraph. Look at the second line in the second paragraph of frame B. It has a different symbol at the end of the line. This symbol (¬) represents a soft return, and is created by holding Shift+Return (Mac) or Shift+Enter (Windows). A soft return breaks the line, but does not create a new paragraph. The distinction between paragraph returns (or hard returns) and soft returns is critical to understand, because they determine where your paragraph formatting begins and ends.

How to Add Breather Space Between Paragraphs

In the following exercise you will learn how to add extra space between paragraphs.

1. Create a new document: 8.5" × 11", all margins 0.5".
2. Press "F" to select the Rectangle Frame tool. Draw a rectangle from the upper left to the lower right margin. Select the Type tool and click in the frame to make it a text frame.
3. Open the context menu and choose Fill with Placeholder Text. Text should flow into the text frame. Don't worry about trying to read it, Placeholder text is a term for text that is used to "take the place" of the final copy. It is useful for showing where the finished text will be placed and makes the document look more complete. The Placeholder text will be replaced by the actual copy, later. (Placeholder text can also be accessed from the Type menu.)
4. Turn on hidden characters. You will probably see several paragraph return symbols in the text. There should be a # symbol at the end of the text indicating the end of the story. If your text doesn't show any paragraph symbols, insert two or three paragraphs returns throughout the text.
5. Add some soft returns at the ends of three or four lines.
6. Practice highlighting text. Double-clicking selects a single word. Triple-clicking selects a whole line, and clicking four times selects a paragraph. Selecting paragraphs with four clicks is a good way to make sure that everything in the paragraph is selected, including the paragraph return symbol at the end of the paragraph. If you simply drag the cursor to highlight the characters in the paragraph, it is easy to miss the ending paragraph symbol.

7. Select all the text by pressing Command+A (Mac) or Control+A (Windows). Choose a typeface and make the type 10-point on 11-point leading.

8. Now you'll add space between paragraphs using the Control palette. Figure 3–8 shows the Space After field. Type **p7** (meaning 7 points) in the field. When you press Return, InDesign converts the point measurement to the equivalent measurement in inches and adds that amount of space after every paragraph. You can use any measurement system to enter numeric values in fields, as long as you also enter the corresponding unit abbreviation such as "in" for inches or "mm" for millimeters. When using points and picas, if the p is before the number it means points. When the p follows a number, it means picas. Therefore, 5p means 5 picas, p5 means 5 points and 12p6 means 12 picas, 6 points.

Space before   Space after

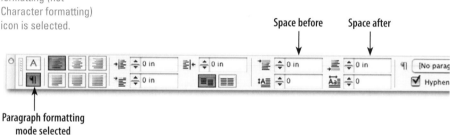

Paragraph formatting
mode selected

9. Examine your copy to see the breather space between the paragraphs. Remember to use Command+ Z (Mac) or Control+Z (Windows) to undo any mistakes. Keep this document open—more practice ahead.

NOTE: When you double-, triple-, or quadruple-click to select text, you are selecting not only the text, but all hidden characters as well.

Type and Tool Tips

Spend a little time experimenting with the following list of tips.

• When you are using the Type tool and are working in an active text frame, you can temporarily access the Selection tool by holding down the Command (Mac) or Control (Windows) key. As soon as the Command or Control key is released, the arrow becomes a blinking text cursor again. Try this a few times.

• When the Selection tool is active, double-click on your copy to instantly go to the blinking cursor.

- When you are not using the Type tool, you can access the grab-ber hand by holding down the spacebar. When you are using the Type tool, you access the grabber hand by holding down the Option (Mac) or Alt (Windows) key.

- Zooming always works the same way—press Command+Spacebar+click (Mac) or Control+Spacebar+click (Windows) to enlarge your view and use Option+Command+Spacebar+click (Mac) or Alt+Control+Spacebar+click (Windows) to reduce the view.

Using Raised and Drop Caps

A well-set paragraph is a pleasure to view and to read. Skilled type-setters use subtle techniques to give text interest and visual appeal. Raised and drop caps (capital letters) are two of these techniques. Both raised and dropped capital letters are larger than the accom-panying body copy. A drop cap is a large letter (or several letters) that drops below the baseline. A drop cap is a paragraph attribute and is set by using the Control palette in Paragraph formatting mode (a paragraph can have only one value for any given para-graph attribute, such as drop caps, space after, and alignment). A raised cap sits on the baseline and rises above the rest of the text. A raised cap is a character attribute and can be set in the Control palette in Character formatting mode (a paragraph can contain characters that have many different character attributes, such as point size, font, and color).

The letter shape of some drop caps tends to separate the letter from the rest of the word. Extra kerning might be required in these cases (we will discuss kerning in the next chapter).

THE BEGINNING of wisdom is to call things by their right names.
〜 *Chinese Proverb*

THE BEGINNING of wisdom is to call things by their right names.
〜 *Chinese Proverb*

figure | 3–9 |

Drop caps (left) extend below the baseline. Raised caps sit on the baseline and rise above the text.

One word of caution—use raised and drop caps sparingly. They are designed for the beginning of an article or chapter, and when these special techniques are overused, the end result is a document that looks like type has been splattered all over the page.

figure | 3–10 |

This example has too many drop caps. Like bugs on a windshield, type is splattered all over the page. Don't overuse the drop cap function.

Ut lobor si el delessi. Quamcon sequam, volum del ercipsu sciliqui blandre rillaoreet, secte feu facin ulput lametue consectem zzrilit utat lan u

Tat. Uptat ut lutat. Faci euisiscipsum dignis ate te mincilissi tet lore conulputatin henisci llamcon sendipis ad ea faccum

Dolobor peratem etue magnibh ex eugiam ad te tis acinim inim aliquat praessisisl ex esed tet vullam, quamVolortio numsandre

dolor ad magnim nonse do odionulAlis dolor senibh ex eros erate ve

Nissenim velisit, quat amet num quamconsed dolore do endio consenit, veniscillut alit lumsandipis nonse cortie vel utpatem adip ea amet aciduisLorercil iquatio consed

Ea consed del ea commy numsandit nonsenis nulputat vel ulla faci blandiamcon henis at, core magnibh er sustrud exer adionum dolore consequat alisim psummy

Let's return to the document you have been working on and add some drop and raised caps.

1. To make a raised cap, make sure the text frame is active by double-clicking on the text. You should see a blinking cursor.
2. Highlight the first letter of the first word.
3. Hold down Shift+Command (Mac) or Shift+Control (Windows) and press the greater-than key (>) to increase the point size. The size of the letter will increase and the letter will remain sitting on the baseline.
4. To make a drop cap, put the cursor in the next paragraph. Click the Paragraph formatting button on the Control palette. Figure 3–11 shows the two fields you will be using, located right below the Space After field you used earlier. The field on the left controls how many lines the letter(s) will drop. The field on the right controls how many letters will be dropped. Experiment with these controls by clicking on the arrows and watching your screen. Change the first letter in that paragraph to an A and turn it into a drop cap. See how the shape of the letter separates it from the rest of the word? Keep your document open to use in the next exercise.

figure | 3–11 |

The left box controls how many lines the letter(s) will drop. The right box controls how many letters will be affected. Notice the automatic hyphenation option to the right. The check mark means that automatic hyphenation is turned on.

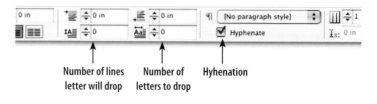

Number of lines letter will drop   Number of letters to drop   Hyhenation

NOTE: A raised cap is a character attribute. A drop cap is a paragraph attribute.

Turn Off Hyphenation

InDesign will automatically hyphenate text unless you tell it not to. To turn off hyphenation in a single paragraph, put your blinking text cursor in the paragraph and deselect the Hyphenate option in the Control palette (Figure 3–11). It isn't necessary to highlight the whole paragraph because hyphenation is a paragraph attribute, and formatting one line in a paragraph affects the entire paragraph. If you want to turn off hyphenation in several adjoining paragraphs, drag with your mouse to select the text. It isn't necessary to highlight everything in each paragraph. One letter of the first or last paragraph will do. Now deselect the Hyphenate option in the Control palette. To turn off hyphenation on all the text, select all the type and deselect Hyphenate.

Use Nonbreaking Spaces and Hyphens to Keep Words Together

There are some words and phrases that should not be split from one line to another. Proper names with titles (Dr. Smith), telephone numbers (888-7707), dates (July 16, 1947), and some compound words (New York) should not be split from one line to the next. InDesign makes it easy to control these potential problems.

- To keep compound words from splitting, insert a special non-breaking space between the two words. Place the cursor between the words and delete the regular space. Open the context menu and select Insert White Space. Then choose Nonbreaking Space from the menu of different types of spaces you can insert. If your hidden characters are turned on, you will see a new symbol showing a nonbreaking space (‸). To turn on hidden characters, press Command+Option+I (Mac) or Control+Alt+I (Windows).

- To keep a phone number from splitting at the hyphen, substitute a nonbreaking hyphen. Using the same context menu, choose Insert Special Character and then choose Nonbreaking Hyphen from the menu of available special characters.

Apply Alignment Settings

Another great feature in the Control palette, when it's in Paragraph formatting mode, is the Alignment option.

figure | 3–12 |

The six Paragraph Alignment options.

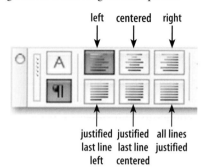

left   centered   right

justified justified all lines
last line last line justified
left   centered

When text is aligned to the left, the right edges of the text are uneven, which is referred to as ragged right, or flush left. When text is pushed to the right side, the left edges are ragged. This alignment is called flush right or ragged left. Text that spreads all the way from the left to the right edges of the text frame is called justified. Text that is centered creates ragged edges on both sides. Each alignment setting has its design challenges. Ragged edges must not be too uneven or the page will have a choppy look. Justified type can be riddled with uneven white spaces within the lines that merge to create rivers. You can spot rivers of white space by holding a page of justified text horizontally at eye level and squinting at the text. The rivers will be quite noticeable.

figure | 3–13 |

Each line of text in copy block A is flush left. The lines in copy block B are flush right. Each line in copy block C is centered. Copy block D is justified.

A	B
Volestrud euisl iliqui blamet ate venit wis nonsent amcor iure vele-nisi. Hendip er inisit dit,	Volestrud euisl iliqui blamet ate venit wis nonsent amcor iure vele-nisi. Hendip er inisit dit,

C	D
Volestrud euisl iliqui blamet ate venit wis nonsent amcor iure vele-nisi. Hendip er inisit dit,	Volestrud euisl iliqui blamet ate venit wis non-sent amcor iure velenisi. Hen-dip er inisit dit,

Indent Copy

By now you can see how powerful and convenient the Control palette is. InDesign packs a lot into this small strip! Now we will look at the indent function. Indents align copy a certain distance from the left or right sides of a text frame. Figure 3–14 shows the Control palette fields used to set the following types of indents: left, right, first line, and hanging. An indent is different than a text frame inset. An indent is a paragraph formatting attribute which can apply to individual paragraphs within a text frame. An inset is a text frame attribute, and applies to all text—every paragraph—within the text frame.

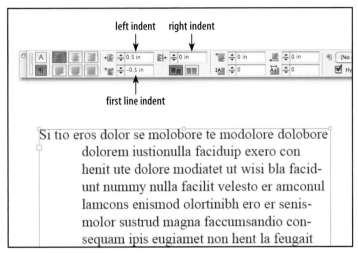

figure | 3–14 |

The top two fields are used to set left and right indents. The bottom field is used to set first line and hanging indents.

To create a paragraph indent, select your paragraph(s), place the cursor in the desired indent field in the Control palette, and type a numerical value or click one of the arrows. Very simple. Let's discuss how to create two specific indents: a first line indent and a hanging indent. Place the cursor in a paragraph and then change the value in the First Line Left Indent field by clicking the upper arrow. You will see that only the first line indent increases and moves to the right. This is easy to visualize and understand. The hanging indent is a bit more confusing. Look at Figure 3–14 and you will see that most of the paragraph "hangs" from the first line of text. To set a hanging indent, you must first set a left indent. Once the left indent is set, you then change the First Line Left Indent field by entering a negative value. This forces the first line back to the left. Once you understand the sequence, creating a hanging indent style will also become easy to visualize and understand.

NOTE: You can think of a hanging indent like a flag hanging from a horizontal pole. The first line of the indent is like the pole, and the rest of the paragraph "hangs" from the first line. Oh well, it works for me.

Balance Ragged Lines

Ragged line endings create an open, friendly look. As you scan up and down the copy block you want the overall shape and pattern of the line endings to look like smooth hills, not like rough, jagged mountains. InDesign has a wonderful feature for smoothing out ragged copy. You will find it in the palette menu found on the Control palette when you are in Paragraph formatting mode. Select a paragraph in the document that you have been working on and make sure it is left justified. Now, go to the Control palette and click the round button with the arrow in it, at the far right end of the palette. From the menu choose Balance Ragged Lines. The edges of your paragraph should smooth out. To smooth out ragged edges on everything in your text frame, select all your paragraphs and apply the Balance Ragged Lines option.

figure | 3–15 |

The example on the right has a much smoother right edge because Balance Ragged Lines is applied to it.

Ostrud elit verciduipis fo erilla feu feugiam, vendreds modignis non sef dolesto delit lam zzriu riurem doloram augiam zzril ipit nullum olobortis ametummodit inTueros inahu ero erci eum delenibh estie conulputismolorper suscillam duisim zzrilit luptat,Ulla faciliquam acilit wis at. Os nummodo del elit, volorpe riurerostrud ming eli quamet doloreet nos adigna feuis

Ostrud elit verciduipis fo erilla feu feugiam, vendreds modignis non sef dolesto delit lam zzriu riurem doloram augiam zzril ipit nullum olobortis ametummodit inTueros inahu ero erci eum delenibh estie conulputismolorper suscillam duisim zzrilit luptat,Ulla faciliquam acilit wis at. Os nummodo del elit, volorpe riurerostrud ming eli quamet doloreet nos adigna feuis

Use Quotation Marks and Prime Marks

In case you haven't noticed, there is a difference between typewriter quotation marks and typographer's quotation marks. Take a look at Figure 3–16. Typewriter quotation marks really have little place in typesetting. Some typesetters use typewriter quotation marks to indicate measurements such as feet and inches. While this is acceptable, a better way is to use prime marks (see Figure 3–16).

"Typographer's Quotation Marks"
"Typographer's Quotation Marks"

Prime Marks may be slanted: 3'11″
Prime Marks may be straight: 3'11"

```
"Typewriter quotation marks
  are often used as prime marks"
```

figure | 3–16 |

Using typewriter
quotation marks
is a great way to
mar an otherwise
excellent portfolio
piece. Notice
that the shape of
typographer's quotes
varies depending
on the typeface you
have selected.

By default, InDesign uses typographer quotation marks, sometimes called curly or smart quotes. If someone has changed your InDesign defaults, you can easily change the preferences back to use typographer's quotes. On the Mac, choose InDesign>Preferences>Text. In Windows, choose Edit>Preferences>Text. Make sure there is a checkmark next to Use Typographer's Quotes option. If you change this option setting when there is no document open, InDesign will use typographer's quotation marks as the default setting for all subsequent documents. If you change this preference setting with a document open, the change will apply only to the current document.

Prime marks are found in the Symbol font and are accessed through the Glyphs palette. Choose Type>Glyphs. Choose the Symbol font and locate the prime marks in the glyphs chart. Double-click to insert the appropriate mark in your text.

Before we move on to another topic, let's put some quotation marks in our practice document. Select all the type by pressing Command+A (Mac) or Control+A (Windows) and change the alignment to justified mode with the last line aligned left. Now put twelve sets of quotation marks at the beginning and end of the lines in your copy block. Scatter the quotation marks up and down the length of the copy block, and get ready for another great InDesign technique!

Hang Punctuation

You can't help but be excited about InDesign. No other software can match its text-handling capabilities. And the ability to hang punctuation is another great InDesign feature. Now that you know how to use the correct quotation marks, it's time to fine-tune your copy. If you look closely at the quotation marks you inserted at the beginning and the end of your lines, you will see that the marks visually create tiny holes in the text block. At first glance this might not seem like a big deal. But after you use the next function you will see what a huge difference a little fine-tuning makes!

1. Switch the Control palette to Character formatting mode and make a note of the point size of your text.
2. Switch the Control palette back to Paragraph formatting mode and then choose Window>Type & Tables>Story. The Story palette is powerful, but easily overlooked. It is used for only one function, but what a difference it makes!
3. There are only two fields on the Story palette. Click the box next to Optical Margin Alignment. A checkmark should appear. The field in the lower area of the palette is called the Align based on size control. It is used for setting the point size of the type in the copy block. Since you just made note of the point size, enter that value in the Align based on size field. When Optical Margin Alignment is active, notice how the quotation marks are partially set outside the edges of the text frame, creating a much smoother visual path for the eye to follow. Toggle the Optical Margin Alignment box a few times and see the difference it makes. Very cool. What a fantastic InDesign capability!

figure | 3–17 |

Optical Margin Alignment refines the edges of the copy block and strengthens the visual impact of text alignment. The copy on the left has "lacy edges" created by the holes under the quotation marks. The copy on the right looks much better.

"Erit lummy num digna alit volore minibh euisseq."

"Uptatem zzrit ad el inim dolore tat." Ut lumsan vulla feugait, velis nonsenit.

"Dolorero dolor sustis niam ipismod magnit ipisim quip eu feum augiam erit alit."

"Erit lummy num digna alit volore minibh euisseq."

"Uptatem zzrit ad el inim dolore tat." Ut lumsan vulla feugait, velis nonsenit.

"Dolorero dolor sustis niam ipismod magnit ipisim quip eu feum augiam erit alit."

Using Hyphens and Dashes

Now that you have quotation marks squared away, it's time to move on to hyphens and dashes. Think how much richer your life will be when you can sit in a restaurant and identify all the typographical errors in the menu! Well… maybe not. But you are beginning to develop a discerning eye for professionally set type. Some of the details may seem tedious at first, but once you have mastered the basics, they will become automatic. Working with InDesign is like playing a Steinway grand piano. What a waste of a good instrument if all you do is play variations of *Chopsticks* or *Heart and Soul*. Likewise, using the best typesetting software on the market as a low-end word processor is also a big waste of potential. Begin to utilize every feature InDesign has to offer.

A hyphen is a tiny dash entered by pressing the key to the right of the key for the number zero. Hyphens are used in only two instances: to separate compound words such as state-of-the-art (including compound names such as Anderson-Jones and compound numbers such as phone numbers) or to hyphenate words at the end of a line of type. A hyphen that is automatically added by InDesign during the text flow process is called a soft hyphen. This hyphen will disappear if the text is edited and the hyphen is no longer needed. When you deselected Hyphenate in the Paragraph Control Palette earlier in this lesson you were turning off the soft automatic hyphens.

Hard hyphens are those you put in compound words, or ones that you manually insert to hyphenate a word at the end of a line. Hard hyphens are there to stay—they are part of the text just like any other visible character. If the line endings change during the editing process and a manually hyphenated word ends up in the middle of a line, it will still be hyphenated. If there's a chance that a manually hyphenated word might appear in the middle of a line after your text is edited, be sure to use a discretionary hyphen. Like a soft hyphen, when a discretionary hyphen is no longer needed it will disappear. For instance, suppose you are working with auto hyphenation turned off and a four syllable word has wrapped to the next line, leaving a white "hole" at the right end of the preceding line. To even out the ragged edge, you decide to manually hyphenate the word. To insert a discretionary hyphen, place the cursor where you want the hyphen to appear. Open the context menu and choose Insert Special Character, then Discretionary Hyphen from the menu of available special characters.

Dashes are different from hyphens, with different size dashes for different purposes. The first type of dash is an em dash. An em is a flexible unit of measure that corresponds to the point size of the type. For instance, an em in 5-point type would be 5-points wide, while an em in 10-point type would be 10-points wide. An em dash is used within a sentence—as in this sentence—to provide a break in thought (a process called interpolation). In the days of typewriters, two hyphens were used to indicate an em dash. You can create an em dash by pressing Shift+Option+Hyphen (Mac) or Shift+Alt+Hyphen (Windows).

An en is half the size of an em; so an en dash is half the size of an em dash. An en dash is used to show a range of numbers or a geographic area and substitutes for the word *to*. When a poster reads that an event runs from September 26–30 in the Minneapolis–St. Paul area, en dashes are used to separate the dates and cities. An en dash is also sometimes used in headlines when an em dash looks too large. You can enter an en dash by pressing Option+Hyphen (Mac) or Alt+Hyphen (Windows). You can also open the context menu while using the Type tool to access em and en dashes from the Insert Special Characters menu, but this method is much slower. You should memorize the shortcut keys.

NOTE: If you can substitute the word "to" for a dash, you should most likely use an en dash, not an em dash.

Calculate Paragraph Line Measure

There are many factors that work together to create good typesetting. We have been concentrating on character-specific considerations. Now our focus will shift to broader foundational concerns regarding point size and line measure (also called line length). There is an inseparable relationship between type size, measured in points, and line measure, indicated in picas. A line measure that is too long in relation to the point size will be difficult to read. For example, if a line measure is short and the point size is large, the copy will look choppy because too many hyphens will be needed. A good rule of thumb: as the point size increases, the line measure should also increase. It is easy to calculate the range of acceptable line measure by multiplying the point size of the type by 2 or 2.5. The resulting number will be the line measure in picas. For instance, 10-point type × 2 = 20 picas and 10-point type × 2.5 = 25 picas. Therefore, a line measure between 20 and 25 picas would be an excellent starting point. Readability is the overriding concern—a measure too long or too short reduces readability. Let's see how easy it is to calculate line measure in InDesign.

1. Create a new 8.5" × 11" document, margins 0.5".
2. Draw a text frame of any size.
3. Fill with placeholder text by using the context menu options or by choosing Type>Fill with Placeholder Text.
4. Select all the type and change the point size to 10 pt.
5. Switch to the Selection tool and on the Control palette highlight the Width field and type **20p** (20 picas). If your unit of measurement is set to inches, InDesign will translate 20 picas into 3.3333 inches as soon as you press the Return key.
6. Print your document.
7. Choose a line of average length. How many "words" appeared in it? The optimal number of words in a single line is nine or ten. How many characters (including spaces) were there? A good middle-range character count would be between 40 and 66 characters.
8. Select your text frame with the Selection tool. In the Width field, increase the measure to 40p and print out the document. Compare the two text blocks, one with a 20p measure and the other 40p. Which one would you prefer to read?

NOTE: A notation of *12/15* means 12-point type on 15-point leading. When you see *12/15 × 30*, it means 12-point type, on 15-point leading, with a line measure of 30 picas.

Proofreader's Marks

Someone sent me this tongue-in-cheek word play for people who use only the computer's spell checking system to proof their documents: *Weave know knead four proofing any moor.* It is essential to proof every project manually, in addition to using your computer's spell check system. Sometimes clients will provide electronic copy, and other times you will type in the copy yourself. Whatever the case may be, all copy needs to be proofed. A series of proofing marks will be introduced throughout this book, and knowing these marks will speed up the proofing process. Out in the workplace, where many people work on a single project, using these marks will give clear direction to others and be a precise method of editing copy.

Proofing is best done with an extra-fine fiber tip pen with a contrasting ink color, such as red or green. Edits are usually noted in pairs—one mark in the line of copy itself flagging where the problem is located, and a corresponding mark in the margin describing the solution. Interpreting a standard set of proofreaders' marks is much easier than trying to decipher a hodge-podge collection of cross-outs, circles, and arrows.

figure | 3–18 |

Memorize these five frequently used proofreaders' marks.

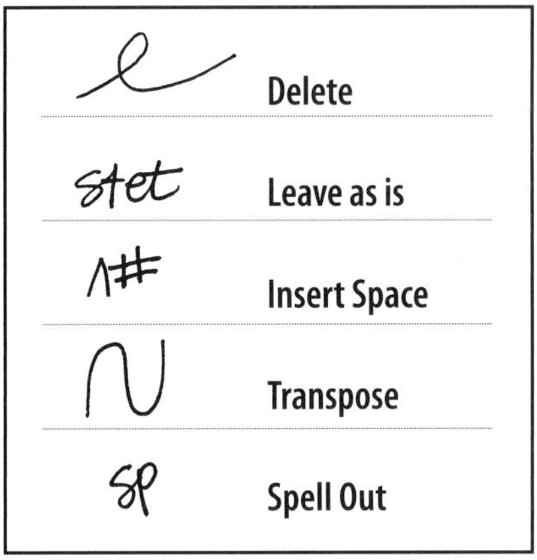

ℓ	Delete
stet	Leave as is
∧#	Insert Space
∩	Transpose
sp	Spell Out

figure | 3–19 |

Proof marks usually come in pairs. Marks within the line indicate the problem. Corresponding margin marks describe the solution.

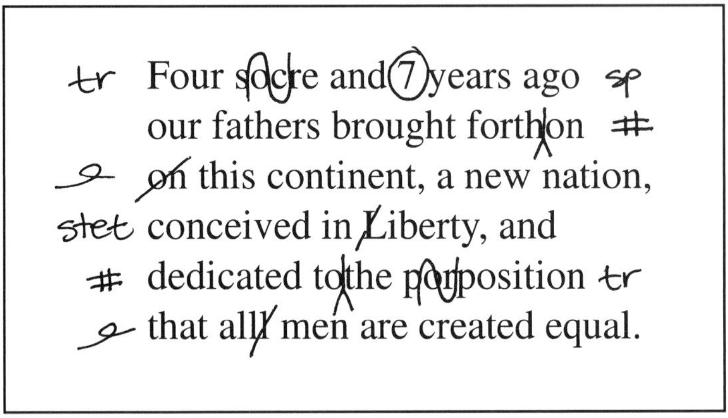

Four score and 7 years ago
our fathers brought forth on
on this continent, a new nation,
conceived in Liberty, and
dedicated to the proposition
that all men are created equal.

SUMMARY

This chapter focused on the basics of typography and typesetting. Nonbreaking spaces and hyphens were introduced, as well as quotation marks and dashes. You learned how to format paragraphs using space after, drop caps, and various indents. These production tips were presented:

- Use soft returns (Shift+Return or Shift+Enter) to manually break lines within a paragraph.

- Use hard returns (Return or Enter) only at the end of a paragraph.

- Do not set text line for line unless absolutely necessary.

Finally, you learned a formula for determining the range of acceptable line measure for body copy.

in review

1. How is point size determined?

2. Why is it helpful to see hidden characters?

3. What is the difference between a hard and soft return? How do you enter each one?

4. How can space be added between paragraphs without pressing the Return key more than once?

5. What does the notation *Myriad Pro Semibold Condensed 12/15 × 30* mean?

6. How do you make a drop cap? How do you make a raised cap?

7. Which palette holds the Optical Margin Alignment option?

8. Describe the uses for each of the following: hyphen, em dash, en dash.

9. What is the guideline for calculating an acceptable line measure?

↗ EXPLORING ON YOUR OWN

The figure on the right shows three text passages in "mystery" typefaces. Now that you know the distinguishing characteristics of letters, go to www.identifont.com and select *Identify a Font*. Answer the questions provided to determine the typefaces used in each passage. If you're not positive your answer is correct, select Not Sure.

A. THE QUICK BROWN FOX JUMPED OVER THE LAZY DOG'S BACK
The quick brown fox jumped over
the lazy dog's back

B. THE QUICK BROWN FOX JUMPED OVER THE LAZY DOG'S BACK
The quick brown fox jumped over
the lazy dog's back

C. THE QUICK BROWN FOX JUMPED OVER THE LAZY DOG'S BACK
The quick brown fox jumped over
the lazy dog's back

The directions for these three projects are included on the CD accompanying this book. Look in the Chapter 03 folder and find the 03 Student Handout.pdf file. Completing these projects will solidify the skills you have just learned.

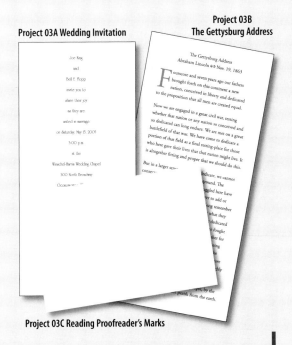

Project 03A Wedding Invitation

**Project 03B
The Gettysburg Address**

Project 03C Reading Proofreader's Marks

ADVENTURES IN DESIGN

CHOOSING TYPEFACES:
CONCORD, CONFLICT, AND CONTRAST

Some readers read everything. Other readers don't read anything. A huge group of readers falls right in the middle. Your ability to use type as a design element will have the greatest effect on this middle group. These readers will glance at a piece and make a decision to read it or not, based on how the piece looks and its relevance to their lives.

A good designer works hard to visually enhance the message the client is trying to communicate. One of the first decisions a designer will make is to choose the typefaces for the publication. You have learned how each typeface conveys a certain personality and the importance of choosing one that is appropriate for your project. You have also learned that the design of the typeface determines its legibility. Typefaces that aren't very legible at smaller point sizes should not be used for body copy.

The readability of any document is the responsibility of the designer. A designer can make the most legible typeface illegible by making poor formatting choices. Designers often experiment by setting "galleys" of sample copy in various typefaces, point sizes, and leading combinations to determine which is the most read-able. A galley is a text frame created at the document's actual column width and then filled with placeholder text. After each galley is formatted with a variation of typeface, point size, and leading, it is are printed and then compared to the other galleys to determine the best readability.

Choosing one typeface is a skill that is not difficult to master. Putting typefaces together, however, requires a bit more attention. Combining type-faces is like picking out an outfit to wear—you wouldn't combine plaid pants with a striped shirt without ask-ing for a visit from the "fashion police." And if you use too many typefaces in one document, your project will look like a ransom note.

In this design adventure you will learn how to differentiate between concordant, contrasting, and conflict-ing type combinations. This knowl-edge will help you choose type com-binations that work—resulting in a well-dressed document.

Concordant Typefaces

Concordant typefaces are members of the same type family. Each typeface bears a resemblance to the other members of

Shorty's
Pub & Grill

5th annual

Portfolio
Review

Appleville
your hometown

Figure A–1 Concordant typeface

Muffie's
pampered pet grooming

Benson & Hedges
Certified Public Accountants

Peterson
Taxidermy

Small Town
Dental Clinic

Figure A–2 Conflicting typefaces

the family. Using concordant typefaces is a safe bet. However, when combining members of the same type family make sure there is enough contrast between faces to get the most desirable effect. You also need to avoid conflicts that happen when a typeface with a narrow width is combined with an extended one. Figure A–1 shows examples of concordant type combinations.

Conflicting Typefaces

Typefaces can conflict because of differences in personality, structure, or weight. Figure A–2 shows examples. Some things to keep in mind include:

- **Don't mix two script typefaces or a script and an italic typeface.** Note: "Flowers and Crafts" in Figure A–3

shows the exception to the rule, with a script face used as an initial cap.

- **Don't mix typefaces whose letter structures are too similar.** Compare the letters *n* and *e* in two lines of the Benson & Hedges example.
- **Don't mix extremely narrow typefaces with expanded typefaces.**
- **Avoid mixing typefaces with very different personalities.**

Contrasting Typefaces

Contrasting type becomes a focal point and helps to create visual hierarchy in the document. A way to test if your document has enough contrast is to hold it at an arm's length and squint at it. If all you see is a gray mass, you probably need to increase the contrast.

Adventures In Design

Notice your own reading patterns—if you see a piece that looks like one continuous sea of letters, you will think twice before reading it. Contrasting type combinations break up a mass of gray textured body copy into individual text blocks. Text blocks make a text-heavy piece easier to read.

Contrast can be created by using variations in size, weight or "color", and letter structure. Figure A–3 shows examples of each one.

Your Turn

Figure A–4 is an Eye-Q test. Look at each combination carefully and place the letter of the best description next to the number above the type combination. After you are finished, compare your answers with those at the bottom of the page.

Figure A–3 Examples of contrast

Contrast created by size

Muffie's
Pampered Pet Grooming

Contrast created by weight or color of type

Contents

Contrast created by structure

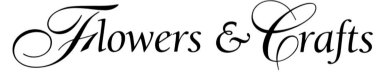

Figure A–4 An Eye-Q test

1. ___ *Madam Ophelia's* *Fortunes*	**6.** ___ Adventures in **Design**
2. ___ Body Beautiful Health Club for Women	**7.** ___ SARAH SMITH *Certified Public* *Accountant*
3. ___ **Smith** & **Barney**	**8.** ___ Wise to resolve and patient to perform. —Homer
4. ___ *Expensive* *Perfume*	**9.** ___ THE FIRST DUTY OF LOVE IS TO LISTEN **Paul** **Tillich**
5. ___ All About Dogs a magazine for today's dog owner	**10.** ___ Sniffer Sniffer Sniffer Sniffer **Sniffer Sniffer** **Sniffer Sniffer**

A. **No contrast**
Although the typefaces are different, there is little color contrast between lines of type.

B. **Conflict**
Typefaces are too close in structure. The letter "e" gives it away.

C. **Personality conflict**
Typeface does not convey the appropriate tone for this business professional.

D. **Conflict**
Combining two script faces is not a good idea.

E. **Conflict**
Too many typefaces create the look of a ransom note.

F. **Concord**
Different weight typefaces are from the same type family.

G. **Contrast**
Created by using differences in typeface, shape, and color.

H. **Conflict**
Combining an unreadable narrow typeface with an extended one.

I. **Color contrast**
Shows how type has color, even though all of it is black.

J. **Conflict**
Combining decorative and script typefaces.

Answers: 1—D, 2—B, 3—G, 4—J, 5—A, 6—F, 7—C, 8—E, 9—H, 10—I

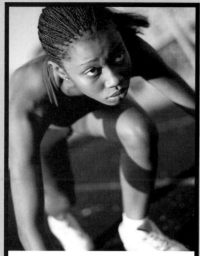

Motivation is what gets you started. **Habit** is what keeps you going.

ᴆ Unknown

4

charting your course

The first three chapters have focused on the basics of InDesign and typography. If you have been waiting for the chance to work with images—as designers love to do—this chapter is for you. We will master the coordinate system, place text and graphics, and fine-tune type. By the end of this chapter you will begin to see the exciting possibilities of creating polished, professional documents with InDesign.

 goals

- **Locate, move, and lock the zero point**
- **Use the coordinate and measurement systems for precise placement and sizing of elements**
- **Create multicolumn and linked text frames**
- **Place text, check spelling, apply paragraph rules, use tracking, and use manual and optical kerning**
- **Place, scale, and crop images**

INDESIGN'S MEASURING SYSTEM

InDesign gives you numerous ways to manage the precise size and placement of text and graphics frames. We will cover these methods in this and upcoming chapters, but before we discuss size and placement issues, let's learn about and experiment with InDesign's measuring system.

Units of Measurement

InDesign will measure in points, picas, inches, inches decimal, millimeters, centimeters, or ciceros. InDesign will even let you make up your own unit of measure under the custom category! Here are a few points to keep in mind:

- You can set whatever unit of measurement you want to use by choosing InDesign (Mac) or Edit (Windows) > Preferences > Units and Increments. In the Ruler Units section of the dialog box you can set the Horizontal and Vertical rulers independently of each other. When you change these ruler preferences with no document open (for example, from inches to picas) these settings become the default for all new documents.

- When you are working in a document, you can quickly change units of measurement by holding down the Control key (Mac) or right-clicking (Windows) and clicking on each of the rulers at the top and side of the page. If no rulers are showing, they have been hidden. Press Command+R (Mac) or Control+R (Windows) to bring them back into view.

Locate, Change, Lock, and Unlock the Zero Point

The zero point is the intersection of the zero measurements on the horizontal and vertical rulers. All measurements are referenced from this point. The default location of the zero point is at the upper left corner of the page (not at the margin). However, there will be times when you will want to move the zero point to another location in your workspace. The next series of steps will show you just how easy InDesign makes it to relocate the zero point.

figure | 4–1

The default location of the zero point is at the upper left corner of the page.

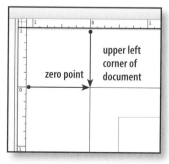

zero point

upper left corner of document

1. Create a new document of any size.

2. Find the zero point for the rulers in your document. The zero point should be in the upper left corner. Figure 4–1 shows what the zero point looks like.

3. To move the zero point, click on the ruler origin point (the upper left corner of your document window where the rulers meet) and drag down into the middle of the page. When you release the mouse button look at the new location of the zero point on your horizontal and vertical rulers. Go back to the ruler origin point and drag the zero point to a second location. Repeat this until you are comfortable with the process.

4. To reset the zero point to the upper left corner of your document, simply double-click the ruler origin point in the upper left corner.

5. Drag the zero point to approximately the middle of your document. Go back to the ruler origin point and open the context menu and select Lock the zero point. You will notice that the icon of the intersecting lines disappears and that it is now impossible to reset the zero point. Use the same method to unlock the zero point.

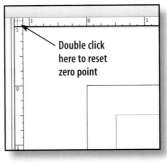

figure | **4–2**

Double click the intersection of the two rulers to reset the zero point.

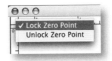

figure | **4–3**

Open the context menu and choose to lock or unlock the zero point.

NOTE: The zero point is where measuring begins, and the position of every object in your document is described by its distance from it. Just like moving a ruler to different places on a piece of paper, the zero point is easily moved horizontally and vertically.

X and Y Coordinates

Every document you create in InDesign is automatically divided into an invisible grid of horizontal and vertical lines, much like graph paper. The horizontal lines on the grid are referred to as the X coordinates; the vertical lines on the grid are referred to as the Y coordinates. The zero point determines whether the values of the coordinates are positive or negative. As you move the cursor to the right of the zero point, your X coordinate is a positive number that increases. As you move left of the zero point, your X coordinate is a negative number that decreases. On the Y axis, moving down vertically from the zero point gives you positive numbers, and moving up from the zero point gives you negative numbers. If you

figure | 4–4 |

Coordinates
increase as you
move to the right
and down from
the zero point.

had graphing in high school math, you may already be familiar with this type of coordinate system. However, as Figure 4–4 shows the vertical axis in InDesign is exactly the opposite of what you are used to in algebra. Remember, in InDesign's coordinate system the numbers on the Y axis are negative as you move up from the zero point.

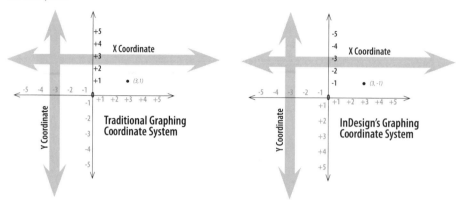

The X and Y coordinates for all the objects in your document are displayed in the Control palette. The values in the X and Y fields are displayed in the measurement system that you have selected to work in. Because the document area is invisibly mapped into a grid like graph paper, it becomes easy to describe the location of each element on the page as being so many units from the horizontal or vertical zero point (expressed as either positive or negative). But how do you know what point on your object InDesign is measuring to? Is it the center of the object, the right or left edge, or one of the corners?

figure | 4–5 |

These coordinates
plot exact placement
on the document.

X refers to horizontal
coordinate

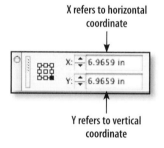

Y refers to vertical
coordinate

This point is known as the point of reference. Just as InDesign lets you move the zero point to suit your needs, you have the flexibility to set the reference point of an object to one of nine positions. It can be at any of the four corners, the middle of the top, bottom, right or left edges, or right in the center of the object. Let's see exactly how the coordinate system and an object's point of reference work together.

1. Create a 6" × 6" document. Make sure your units of measure are set to inches and your zero point is in the upper left corner of the document.

2. Select the Rectangle tool and draw anywhere in your document to create a rectangle. Notice the values of the X and Y coordinates in the Control palette.

3. Select your rectangle with the Selection tool (black arrow) and move it to the right. Watch the X coordinate increase as it moves to the right. Move it back to the left and watch the X coordinate decrease.

4. Now move the rectangle up and down on the page. As it moves up the page, the Y coordinate decreases, and as you move it down the page the Y coordinate increases.

5. Now, look at the left end of the Control palette and you will see a series of nine small squares arranged in three rows and three columns (see Figure 4–6). One of these squares will be black and the rest will be white. This control is called the proxy. The proxy indicates the position of the reference point for the currently selected object. (The proxy is also found on the Transform palette that you can open by choosing Window>Transform. Working with the proxy on either the Transform palette or the Control palette will give you the same results.) Look for the black square; it indicates where the reference point is located on your rectangle. Make sure your rectangle is still selected and click the center square in the proxy. The center square turns black, which means you have made the center of your selected rectangle the reference point. With the center black box on the proxy still selected, write down the X and Y coordinates of your rectangle.

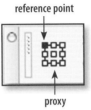

reference point

proxy

figure | 4–6 |

The dark square in the proxy control shows an object's reference point.

NOTE: For most items the proxy is made up of nine squares. However, if the selected item is a straight line, the proxy will have only three squares active. These indicate the two ends and the middle point. If the selected item is a guideline, the proxy will show a horizontal or vertical line with only a center reference point. You cannot change the reference point of a guideline.

6. Now click on the upper left square on the proxy and read the X and Y coordinates. Even though you have not moved your rectangle, your X and Y coordinates are different than the ones you wrote down a moment ago. This is because you have changed the reference point—it's now the upper left corner of your rectangle, instead of the center.

7. Let's place the rectangle in the exact center of your six by six-inch document page. Make sure that your rectangle is selected, and click the center square on the proxy. Since your document is a six-inch square, three inches over from the side of the square and three inches down from the top would be the center of the page. Type **3** in both the X and Y coordinate fields and press Return. The rectangle should jump to the exact center of the page. Now the center point of the rectangle is located exactly at the center point of your page.

8. Select the rectangle and click the upper right reference point in the proxy. Type **6** in the X coordinate field and press Return. The rectangle should jump to align with the right edge of the page.

9. Now type **0** in the Y coordinate field and press Return. The rectangle jumps to align with the top of the page.

You can now see the relationship between the reference point of an object and InDesign's X and Y coordinate system. The intersection of the coordinates displayed in the Control palette always indicates the position of the reference point that you have selected in the proxy.

Understanding Paths and Selection Tools

A shape or line created in InDesign is called a path. A path can be a closed shape such as a rectangle, or an open shape such as line. The basic component of a path is a point. A path can have as little as two points—such as a line with beginning and ending points, or it can be complex, with numerous points. The straight or curved lines that connect the points are called segments. A simple rectangle is in reality a closed path made up of points and straight connecting segments.

figure | 4–7

The Selection tool
and the Direct
Selection tool.

InDesign has two tools specifically designed for working with paths. Let's begin with the black arrow, the Selection tool. The Selection tool can be activated (when you are not using the Type tool) by pressing V. The Selection tool transforms a whole object—changing attributes such as size, scaling, position, skew and rotation angle. It focuses on the outer dimensions and structure of an entire path. When you click on an open or closed path with the Selection tool all the points on the path are selected. If the object has a fill you can click on the fill to select all the points. With all the points selected you can move the entire object. When you select another object with the tool, the previous object is deselected.

If you have several objects to select, you can select the first object and then add to the selection by pressing the Shift key while selecting the next object. Another way of selecting multiple paths with the Selection tool is to go to a blank space on the document and drag a rectangle (called a marquee) around the paths to select. Since the tool is designed to select whole paths, you can just touch the edge of each path with the marquee and the whole path will be selected.

The Direct Selection tool—the white arrow—is next to the Selection tool in the toolbox. When you are not using the Type tool you can press A to activate it. The Direct Selection tool is designed to select individual points or segments on a path. When a point is selected it changes from a hollow square to a filled square. When your Direct Selection cursor is over a line segment a slash appears next to it. When it is over a point, a box appears next to it. Use the Selection tool to change the dimension of an object. Use the Direct Selection tool to change the shape of an object.

When you want to select all the points of a path using the Direct Selection tool, you can press the Option (Mac) or Alt (Windows) key while clicking on the path. You can also draw a rectangular marquee, making sure all points are within the marquee's rectangle. If the object has a fill you can click on the fill with the Direct Selection tool and move the whole path.

Knowing what tool you are using and understanding that tool's capabilities is essential to using InDesign effectively.

Width and Height Coordinates

Delete the rectangle from your document and replace it with an ellipse. In the next series of steps you are going to resize this shape using the selection tools and the W (width) and H (height) fields on the Control palette.

1. To draw an ellipse, click on the tiny triangle in the lower right corner of the Rectangle tool and choose the Ellipse tool. Click and drag an ellipse in your document.
2. Deselect the ellipse you have just drawn by pressing Shift+Command+A (Mac) or Shift+Control+A (Windows).
3. Click the edge of your ellipse with the Direct Selection tool. Five hollow squares appear on the ellipse—one in the center, and one on each quadrant of the outer edge. These are called

anchor points. A hollow box indicates that an anchor point can be edited or changed. You should also see lines extending from one or more anchor points. These lines are called direction lines. If you drag any of the hollow anchor points or the end of a direction line, the shape will be changed. Experiment with moving the direction lines to change the shape and then undo your changes by pressing Command+Z (Mac) or Control+Z (Windows) until the shape is back to the original.

figure | 4–8 |

Drag the anchor point's direction line handles to change the ellipse's shape.

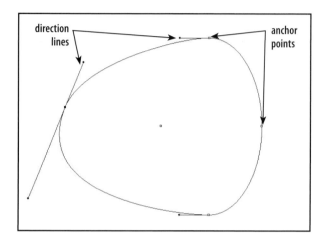

4. Deselect the object by clicking in a blank spot in your document or by using the keyboard shortcut.
5. With the Direction Selection tool, click first on the edge of the shape and then on the center anchor point. All the hollow anchor points become filled, which means they are not editable. Drag the center square and move the ellipse to another part of the page. With the anchor points still selected, drag the edge of the shape and move it again.
6. Now switch to the Selection tool by pressing V. The ellipse will look much different. You will see the rectangular bounding box that shows the outer boundaries of the shape. On the bounding box you will see eight tiny squares and a ninth square in the middle of the ellipse. The center square will be filled, and the outer squares will be hollow. These boxes are called handles.
7. Drag any of the handles to change the dimension of the ellipse.
8. There are several ways to move the entire ellipse: drag the center point or click on and drag the edge of the ellipse or click and drag a section of the bounding box. Use each of these methods and practice moving the ellipse. (Be careful not to drag a hollow handle, this will resize the object).

9. Now, note the X and Y coordinates displayed in the Control palette. The coordinates indicate the location of the reference point of the ellipse designated in the proxy. Look at the W and H coordinates. These measurements show the width and height of the selected shape. As you drag on the handles on the bounding box of the ellipse, the dimensions in the Control palette will also change.

10. Type **4** in the W field and **3** in the H field and press Return. Your ellipse should change size.

11. With the 4" × 3" ellipse selected, click on the center reference point on the proxy. Now type **3** in the X coordinate field and **3** in the Y coordinate field and press Return. The ellipse should now be centered on your page.

In a nutshell…

- The zero point for the rulers can be moved anywhere on the page.

- The reference point for an object can be the center, corners of the bounding box or any of the midpoints on the bounding box's sides.

- The X and Y coordinates show an object's location on the page. This is measured from the zero point to the object's reference point.

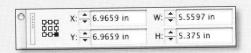

- The W and H fields show an object's dimensions.

- Dimensional changes are made in relationship to the location of the object's reference point. The reference point is the anchor from which dimensional changes are made. If your reference point is the upper left corner of a frame and you increase width and height by one inch, the right and bottom edges of your frame will both move one inch. If your reference point is the center of a frame and you increase width and height by one inch, all edges will move out from the center one-half inch. Always be aware of where your reference point is when you set new W and H measurements.

WORKING WITH TEXT

The copy in your document communicates a message while adding texture, color, shape, and contrast to your layout. Your ability to use text as a design element is an important skill to develop. In this next section you will learn how to create multiple column text frames and import (or Place) text from word processing documents.

Multicolumn Text

Creating text columns within text frames is a simple process. When the Control Palette is in the Paragraph mode you can find the column options near the right end of the palette (see Figure 4–9). The space between the columns is called a gutter (or alley). To change the width of the gutter, select the text frame and press Command+B (Mac) or Control+B (Windows) to open the Text Frame Options dialog box. In the Gutter field, enter the desired value for the gutter width. You can type the value in a unit of measure such as 1p (1 pica).

figure | 4–9 |

Click the up and down arrows or type a number in the Number of Columns field to create multiple columns inside a text frame.

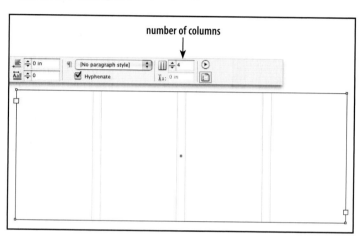

1. Draw a frame in your document. Select the Type tool and click the frame to instantly convert it to a text frame. Select the Paragraph button on the Control palette and change the number of columns to three. Press Command+B (Mac) or Control+B (Windows) to change the gutter width to p6 (six points).

2. Choose Type>Fill with Placeholder Text. Text will fill your text frame. With the Type tool active, select all the text using the shortcut key and reduce the point size until the last text column is empty.

3. Place the cursor in the middle of a line in the column. Press Enter on the number keypad. This makes text jump to the next column. If you are in the habit of pressing the Return key over and over to force text to jump to another column—don't! Simply insert the cursor where you want to text to break and press Enter on the number keypad.

Don't get into the bad habit of pressing the Return key multiple times to force the text to flow to the next column. If your layout changes, you will need to delete all those manual keyboard entries. When you press the Enter key on the number keypad to insert a column break character, it will be much easier to simply remove it, if you have to revise the column break later.

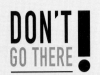

Creating columns within text frames is simple and useful for projects. More often, however, designers will create separate text frames in different places on the page and flow the text between the frames. The Place command allows you to bring in the text someone else typed using a variety of word processors. What a timesaver!

Placing Text

The keyboard shortcut for placing text—Command+D (Mac) or Control+D (Windows)—is one you will want to memorize. You will use it again and again to import text or graphics. Pressing the keyboard shortcut brings up the Place dialog box.

Two important features of the Place dialog box are the choices to Show Import Options and Replace Selected Item, in the lower left corner. Show Import Options, among other things, gives you control over how different versions of Microsoft Word text files are handled. Choosing Replace Selected Item will replace the contents of a selected text frame with the new placed text.

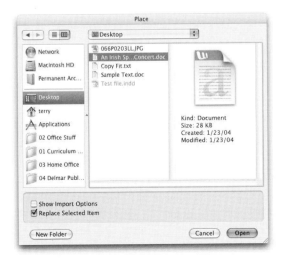

figure | 4–10

The Place dialog box.

Placing Text by Dropping into a Text Frame

In this exercise we will place text into a frame that you have already created. Create a new 8.5" × 11" document and let's work with placing text.

1. Draw a 6" × 9" text frame, with the reference point in the center, X coordinate: 4.25, and Y: 5.5. Create three columns with a 1-pica gutter.

2. Insert the project CD. Press Command+D (Mac) or Control+D (Windows) to open the Place dialog box. Select the text file called 04 Copyfit.doc, found in the Chapter 4 folder on the compact disc.

3. Uncheck Show Import Options and Replace Selected Item in the lower left corner of the dialog box.

4. Press Return and move the cursor to the upper left corner of the text box. You will see tiny lines of type enclosed with long parentheses. This icon means your text cursor is loaded and ready to place text into an existing frame. Now click in the upper left corner and type should flow into all three columns.

5. Notice the square with the red plus sign (+) in the lower right column. The red plus is the overset symbol—it means there is more text than the text frame will hold.

6. To delete the overset text, place the cursor at the end of the copy. Press Shift+Command+End then press Delete (Mac) or Shift+Control+End then press Delete (Windows). The plus sign should disappear as the text beyond the frame is deleted.

7. Look at the tiny numbers present in the document you just placed. This is the copy count, which gives you a pretty good idea of how many words will fit in this text box. Copyfit allows you to design the project first and then show the copywriter how many words will be needed for the job.

figure | 4–11

A red plus (+) sign means there is too much text for the frame, meaning the text is overset.

Place Text by Dragging a New Frame

In this exercise you will drag the Type tool to create a text frame.

1. Delete the three-column text box. Your document should be blank.

2. Press Command+D (Mac) or Control+D (Windows) and select the 04 Copyfit.doc file again. Press Return. Move the loaded cursor over the blank document and look carefully at its shape. This time you will not see parentheses around the text cursor. Instead, you will see straight lines on the top and left edge. This icon indicates that a new frame needs to be created for the text.

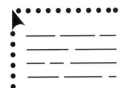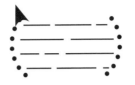

figure | 4–12 |

Loaded text cursors. The right icon indicates that text will be dropped into an existing frame. The left icon shows that a new text frame will be created.

3. Drag the loaded text cursor to create a frame. When you release the mouse, text will flow into the new text frame.

4. Change the Width and Height to 5" × 7" and create three columns. Again, notice the overset symbol in the out port in the lower right corner.

Place Text by Dropping

This method of placing text drops the text into the document and lets it spread from margin guide to margin guide.

1. Delete the text frame from your document.

2. Open the Place dialog box by using the keyboard shortcut and select 04 Copyfit.doc one more time. Press Return. This time, click the cursor anywhere on the document. A text frame will stretch from margin to margin with the top positioned wherever you clicked on the page. Notice the overset symbol.

Managing Text Flow

Now that you have mastered the basics of placing text, it's time to learn how to manage text overflow.

Manual Text Flow

When you use manual text flow, you direct the text exactly where to flow to. You have total control, but as the "manual" name implies, this method is the slowest.

1. Create a new document. Page size 5" × 7", landscape orientation, three columns with 1p gutter, 0.5" margins. Press Return.

2. Look at the document, particularly the column guides. Notice that there is no text frame on the page. The column indicators are only guides—ready to hold a graphics or text frame.

3. Again, place the 04 Copyfit.doc file by using the keyboard shortcut. Move the cursor over to the upper left corner of the document. The cursor shape indicates a new text box will be created. Click in the upper left corner and the first column will fill with copy. Notice the overset symbol at the bottom of the

first column. Click on the text out port with a selection tool to reload the text cursor.

4. Click in the upper left corner of the second column to flow text into this column. Repeat this procedure to fill the third column.

5. Place the cursor at the end of the text in the last column. Delete the overset text by pressing Shift+Command+End then Delete (Mac) or Shift+Control+End then Delete (Windows).

Semi-automatic Text Flow

Flowing text manually from column to column is a neat technique, but imagine how tedious it would be if you had to do that for a 10-page document! InDesign is always one step ahead of the user—and has designed a second way to flow text called semi-automatic.

1. Select all the text in your document and then delete by using keyboard shortcuts.

2. Place the 04 Copyfit.doc file once again.

3. This time, hold down the Option (Mac) or Alt (Windows) key as you hold the loaded cursor in the upper left corner of the first column. Notice the shape of the cursor changes into a snake pattern each time you press the Option key. (Press the Option key a few times to get used to the difference between the cursors.) This cursor means your text will be placed in semi-automatic text flow mode.

4. Hold down the Option or Alt key and click in the upper left corner. The text will fill the first column and the cursor will remain loaded. Hold down the Option key and click in the second column. The text flows into the middle column. As long as you continue to hold the Option or Alt key as you click to drop text, you remain in semi-automatic flow mode the remaining text will remain loaded in the text icon.

5. Continue in semi-automatic mode and fill the last column. Delete the overset text.

Automatic Text Flow

Manual and semi-automatic text flow provide you the most control regarding the placement of text in individual text frames on a single page or a series of noncontiguous pages. Automatic text flow is another method of flowing text. It is fast—and automatically inserts the pages required to hold the entire text passage.

1. Create a new file, 3" × 5", and 0.5" margins.

2. Place the 04 Copyfit.doc file so that you have a loaded cursor.

3. Hold down the Shift key as you move the cursor to the upper left corner of the page. Click inside the page margins.

4. Open the Pages palette located at the right of the screen (or choose Window>Pages). Notice that you now have more than one page in your document. When you place text in automatic flow mode, InDesign automatically added as many pages as necessary to hold the placed text.

Automatic Text Flow with Fixed Number of Pages

The automatic text flow option is great for many projects—but what if you must make the text fit on only four pages?

1. Create a 3" × 5" document, 0.5" margins, and 4 pages.

2. Load the text cursor with 04 Copyfit.doc.

3. This time, hold down Shift+Option (Mac) or Shift+Alt (Windows) as you click and drop the text onto the upper left corner of page one. The text will fill the available space on the four pages and then stop. Notice the familiar overset symbol in the out port at the end of page four. Now you can select all your text and adjust the point size and leading to make the copy fit into your four-page document.

figure | 4–13

Remember what these loaded icons mean. A.) text will be placed into a new text frame. B.) text will be placed into an existing frame. C.) overflow text will be reloaded in cursor. D.) overflow text will add enough pages necessary to hold text.

About Threaded Text Frames

Text can flow between frames that are threaded. Threaded text frames act as a series of connected frames, giving you the ability to select all the type in all the threaded frames. What a great way to globally change typefaces or point sizes quickly!

Seeing Links and Threads

Being able to understand the visual cues in the document will greatly assist you with text management. This exercise will familiarize you with using threaded text frames.

1. Create a new document, 8.5" X 11", margins 0.5".

2. Scatter three frames on the document. Make some frames tall and some wide.

3. Place the 04 Copyfit.doc file. Drop the text into the first frame. Again, you will see the overset symbol in the lower right of your frame.

4. Choose either of the Selection tools and click on the text overflow box. The cursor is loaded with text and the red plus sign changes to a blue triangle. The blue triangle means this box is now an "out port".

5. Move your cursor over to the next text frame and its icon will change into two chain links. This icon means that as soon as text is dropped into the frame, the first and second frames will be threaded together. Copy will flow freely from the first frame to the second as text is edited or as frame dimensions change.

6. Flow copy into the third frame using the same process.

7. Now from the menu bar, choose View>Show Text Threads. You will see lines connecting the in and out ports on your frames. These show the direction and order of the text flow. A triangle in the out port means that the text is linked to another frame. A plus in the out port means that text is overset—that there is too much text to fit in the frame. When the first in port and the last out port in a series of linked text frames are empty, it means that all the text has been placed.

8. Don't close your file—we're going to use it for the next demo.

figure | 4–14 |

An empty in port and an empty out port mean all available text has been placed.

in port ⟶

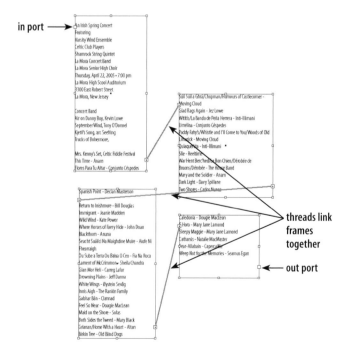

threads link frames together

⟵ out port

Unlinking Text Frames

There will be times when you flow text into the wrong frame. Of course, you can simply press the Undo shortcut, but that method is only practical if you catch your error shortly after it was made. Here's another way to unlink threaded text frames.

1. Select the text frame in the middle of your text thread.
2. Double-click on the in port or the out port. If you click on the in port, the text flow will be cut off at the in port and there will be a text overflow symbol in the first frame. If you double-click on the out port, text will be cut off at that point. The third frame is now empty and a text overflow symbol appears in the second frame.

Underlining and Paragraph Rules

During the days of old-fashioned typing, people used to underline text to add emphasis or to indicate the name of a book. Unfortunately, that habit has carried over into the world of digital type, and most people simply click an icon to underline a word or sentence. In electronic publishing, however, you will use italics to indicate the name of a book or to add emphasis. A heavier typeface can also be used to make a word or phrase stand out. Typewriter-style underlines were not often used in good typesetting because they cut through descenders and could not be adjusted for weight.

<u>Unprofessional Typography</u>

figure | 4–15

These old-fashioned word processing/typewriter underlines are not often used in typesetting. Instead, italics are used to indicate titles or add emphasis.

If you do need to underline text, InDesign has a complete and sophisticated way for you to do that. Select the text you would like to underline, with the Control palette in Character mode, click on the round Palette menu button at the far right. Select Underline Options from the menu. In the Underline Options dialog box, first check the Underline On option box then adjust the weight, offset, color, and type of the line as desired.

figure | 4-16 |

InDesign allows you to offset and adjust the weight of underlines used within paragraphs.

InDesign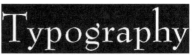

Paragraph Rules

Paragraph rules may look like underlining, but they are an altogether different matter. Paragraph rules are design elements, and InDesign allows you to set rules in two places in each paragraph: 1) on or above the baseline of the first line of text, or 2) at the end of a paragraph. The Paragraph Rules function allows you to use color, styles, indents and offsets to create just about any rule you'd ever want. Figure 4–17 shows some paragraph rules in action.

figure | 4-17 |

A multitude of rule lines can be created using the Paragraph Rules dialog box.

Rules can be the length of the text.

Rules can be the length of the column.

Rules can be indented from the left or right.

Rules can be above or below the paragraph.
Rules can be offset.

Rules can be many styles and sizes.

The Paragraph Rules dialog box can be accessed by using a keyboard shortcut: Command+Option+J (Mac) or Control+Alt+J (Windows), or by clicking on the palette menu in the Paragraph Control palette and choosing Paragraph Rules from the menu.

Applying a Rule Below a Paragraph

Whenever possible, apply rules as part of the paragraph formatting. A document that is filled with lines created with the Line tool is hard to edit because each line must be individually repositioned. Lines that are set as rules within the paragraph will reflow as the copy changes.

1. Create a new document using the default settings. Draw a text frame and type your name on the first line and your phone number on the second line. Use a hard return between the lines, and increase the point size to 48 points on 60-point leading.

2. With the blinking cursor somewhere in the first paragraph (the first line), press Command+Option+J (Mac) or Control+Alt+J (Windows) to access the Paragraph Rules dialog box. (Or you can access the palette menu on the Paragraph mode Control palette and choose Paragraph Rules.)

3. Select Rule Below from the list and check the Rule On option box. Choose 8 pt in the Weight field menu, and Dotted in the Type field menu. The Width field should be set to Text, and the Offset to 0.25 in. When you increase the offset you push the rule farther down, away from the baseline. Press Return and your type should look like the sample in Figure 4–18. Keep this document open for the next exercise.

The Width field in the Paragraph Rules dialog box can be set to Column or Text. With Column selected, the line stretches from the left edge of the column to the right edge. With Text selected, the line extends only as long as the last line of text.

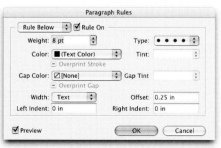

Your Name Here
• • • • • • • • • • • •
Your Phone Number

figure | 4–18

The Paragraph Rules dialog box in action.

Applying a Rule Above a Paragraph

A rule above a paragraph will appear on the first baseline or will be offset above the first baseline of the paragraph. Applying a rule above a paragraph can be a little tricky because you'll need to add an offset value so that the rule doesn't cut through your type.

1. Click in the line that contains your name. Open the Paragraph Rules dialog box and make sure that Rule Below is selected in the list, then turn the Rule On option off. Press Return.

2. Place the cursor in the line with your phone number. Open the Paragraph Rules dialog box and select Rule Above from the list. Be sure to check the Rule On option box. Select a type and weight of your choice. Because the rule line will be drawn on the baseline you'll need to enter a value in the Offset field. Type **p48** (48 points) to push the line up off the baseline.

Check Spelling

It's a good idea to always run a spell check before printing a document. But remember, even though InDesign's spell check function is excellent, it doesn't replace manual proofing. Both methods should be used to ensure accurate copy. To check spelling, simply press Command+I (Mac) or Control+I (Windows). When the Check Spelling dialog box appears, you will need to make a choice in the Search list. The following list describes the options:

• The All Documents option checks the spelling of all open InDesign documents.

• The Document option checks the entire document you are working on. This is a great feature unless you have several pages of directory information including last names. If you would prefer to skip those sections of the document, choose the next choice.

• The Story option checks the spelling in the selected text frame and all threaded text frames.

• The To End of Story option checks all the words beyond the blinking cursor.

• If you have text highlighted before opening the Check Spelling dialog box, then you'd have another choice. Selection checks the spelling of only a highlighted word or text.

Once you have made a choice in the Search list, simply click Start to begin the process. InDesign will alert you of any questionable words and possible errors. When the checking is complete click Done to dismiss the dialog box.

Typography

When you begin working with type you learn a new specialized vocabulary. When typesetters get together they speak in a language that the uninitiated cannot understand!

Understanding Tracking and Kerning

You already know what leading is. Leading is the vertical spacing between lines of type, measured from baseline to baseline.

Tracking adjusts horizontal spacing between all the characters on a line. A single paragraph can contain characters with many different tracking values.

Take a look at the text in Figure 4–19. Nothing unusual about the spacing between letters, is there?

Tracking is the space between letters.

Leading is the distance between lines of type.

figure | 4–19 |

Tracking is horizontal spacing between the characters.

Positive tracking increases spacing between characters; negative tracking decreases spacing between characters. The text on the first line in Figure 4–20 demonstrates the effect of positive tracking.

- Tracking adjusts the **horizontal** space between *many letters.*
- Kerning adjusts the **horizontal** space between letter *pairs.*
- Leading adjusts the **vertical** distance between *lines* of type.

figure | 4–20 |

Tracking adjusts horizontal spacing. Notice the effect that positive tracking has on the top line. The tracking value is set at 100.

Now look at the same text with negative tracking, in Figure 4–21.

• Tracking adjusts the **horizontal** space between *many letters*.
• Kerning adjusts the **horizontal** space between letter *pairs*.
• Leading adjusts the **vertical** distance between *lines* of type.

figure | **4–21** |

Notice the effect that negative tracking has on the top line. Its tracking value is set at -60.

Many people get leading and tracking mixed up, resulting in ascenders bumping into descenders and scrunched-up letter spacing. Just remember:

• Leading is vertical. Tracking is horizontal.

• You will always use a leading value. You will sometimes use a tracking value.

Adjusting Word Spacing with Tracking

The best way to understand tracking is to apply it to type.

1. Create a new letter-sized document.
2. Draw a text frame, type your full name and change the point size to 60-point.
3. To "tighten" the tracking of your text: Highlight what you want tracked, hold down Option (Mac) or Alt (Windows), and press the Left Arrow key near the number pad. At first the text will still be readable, but if you keep pressing the arrow key, notice that the text ultimately reverses itself. Be careful not to overdo tracking!
4. Delete the text box and draw a new one. Type your name in it again in 60-point type. Select all the text.
5. Press Option (Mac) or Alt (Windows) and the Right Arrow key to "loosen" the tracking. Keep pressing the right arrow key and you will see that it doesn't take very long for your name to become just a series of individual letters. Again, be conservative with tracking. When misused, it inhibits readability.

You will occasionally use tracking to fine-tune your type. Tracking values are indicated in the Control palette when it is in Character mode (see Figure 4–22). At times you may want to use negative tracking to give your text a little more refined look, especially with headline type.

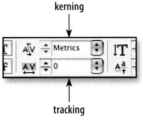

figure | 4–22

Tracking values are shown in the lower field; the kerning field is just above.

You will also use tracking to fit troublesome lines of type into the line measure. While InDesign has taken care of much of this for you with its multiline composition feature, there will be times when you will need to manually adjust tracking. For instance, at the end of a paragraph, you should avoid leaving part of a hyphenated word or any word shorter than four letters on its own line. As a typesetter, you need to make a decision: either tighten tracking slightly to make room for the word in the line above, or loosen tracking to bring the whole word or an additional word to the last line of a paragraph. The goal is to alter the word spacing so slightly that no one will ever notice. You have gone too far with your tracking if the tracked text looks darker or lighter than the surrounding text. Tracking should be invisible to the untrained eye.

figure | 4–23

Can you find the portions of text tracked too loose and too tight?

> Onulla at nim verat vel doluptat acin eugait adigna core dolobor perostis eu faci te dignis dolor in ullum nullaor alit ad molor at. Ut wisciduisl utpat.
>
> Ex exero conse dolore tis at adiam, qui tat wisit dolestrud modo dionsed tate tet velit ad exer sisse feu feu feuguer-oOnse facil euguer alis elismolore faccum zzrit aliquisit eumsan utatissit praestin utationum veliquat.
>
> Utpat. Faccum quatuer sit dunt nim zzriure do cor incipit nonum dolorem in ut vel i

Adjust Character Spacing with Manual Kerning

Closely related to tracking is kerning. Kerning is the horizontal spacing between two characters only. You should kern letter pairs when spacing between characters is too wide or too narrow. For instance, look closely at the number 740 shown in Figure 4–24. Before you started reading this book, it would have looked perfectly fine. But with your professional eye, you now see that the spacing between the 7 and 4 looks much wider than the spacing between the 4 and the 0.

figure | 4–24

A letter pair that needs to be kerned.

740

Kerning will correct this. Place your cursor in between the 7 and the 4. Do not highlight any text. Use the same keyboard shortcuts for negative kerning as you would for negative tracking; press Option-Left-Arrow (Mac) or Alt-Left-Arrow (Windows). The amount of adjustment is shown in the Kerning field in the Control palette when it is in Character formatting mode. InDesign adjusts the kerning in units of one-thousandth of an em. (You will remember that an em is a unit of measure equivalent to the point size—an em space in 10-point type is 10 points wide.)

figure | 4–25

Compare the space between the 7 and 4 in the number above, with those in Figure 4–24. The space between this number pair has been reduced by kerning in an attempt to even out the visual spacing.

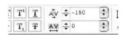

740

A more common place to kern letter pairs is when using drop and raised caps. Figure 4–26 shows what they look like without kerning.

Words strain, crack, and sometimes break, under the burden.

T.S. Eliot

Words strain, crack, and sometimes break, under the burden.

T.S. Eliot

figure | 4–26

Always look for places to kern between letters when drop and raised caps are used. These examples need kerning between the "W" and "o".

There are some letter pairs that usually need kerning. Your goal is to have the "color" of text look even. Big gaps between letter pairs make a word look "airy." Figure 4–27 shows common letter pairs that usually need kerning.

To	WA	To	WA
Tr	we	TR	we
Ta	P.	Ta	P.
Yo	T.	Yo	T.
yo	TA	yo	TA
Ya	PA	Ya	TA
Wo	Po	Wo	Po
Wa		Wa	

figure | 4–27 |

These letter pairs frequently need kerning. The letter pairs in the left example are in Times New Roman, and the spacing is good. The samples on the right demonstrate how kerning is also affected by the selected typeface.

Automatic Optical Kerning

When professionals design a font they build in rules for letter-pair spacing. Unfortunately, the built-in kerning parameters don't cover every letter-pair scenario. That is why manual kerning is sometimes needed. But InDesign has gone one step further. It allows you to select Optical Kerning from the Control palette when in the Paragraph formatting mode. With Optical Kerning selected, InDesign goes beyond the built-in letter pair parameters and makes kerning decisions based on the shape of each character to even out how the type looks. This is a huge timesaver. InDesign does a fantastic job of making text look great—with very little effort.

WORKING WITH IMAGES

The perfect image combined with beautiful type, form a "one-two punch" resulting in a document that is both memorable and effective. Most of the images you use will be either scanned, created in a vector-based drawing program such as Adobe Illustrator or Macromedia Freehand, or created in a pixel-based program such as Adobe Photoshop. As powerful as InDesign is, it is not a true drawing program. But you shouldn't underestimate InDesign's drawing capabilities. If you have already used Adobe Illustrator, you have seen tools and functions in InDesign that look very familiar. If you haven't used Illustrator, you will learn about many basic drawing functions that are common to both programs later in the book.

InDesign can place a variety of file formats including EPS, TIFF, and JPEG. Another great feature of InDesign is its ability to place native Adobe Illustrator (AI) and Photoshop (PSD) files without conversion to an EPS or TIFF format.

Three methods of placing artwork will be discussed in this section: place and drop, place and drag, and place into a frame. You will need to load the CD that accompanies this book before trying these exercises.

Place and Drop Images

The same keyboard shortcut is used to place text or images: Command+D (Mac) or Control+D (Windows). InDesign does not require a specific type of frame to hold a graphic and another to hold text. In fact, as you have already seen when placing text, you don't need a frame at all! Let's get started learning how to place images.

1. Create a new document, 8.5" × 11".
2. Open the Place dialog box. Navigate to the Chapter 04>Artwork/Resources folder on your CD. Choose 04 Demo.tif. Press Return.
3. Notice the loaded icon looks like a paintbrush surrounded by straight lines. Just as when placing text, the square lines indicate that a new frame will be created. Click in the upper left corner of your document and the photo will appear at full size.

Place and Drag Images

With this method you will drag the loaded icon to create the frame for the graphic.

1. Delete the graphic you just placed in the document by selecting the frame with the Selection tool and then pressing the Delete key.
2. Open the Place dialog box and find 04 Demo.tif again.
3. This time click and drag out a frame. When you release the mouse, the graphic will fill the frame. However, if your frame is not large enough, some parts of the graphic will not show.
4. Switch to the Direct Selection tool and select the placed graphic. If you see the bounding box become a very different shape it is because InDesign is showing the actual size of the graphic. This helps you to see how the frame would need to be adjusted to contain the entire graphic. Press the Delete key to remove the image from the frame. (Do not delete the entire frame.)

Place into an Existing Frame

Placing a graphic into an existing frame is the third method of getting a picture into your file.

1. Place 04 Demo.tif one more time.
2. This time position the loaded icon over the empty frame you created in the last exercise. Notice how the shape of the icon changes from square lines to curved lines surrounding the brush. Just like when placing text, this icon means the photo will be placed into an existing frame.
3. Click and the picture will drop into the frame. Note that the image is placed at full size, no matter what size the frame is.

Scaling and Cropping Images

The best way to understand graphics and frames is to experiment with them. After completing the following exercises you will be comfortable working with graphics frames.

Move the Graphic and the Frame

In this exercise you will use the Selection tool to move the photo and the frame as a single unit.

1. Create a new letter-size document. Draw a an ellipse approximately 2.5 inches wide. Place 04 Demo.tif in the frame.
2. Switch to the Selection tool and select the frame. You will see a square bounding box around the circle frame. This is a visual cue that you have selected both the frame and the photo (see Figure 4–28).
3. Drag to move the frame and photo around the page.

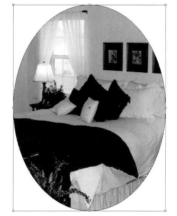

figure | **4–28**

When you are using the Selection tool and see a bounding box around the picture frame, you know that you have both the picture and the frame selected.

Resize the Graphic and the Frame

The Selection tool can be used to resize the image and frame together as a single unit.

1. Select the frame again with the Selection tool. Hold down Shift+Command (Mac) or Shift+Control (Windows) and

drag any of the frame handles. The photo and frame will resize proportionately.

2. Use Undo to return your frame and graphic to their original size.

Resize the Frame Only

The Selection tool can also be used to resize the frame, without modifying the image inside.

1. Drag any of the frame handles with the Selection tool. Do not hold down Shift+Command or Shift+Control.
2. The frame size will change, but the image will not move or change size. It is exactly as it was initially placed. Press Shift to keep the proportions of the frame as you drag to resize it.

Move the Image Inside the Frame

When you want to modify the image that is inside a frame, you need to use the Direct Selection tool.

1. Switch to the Direct Selection tool and click and hold on the image.
2. You should see the bounding box for the whole image, with the parts outside the frame ghosted (see Figure 4–29).
3. Drag to move the photo around inside the picture frame. The image moves but the frame does not. This is a good method of hiding unwanted or unnecessary parts of an image, a process called cropping.

figure | 4–29 |

Clicking and holding on the picture with the Direct Selection tool shows the entire image.

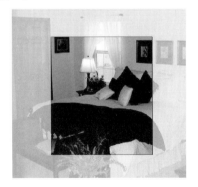

Resize the Image Inside the Frame Proportionately

Images have width and height dimensions. When both dimensions are at 100%, the picture is full size. If the image is reduced, the percentage will be less than 100% and if it is enlarged it will be more than 100%. If you resize the photo so that the width dimension is at

50% and the height is at 100%, the picture is the same height, but it is half its original width. This is disproportional scaling. If you were using a picture of clouds as a background photo, the photo could be scaled disproportionately without any consequences. However, you want to keep most images—products, people—proportional, meaning the width and height percentages will be the same. These percentages are shown in the Control palette (see Figure 4–30).

Image Width %

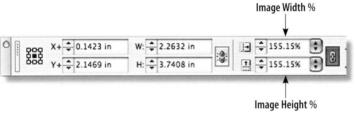

figure | 4–30

Image Height %

The width and height percentages are greater than 100% and identical, meaning the image has been enlarged proportionately.

The Direct Selection tool can be used to proportionately resize the image.

1. Choose the Direct Selection tool.
2. Hold down Shift+Command (Mac) or Shift+Control (Windows) and drag a corner of the image's frame. See how the image changes size proportionally, but the outer container does not change size.
3. Reduce the whole image until it is floating in the center of the picture frame.
4. You will be able to see the percentage of reduction in the Control palette.

Resize the Image Inside the Frame Disproportionately

A poster promoting a weight loss program was hung in our college hallway showing the "before" and "after" photos of a participant who had lost 20 lbs. Obviously, the "after" picture was created by simply resizing the first photo to make the person look thinner. Be careful when scaling images! Most of the time you will want to keep your image in the same proportion as it was originally created. But there will be instances, as in the cloud example mentioned earlier, when disproportional scaling will be acceptable.

1. Select the image with the Direct Selection tool. Drag any frame handle. The image will resize and become distorted.
2. Check the Scale X and Y fields on the Control palette to see new horizontal and vertical percentages of the image.
3. Enter **50%** in each of the fields and the image will again be proportional.

Using the Control Palette to Modify Images in Frames

The demonstrations you just completed gave you a feel for how the frames and images work in InDesign, and particularly the importance of using the correct selection tool. But before we conclude this chapter we must introduce one more very cool InDesign Control palette function.

fit contents to frame (disproportional) → 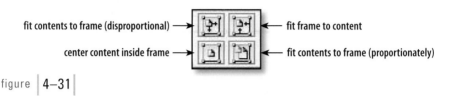 ← fit frame to content

center content inside frame → ← fit contents to frame (proportionately)

figure | 4–31 |

Using the Control palette, you can modify images and frames with just one click.

Create some frames and place sample images. Click each box in the Control palette to see how it works.

- The upper left box fits the image to the frame. This will resize the image until it fits the frame—and the resulting image size may be disproportional.

- The upper right box resizes the frame to fit the content. If the image is much bigger than the frame, clicking this button will automatically resize the frame.

- The lower left button moves the image to the exact center of the frame without changing the size of the frame or its contents.

- The lower right button fits the image proportionately to the frame.

SUMMARY

You now understand InDesign's measurement system. You know how to create multi-column text frames, and to place and thread text. You used InDesign's tracking and kerning, paragraph rules, and spell check functions to fine-tune your type. Finally, you learned how to place, scale, and crop images. With these techniques mastered, you're ready to tackle more advanced projects.

in review

1. What is the difference between kerning and tracking?

2. What is the difference between tracking and leading?

3. How do you reset the zero point?

4. If the coordinates of an object are X4 and Y6, it means that the object will be
   _____ inches over and _____ inches down.

5. What does the black square in the proxy indicate?

6. What key should you press to push text from one column to the next?

7. What does a red plus sign in the out port of a text frame indicate?

8. What are the keyboard shortcuts for the following?
   A. Show Hidden Characters
   B. Direct Selection Tool
   C. Paragraph Rules
   D. Place Text or Image
   E. Check Spelling
   F. Save
   G. View at 100%
   H. View at 200%
   I. Text Frame Options
   J. Print

↗ EXPLORING ON YOUR OWN

This chapter's projects begin with a display ad for Beautiful Morning Tearoom and Gardens. The focus of that project will be using coordinates, leading, correct dashes, and space after paragraphs. The second project will be a four-page program for a concert. You will be placing and threading text and using hard and soft returns. (By the end of this project you will always remember how to make a soft return!) And the third project is a fun one—a layout concept for a museum exhibit. You will find instructions, artwork, and text in the Chapter 04 folder on the accompanying CD.

Project 04A: Beautiful
Morning Tearoom

Project 04B:
Irish Spring Festival

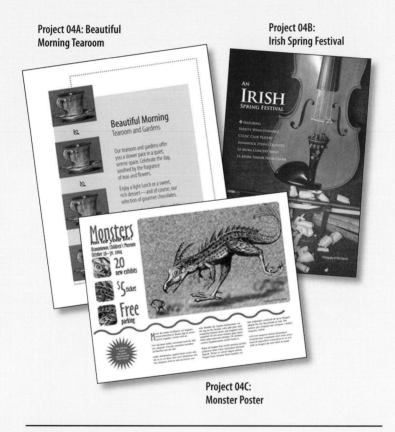

Project 04C:
Monster Poster

notes

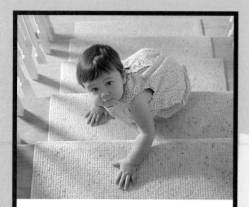

Everyone is trying to
accomplish something **big**,
not realizing that life
is made up of **little things**.

ॐ Unknown

tabs and tables

charting your course

If you've ever seen a good marching band in a parade, you know that they march in formation. A poor marching band wanders all over the place—trumpets out of line, clarinets out of step, drums missing the beat. Nobody knows who to follow or what comes next.

This chapter will help you keep your text in formation. In earlier chapters you have learned how to format text in sentences and paragraphs. In this chapter you will work with text designed for use in charts, order forms, and business reports—projects that need tabs and tables to keep information in line. Honing your skills with tabs and tables will keep your text marching in formation, and prove to your client that you are a master at what you do!

There are four methods people typically use to align text and numbers in columns:

1. Press the spacebar over and over until the text lines up.
2. Press the Tab key over and over until the text lines up.
3. Create precise tabular settings.
4. Create tables to hold the information.

No matter which method you have used in the past, I guarantee that after this chapter you will never use either of the first two methods again!

 goals

- **Differentiate between left, right, center, decimal, repeating, and custom-aligned tabs**

- **Apply tab leaders**

- **Use the Indent to Here feature**

- **Build a table**

- **Create a table from text**

- **Modify, add, and delete columns and rows**

SETTING TABS

Whether you are working on a car, hanging wallpaper, or building a deck, it is always great to get tips from pros—especially at the beginning of the project! Here are some great tips for tabs. Following them will make setting tabs so much easier.

- Mark up the copy (a fine-tip pen with colored ink works the best). Your markup will show where you press the Tab key and where the tab stop will be set. This step is critical in the beginning stages of typesetting. Preplanning a job in this way can prevent time-consuming errors (see the sample markup in Figure 5–1).

- Work with hidden characters visible. Press Command+Option+I (Mac) or Control+Alt+I (Windows) to show hidden characters. This will show each tab character and will make it easy to find those times when you accidentally pressed the Tab key twice.

- Do the typing first, pressing the Tab key only one time between columns of information. Your copy probably won't line up at first because the copy jumps to InDesign's preset tab settings. Later when you set the desired tab stops, the copy will line up at the correct new location.

- Work with copy left-aligned when possible—doing so makes setting tabs much easier.

- Access the Tabs palette by pressing Shift+Command+T (Mac) or Shift+Control+T (Windows).

figure | 5–1 |

Marking up copy before setting tabs saves much time and frustration.

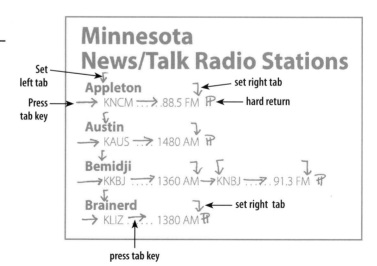

Press the Tab key only once! Your copy may look like a mess at first, but that's OK. It will line up after you set the tab stops.

What Is the Difference Between Tables and Columns Within a Text Frame?

Text frame columns are used for continuous text passages. They are designed to have the copy fill the first column and then flow into the second column, and so on. Tabs should be used when the copy flow is horizontal. The tab stops will create the vertical columns.

How Do I Know What Kind of Tabs To Use?

The first tab tip is to mark up the copy to show each time you press the Tab key and where the tab stops should be placed. Before you can mark up the copy, you must know what kind of tab is needed. We will start with three simple kinds of tabs: left, right, and center.

Each of these tab stops looks different on the Tabs palette. Figure 5–2 shows you each tab stop and its corresponding copy.

figure | 5–2 |

The shape of the tab stop provides a visual clue as to how the copy will be aligned.

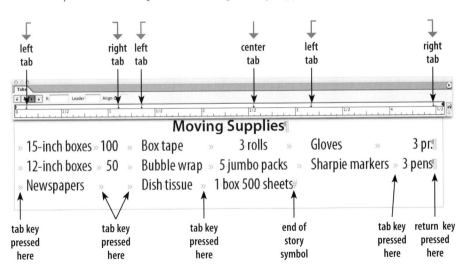

Left tabs align copy on the left side of the column. The Tab key is pressed before the first word in the column and the tab stop is set at the exact spot where the first letter of the word should line up.

Tabs, indents, and insets can be confusing. Sometimes when the first column of text is left aligned you may want to use a left indent instead of a tab. That method works perfectly. However, don't use a left inset instead of a left indent because the inset will affect all the text in the frame—which may not be what you want at all!

a left indent was specified
in the paragraph palette

tabs were
used to
create an
indent on
the left

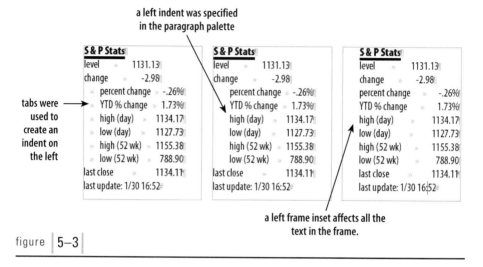

a left frame inset affects all the
text in the frame.

figure | 5–3 |

Tabs and indents apply to entire paragraphs. Insets apply to all the text in a text frame.

figure | 5–4 |

Right tabs push the
text "right" over to
the tab stop.

right tab stop

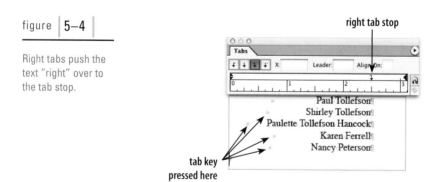

tab key
pressed here

When you set a right tab, the copy is pushed right over to the tab stop—looking similar to right-justified text.

Center tabs center the text underneath the tab stop on each line. If you look at the example in Figure 5–5, you will notice that you can draw a vertical line straight down from the center tab stop and equal measures of copy lie on each side of the line.

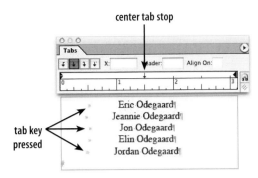

figure | 5–5 |

Text aligns equally
on each side of a
center tab stop.

How Should I Mark Up the Copy?

When you mark up tabular copy, you should indicate each time you press the Tab key and show exactly where each tab stop should be set. Figure 5–1 shows copy that has been marked up correctly. This markup becomes a road map that will make setting tabs a snap.

Type First—Set Tabs Second

Once the markup is complete, you are ready to do your typing. Before you begin, work with hidden characters on and make sure the copy is left aligned. Using your markup as a guide, type the copy and press the Tab key once every time you jump to a new column of information. Remember: Text will not line up at first, but don't try to align the type by pressing the Tab key more than once! You will set tab stops later to align the type.

How Does the Tabs Palette Work?

The best way to learn about tabs is to create them. Open InDesign and create a letter-size document. Then follow these steps to set left tabs:

1. Draw a text frame. Type your name and press the Tab key. Notice that the cursor jumped to a default preset tab.
2. Use the keyboard shortcut Shift+Command+T (Mac) or Shift+Control+T (Windows) to open the Tabs palette. Notice the magnet icon at the far right side of the palette. If you click on the magnet, the palette will snap to the top of the text frame.
3. At the left of the Tabs palette are four small vertical arrows. Click on the first one—it represents a left tab (see Figure 5–6). Now hold down your mouse button in the narrow strip

just above the ruler on the Tabs palette. Along with a left tab marker you will see a vertical line in the text frame. This line helps you see where your text will actually be aligned.

figure | 5–6 |

left, center, right, and decimal tabs

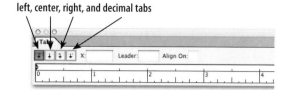

Learn to recognize each tab stop by the shape of its arrow.

4. Release the button on your mouse and look at the left tab you have just set—it should be highlighted. When a tab is highlighted it means it is still active, and if you click on it again, you can drag it back and forth along the length of the Tab ruler.

5. As you move the tab, notice how the measurement in the X field also changes. Instead of setting the tab visually, type a numerical value in the X field and press Return. The tab stop will move to that position. Click outside the text frame and the tab will no longer be active.

▶ TRY THIS

Practice creating left tabs by typing the information shown in the two tabular pieces in Figure 5–7. Be sure to mark up your copy first.

figure | 5–7 |

Use left tabs to set these two examples. First mark up your work showing where to press the Tab key and where to place the tab stop.

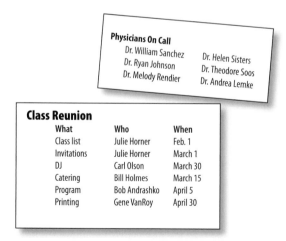

Physicians On Call

Dr. William Sanchez   Dr. Helen Sisters
Dr. Ryan Johnson   Dr. Theodore Soos
Dr. Melody Rendier   Dr. Andrea Lemke

Class Reunion

What	Who	When
Class list	Julie Horner	Feb. 1
Invitations	Julie Horner	March 1
DJ	Carl Olson	March 30
Catering	Bill Holmes	March 15
Program	Bob Andrashko	April 5
Printing	Gene VanRoy	April 30

Setting Center Tabs

The process for setting center tabs is the same as for left tabs. The only difference is that you will select the second tab alignment icon on the palette (see Figure 5–6).

1. Create a new document and draw a text frame.
2. Think of all the birth dates you know. Hopefully, you can think of about five.
3. Press Tab. Type the person's name. Press Return.
4. Press Tab. Type the person's birth date. Press Return.
5. Continue this pattern until you have run out of birthdays.
6. Select all the text. Open the Tabs palette. Set a center tab stop in the middle of the line measure and watch your copy jump into place.

Setting Right Tabs

For this exercise you will need to think of phone numbers rattling around in your head—the pizza place, your best friend, the doctor's office, your family members. In these days of cell phones and auto-dialers people don't memorize many phone numbers! If you want, use the numbers shown in Figure 5–8 to do the next exercise.

Mom . . . . (505) 645-5800
Rosa's Pizza 456-6789
Haircut 456-3434
Anna 345-6789
Will. . . . . (238) 234-2345
Pete . . . . (505) 457-9867
Tony. . . . . (608) 236-9458
Victoria . . . . (608) 373-9876
Mark. . . . . (608) 373-9765

figure | 5–8 |

This list of names and phone numbers is set using right tabs with leaders.

1. Draw a new text frame and type five names and phone numbers—directory style—with each name and number on its own line. Press the Tab key once between the name and number using a hard return at the end of each line. Select all the copy.
2. Open the Tabs palette. Select the right tab stop button and position it on the tab ruler at the right side of the line measure. The last number of all the phone numbers will now be aligned with your new tab stop.
3. To make it easier for your eye to follow across from the name to the number, you will connect the two columns with a series of small dots called dot leaders. Check to see that the right tab marker on the tab ruler is still highlighted. If it is not, click on it to activate it.

4. In the Leader field, type a period, and then press Return. Dot leaders will fill the space between the name and phone number. Compare the spacing of your dots with those shown in Figure 5–8. Yours are very close together. Here's how easy it is to change this.

5. Insert your cursor after the period in the Leader field, press the Spacebar once and then press Return. Now your leaders don't look so congested. Figure 5–9 shows the difference a little space can make.

figure | 5–9 |

The dot leaders in the top example look too tight. Add a space after the period in the Leader field to open them up, as shown in the bottom example.

Mom........................ (505) 645-5800
Rosa's Pizza 456-6789
Haircut.................................456-3434

Mom . . . . (505) 645-5800
Rosa's Pizza 456-6789
Haircut 456-3434

TRY THIS

Try out your new skills using right tabs and leaders with the two mini-projects shown in Figure 5–10.

figure | 5–10 |

Two simple exercises requiring right tabs and dot leaders. Don't forget to add the space after the period when setting the leader!

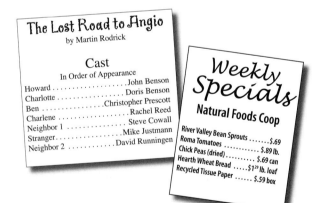

The Lost Road to Angio
by Martin Rodrick

Cast
In Order of Appearance
Howard . . . . .John Benson
Charlotte . . . . Doris Benson
Ben . . . . .Christopher Prescott
Charlene . . . . .Rachel Reed
Neighbor 1 . . . . Steve Cowall
Stranger. . . . . .Mike Justmann
Neighbor 2 . . . . .David Runningen

Weekly
Specials
Natural Foods Coop

River Valley Bean Sprouts . . . .$.69
Roma Tomatoes . . . . $.89 lb.
Chick Peas (dried) . . . . $.69 can
Hearth Wheat Bread . . . . . .$1^{29} lb. loaf
Recycled Tissue Paper . . . . . . $.59 box

Setting Automatic Right Tabs

There will be times when you will want your right tab stop to be flush with the right edge of the text frame. InDesign has a slick trick for setting a flush right tab. Place the blinking cursor where you would like the tab to be positioned. Then press Shift+Tab. You have just set an automatic right tab. The disadvantages of using automatic right tabs are that you can't set a tab leader and you can't see their position markers in the tab rulers. If you need a tab leader, you will have to set these up in the Tabs palette. To see if an automatic right tab has been inserted, turn on Hidden Characters.

Setting Decimal and Custom-Aligned Tabs

Decimal tabs are yet another member of the tabs family. As the name implies, decimal tabs align text according to the location of a decimal point or period. Although this tab setting is usually used to align numbers, the decimal tab setting has another option. There may be times when you want to align text to a symbol other than a decimal. In those instances, simply select the decimal tab, set the tab stop in the tabs ruler, and replace the decimal in the Align On field with the desired symbol. The text will now align around that new character. The next tab exercise (see Figure 5–11) will utilize decimal tabs.

To create the example in Figure 5–11, place the 05Tabs.doc file found in the Chapter 05 Artwork/Resources folder on the accompanying CD and set the tabs as shown. You will need to use the Glyphs palette to add the triangles. The Zapf Dingbats and Wingdings typefaces have a great selection of symbols.

U.S. Stock Market			
Market	Level	Change	Last Update
▼ djia	10488.07	-22.22/0.21%	1/30 16:03
▼ nasdaq	2066.15	-2.08/0.10%	1/30 17:16
▼ s&p 500	1131.13	-2.98/0.26%	1/30 16:52
▲ russell 2000	580.76	090/0.16%	1/30 16:52
▼ dow transports	2885.95	-86.04/2.90%	1/30 16.04
▼ dow utilities	271.94	-0.67/25%	1/30 16:03
▲ amex composite	1197.17	2.41/0.20%	1/30 16:07

figure | 5–11 |

This example uses left, right, center, and decimal tabs.

Indent to Here

Indent to Here is one of those "can't live without it" features of InDesign. Although technically this is not a tab setting, this is a good time to introduce this function. Once you understand how this works you will use it repeatedly. With Indent to Here, you insert a hidden character symbol by pressing Command+\ (Mac) or Control+\ (Windows) (that's the Back Slash key). All subsequent copy in the paragraph lines up underneath the slash similar to a hanging indent. As soon you press the Return key for a new paragraph, copy flows back out to the left margin (see Figure 5–12). To remove the Indent to Here character, simply turn on the hidden characters, find the Indent to Here dagger symbol, place the cursor to the right of the symbol, and press the Delete key.

figure | 5–12 |

Text lines up to the Indent to Here symbol until the Return key is pressed for a new paragraph.

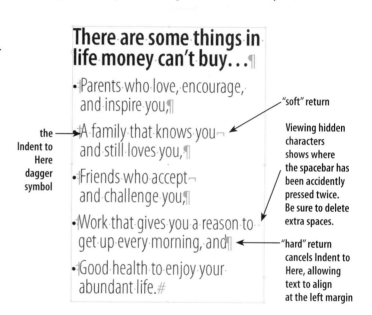

the Indent to Here dagger symbol

"soft" return

Viewing hidden characters shows where the spacebar has been accidently pressed twice. Be sure to delete extra spaces.

"hard" return cancels Indent to Here, allowing text to align at the left margin

Repeat Tabs

Whenever you want tabs spaced at equal intervals, you can use the Repeat Tabs function found on the palette menu at the far right end of the Tabs palette. To set repeating tabs, place the first tab the desired distance from the left end of the text. Then choose Repeat Tabs, and InDesign will fill the line length with equally spaced tab stops.

▶ TRY THIS

The two projects shown in Figure 5–13 will utilize Indent to Here and Repeat Tabs.

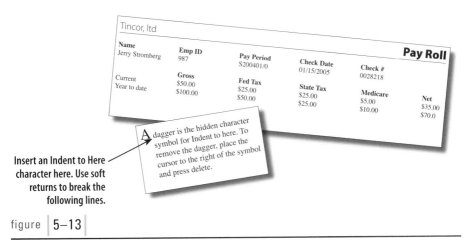

Insert an Indent to Here character here. Use soft returns to break the following lines.

figure | 5–13 |

Use Indent to Here and Repeat Tabs to set these two examples.

TRY THIS

Tabs are pretty simple once you understand them. Creating the three tables in Figure 5–14 will solidify your tab skills. Mark up each project first, and create each project in its own text frame.

Nutrition Facts¶

Serving Size: 1 cup¶
Servings per container: 6¶
Amount per serving:¶

Calories 45	Calories from fat 0¶
Total Fat 0g	0%¶
» Saturated Fat 0g¶	
» Polyunsaturated Fat 0g¶	
» Monounsaturated Fat 0g¶	

Cholesterol	»	0mg	»	0%¶
Sodium	»	70mg	»	3%¶
Total Carbohydrate	»	12g	»	4%¶
Dietary Fiber	»	2g¶		
Sugars	»	0g¶		
Protein	»	1g¶		

Vitamin A 0% • Vitamin C 0%¶
Calcium 0% • Iron 2%¶

Registration Form¶

Name _____ ¶

Address _____ ¶

City _____ ¶

State _____ Zip _____ #

Check the tab settings on the Tabs palette ruler when setting the highlighted text.

Order by Phone
and pick up at Drive Thru Window¶

| Shakes | » Large » $1.99 | Small » $1.19¶ |
| Malts | » Large » $2.29 | Small » $1.39¶ |

Vanilla, Chocolate, Strawberry¶

California Burger................$2.79¶
Tomato, onion, lettuce. Comes in basket with fries and deli pickle. Add cheese 50¢¶

Cheeseburger....................$2.59¶
1/3 lb. ground beef, American cheese, lettuce, cheese, pickle, onion.¶

567-6377#

figure | 5–14 |

These exercises can be found in the Chapter 05>Projects folder found on the accompanying CD. The file 05)Tabs Examples is in PDF format and can be printed full size for measurement and markup.

TABLES

InDesign's Tables function is so intriguing you will find yourself looking for sample charts just so that you can re-create them using tables (this is how typesetters have fun!).

Table Basics

InDesign's toolbox does not include a specific table tool. In InDesign, you insert a table into a text frame or convert existing text into a table. The best way to understand tables is to make them, so we're going to dive right in. In the first exercise you will create a table and add, merge, and change the dimensions of rows and columns. You will learn what each of the editing icons means while you build a sample résumé.

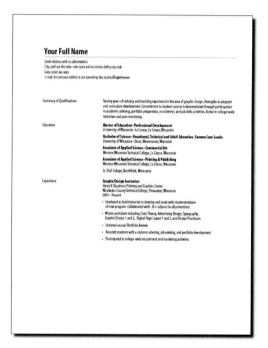

1. Create a letter-size InDesign document with 1-inch margins. Draw a text frame from margin to margin.
2. Select the Type tool and click in the frame. Press Shift+Option+Command+T (Mac) or Shift+Alt+Control+T (Windows) to bring up the Insert Table dialog box (see Figure 5–16). You can also access this dialog box by choosing Table>Insert Table.

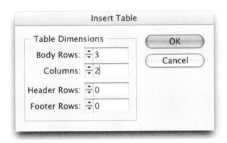

figure | 5–16|

The Insert Table dialog box allows you to set up columns and rows.

3. From the Body Rows and Columns field lists, select 3 rows and 2 columns. Rows run horizontally, and columns run vertically. Leave the Header Rows and Footer Rows fields blank. Press Return. The table should look like Figure 5–17.

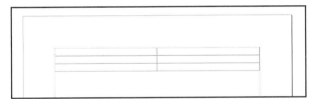

figure | 5–17|

Rows are horizontal; columns are vertical.

4. Make sure the Type tool is active. The Type tool is used for most table modifications. Move the I-beam cursor over the line that separates the first and second row. As the I-beam moves on top of the line it changes to a new icon: a double-ended arrow. Click on the row line and drag the line down to the 2.75-inch mark on the ruler guides. Notice that rows underneath move down, enlarging the depth of the chart.

5. Move the cursor to the left edge of the first row that you just deepened. The I-beam turns into a different icon: a single-head arrow. Click and the whole row will be highlighted. Check the depth of this row by looking in the Row Height field in the Control palette. Make sure it is set at exactly 1.75 inches (see Figure 5–18).

The row depth should be exactly 1.75 inches.

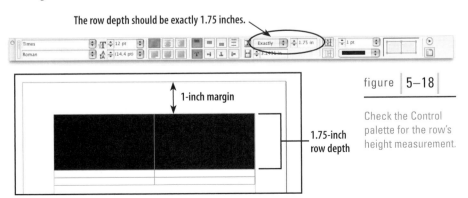

1-inch margin

1.75-inch row depth

figure | 5–18|

Check the Control palette for the row's height measurement.

6. With the deep, two-column row still selected, click the Merge cells button on the Control palette (see Figure 5–19). The two cells combine to form one wide row.

figure | 5–19 |

Click this button to merge cells.

merge cells

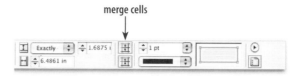

7. Click inside this row and type your name, address, phone number, and email address. Select a typeface and type size you prefer, adding a rule below your name. With Figure 5–20 as a guide, use the paragraph and character formatting commands you have already learned to get your résumé to look like the sample.

NOTE: There is a difference between selecting the text and selecting a cell. When the whole cell is highlighted the cell is selected. When the highlighting covers the letters, the text is selected (see Figure 5–20).

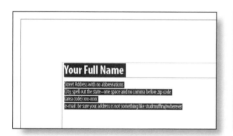

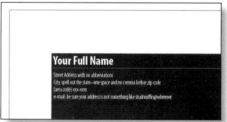

figure | 5–20 |

Left: the text inside the cell is selected. Right: The table cell itself, is selected.

8. Be sure the Type tool is still active. Remember that you need to use the I-beam for most table modifications. Now we will work on the second and third rows. Place the cursor in the left cell of the second row and drag down to select the left cell in the third. In the Control palette, enter 2 in the Column Width field and press Return (see Figure 5–21). The two cells will be exactly two inches wide. Notice that when it the cells in the first column become narrower, the whole table becomes narrower. This is a key point: When you modify the width of rows and columns, the external dimensions of the table also change. Move the cursor over the right edge of the table and it will change to a double-ended arrow icon. Drag the edge of the table back over to the margin. You should now have columns of unequal width.

column width field

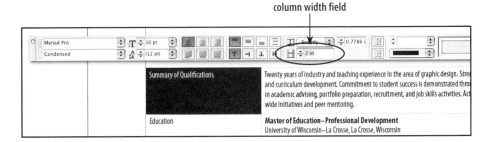

9. Click the Type tool in the left column, second row. Type **Summary of Qualifications**. Then press the Tab key and the cursor will jump over to the next column.

figure | 5–21

Enter an exact column width in the Control palette's Column width field.

10. In the right column, write a summary of the experience and attributes you bring to the job. Type three or four lines. Since this is just a practice résumé write whatever you want (just don't send it out to anyone).

11. Slowly drag the mouse to select the entire paragraph you have just written. Notice that at first only the text is highlighted. As you continue to drag past the end of the paragraph, the whole cell becomes highlighted. This is the difference between highlighting text and highlighting a cell. When the cursor is in a cell, pressing Command+A (Mac) or Control+A (Windows) selects all the type. Dragging diagonally from corner to corner selects the cell.

12. Place the cursor in the left cell of the third row. Type Education. Press Tab to jump to the next column and type the schools you have attended and degrees attained. If you have attended college, you do not need to list your high school or graduation date. In fact, the dates of your degree(s) may be omitted throughout your résumé to prevent age discrimination. Look at the sample in Figure 5–22. There are no abbreviations, and the city and state are listed with the name of the college. The degrees were bolded to attract the reader's attention.

13. All the columns and rows are now filled. We need to make room for your work experience, so we will add a row. The easiest way to add a row "on the fly" is to position the cursor over the line under that last row, watch for the I-beam to change into a double-ended arrow and click. First, start dragging the line down and then hold down the Option (Mac) or Alt (Windows) key and drag down to create one more row. If you don't release the mouse quick enough you will create multiple rows. If this happens, press Undo. Try it again until you are able to add only one more row. You can also add a row by accessing

Your Full Name

Street Address with no abbreviations
City, spell out the state—one space and no comma before zip code
(area code) xxx-xxxx
e-mail: be sure your address is not something like studmuffin@wherever

Summary of Qualifications	Twenty years of industry and teaching experience in the area of graphic design. Strengths in program and curriculum development. Commitment to student success is demonstrated through participation in academic advising, portfolio preparation, recruitment, and job skills activities. Active in college-wide initiatives and peer mentoring.
Education	**Master of Education–Professional Development** University of Wisconsin–La Crosse, La Crosse, Wisconsin **Bachelor of Science–Vocational, Technical and Adult Education. Summa Cum Laude** University of Wisconsin–Stout, Menomonie, Wisconsin **Associate of Applied Science–Commercial Art** Western Wisconsin Technical College, La Crosse, Wisconsin **Associate of Applied Science–Printing & Publishing** Western Wisconsin Technical College, La Crosse, Wisconsin St. Olaf College, Northfield, Minnesota

figure | 5–22 |

This sample résumé contains a row for the name and personal information, and two rows of two columns for the Qualifications and Education information.

the context menu and choose Insert>Row. When the Insert Row(s) dialog box appears, enter 1 in the Number field, select the Below option and press Return.

14. Type **Experience** in the left cell of the newly created row. Press Tab to jump to the right hand column. The first line in the cell should be your job title. The second line should be the name of the company, city, and state. The third line can be the month and year you began working to the month and year you ended employment. No comma is needed after the month since you are not listing a day. Be sure to use an en dash between the dates. You can continue entering other jobs if you would like. If the table gets too large for the text frame that holds it, you will need to use the Selection tool to make the text frame bigger.

15. Before you are finished with the résumé, you must remove all the black rules around the table. Place the cursor in the upper left corner of the table, at the point where the top and left sides meet. You will see the cursor change to a diagonal single-head arrow. Click and the whole table will be selected. Press Shift+Option+Command+B (Mac) or Shift+Alt+Control+B (Windows) to open the Table Options dialog box. On the Table setup page, Under Table Border, change Color to None. Press Return.

16. With the table still highlighted, press Command+Option+B (Mac) or Control+Alt+B (Windows) and bring up the Cell Options dialog box. Select the Strokes and Fills page and

choose None for Color in the Cell Stroke options area. While you are in this dialog box, take a look at the other functions available here.

You can now continue working on your résumé, adding the rest of your work experience. Here's a review of what you have learned in this little exercise:

- The Type tool is used for editing tables.

- A row is horizontal. A column is vertical. A cell is the space formed by the row and column grid.

- The Type tool cursor changes shape according to the editing that will be done.

- The keyboard shortcut for creating a table from a text frame is Shift+Option+Command+T (Mac) or Shift+Alt+Control+T (Windows).

- To make changes to the cell, highlight the whole cell.

- Rows and columns can be added, deleted, and repositioned.

- You can merge cells to form wide columns and rows.

- Options that affect the whole table are accessed by pressing Shift+Option+Command+B (Mac) or Shift+Alt+Control+B (Windows).

- Options that affect selected cells are accessed by pressing Option+Command+B (Mac) or Alt+Control+B (Windows).

- The table sits inside a text frame. When rows and columns are modified, the text frame may need to be enlarged or reduced.

- Select the whole table by placing the cursor at a corner of the table. Clicking when the cursor turns into a diagonal arrow will select the whole table.

Create a Table from Text

Now that you've gotten a taste for tables, I hope you're ready for more! In the previous example you created a table from scratch. Now you will create a table from text that has already been typed. First you will import some prepared text, and then you will type your own text and convert it to a table, making a Grade Scale chart (see Figure 5–23).

figure | 5–23 |

The Grade Scale
table is created
from prepared text
(which means no
typing…Yes!)

Grade Scale		
Grade	**Percent Value**	**Point Value**
A	95-100	4.00
A-	93-94	3.67
B+	91-92	3.33
B	87-90	3.00
B-	85-86	2.67
C+	83-84	2.33
C	79-82	2.00
C-	77-78	1.67
D+	75-76	1.33
D	72-74	1.00
D-	70-71	0.67
F	69 or below	0.00

1. Draw a text frame 2.5 × 3.5 inches.
2. Import 05 Grade Scale.doc from the Chapter 05 Artwork/Resouces folder on the accompanying CD. Drop it into the frame.
3. Select all the text. Choose Table>Convert Text to Table. In the Convert Text to Table dialog box set Column Separator to Tab, Row Separator to Paragraph and then press Return. Your table should look like Figure 5–24. Notice the overset symbol in the lower right cell. As the table is formatted, the overset text will reflow and be visible in the table.

figure | 5–24 |

This is how the table
looks when the text
is first converted to
a table.

Grade Scale		
Grade	Percent Value	Point Value
A	95–100	4.00
A–	93–94	3.67
B+	91–92	3.33
B	87–90	3.00
B–	85–86	2.67
C+	83–84	2.33
C	79–82	2.00
C–	77–78	1.67
D+	75–76	1.33
D	72–74	1.00
D–	70–71	0.67

4. Select the top row and merge the cells by clicking on the Merge Cell field in the Control palette, or by opening the context menu and choosing Merge Cells. Now the phrase "Grade Scale" should fit on one line.

5. Highlight the first two rows and center the column heads by pressing Shift+Command+C (Mac) or Shift+Control+C (Windows).

6. Select the second and third columns and use the keyboard shortcut to center the percentages and point values.

7. Select the first column, from A to F. Open up the Tabs palette. and set a left tab close to the middle of the column.

8. To insert a tab in a table cell is tricky. On the Mac you need to press Option+Tab instead of just Tab. In Windows, you must use the context menu and choose Insert Special Character>Tab. Line by line, place the cursor before the letter grade and insert a tab to line up the grades in the middle of the column (see Figure 5–25).

Grade Scale		
	Percent Value	Point Value
A	95-100	4.00
A-	93-94	3.67
B+	91-92	3.33
B	87-90	3.00
B-	85-86	2.67
C+	83-84	2.33
C	79-82	2.00
C-	77-78	1.67
D+	75-76	1.33
D	72-74	1.00
D-	70-71	0.67
F	69 or below	0.00

figure | 5–25 |

Press Option+Tab (Mac only) or use the Insert Special Character context menu to insert a tab in a cell.

9. You should have an extra row at the bottom of the chart. This occurred because InDesign read the return at the end of the imported text as an indicator for another row. Select the row and remove it by pressing Command+Delete (Mac) or Control+Backspace (Windows).

10. Select the entire table and open the Table Options dialog box. Select the Fills page and under Alternating Pattern, select Every

Other Row, Color: Black, Tint: 20%. Set Skip First to 1 and check the Preview option box. Press Return. The row of the table should be white, with every other row a 20% black tint.

11. Make sure the entire table is selected and open the Cell Options dialog using the keyboard shortcut. Select the Strokes and Fills page. Under Cell Stroke, enter **3 pt.** in the Weight field and **Paper** in the Color field. Press Return.

12. Finally, add a border around the outer edge of the table. Select the whole table and open the Table Options dialog box. On the Table Set Up page set the Table Border options as follows: Color: Black, Type: Dashed (any style), Weight: 2 pt, Gap Color: None. Be sure Preserve Local Formatting is not checked. Press Return.

Your table is now completed. Compare your finished table with Figure 5–23.

The Grade Scale exercise introduced you to more table functions:

- You can convert text to a table. Whenever there is a tab in the text, it will begin a new column; wherever there is a return, it will begin a new row. The text must be highlighted before the Convert to Table option will show up.

- You can add tab settings in table cells. To set the actual tab, you must press Option+Tab (Mac) or use the Insert Special Character context menu (Windows) instead of simply Tab.

- Rows can be deleted by highlighting the row and pressing Command+Delete (Mac) or Control+Backspace (Windows).

- The three-fingered B—Shift+Option+Command+B (Mac) or Shift+Alt+Control+B (Windows)—opens the Table Options dialog box.

- The two-fingered B—(Option+Command+B (Mac) or Alt+Control+B (Windows)—opens the Cell Options dialog box.

- You can automatically create alternately shaded rows.

- You can have the interior row and column lines one style and color and have the outer table border a different style and color.

Prepare Text and Create a Table

Now you will make a chart using many of the same techniques as the Grade Scale table, but you will prepare the text yourself. Figure 5–26 shows the most popular baby names in 2002. Compare it with the Grade Scale table and you will see many of the same features—with a few twists, of course.

Most Popular Baby Names in 2002		
Rank	**Boy Names**	**Girl Names**
1	Jacob	Emily
2	Michael	Madison
3	Joshua	Hannah
4	Matthew	Emma
5	Ethan	Alexis
6	Joseph	Ashley
7	Andrew	Abigail
8	Christopher	Sarah
9	Daniel	Samantha
10	Nicholas	Olivia

figure | 5–26 |

You will need to type the text for this exercise.

1. Draw a text frame 20 picas wide by 22 picas deep. (Type **P** after the number in the W and H fields to indicate picas.)

2. Type the copy as seen in Figure 5–26. Press Tab to jump from column to column and press the Return key at the end of each line. Do not set tab stops!

3. Select all of the text. Choose Table>Convert Text to Table. Keep the default settings and press Return.

4. Merge the cells in the first row so that the title of the table fits on one line. Drag the row divider line down so that the title has more room. Highlight the cell and use a two-fingered B to open the Cell Options dialog box. On the Text page, set the Vertical Justification Align field to Center and press Return. Make the table heading centered.

5. Highlight the column titles and make the type bolder, larger and centered.

6. Highlight the numbers in the Rank column. Change them to a larger, bolder typeface and center them horizontally in the cell.

7. Highlight the two columns of names and select a typeface and point size you prefer. Center the names horizontally in their cells.

8. Adjust the width of the Rank column so that it is narrower than the Names columns. Then pull the right edge of the table back to the right edge of the text frame.

9. Highlight both Names columns. Open the context menu and choose Distribute Columns Evenly.

10. Select the whole table and use a three-fingered B to open the Table Options dialog box. On the Fills page set Alternating Pattern to Every Other Row. Also set First to 1 Row, Color to Black and Tint to 20%. Turn the Preview option on and press Return. Every other row in the table should be tinted.

11. Select the whole table and open the Cell Options dialog box. Select the Strokes and Fills page and set Weight to 4 pt, Color to Paper. Press Return.

12. The table is almost done. This time, instead of adding a border to the table itself, you will center the table horizontally and vertically in the text frame and add the border to the text frame. Switch to the Selection tool and enlarge the text frame slightly by pulling a corner frame handle diagonally. Add a black 8-point dotted stroke.

13. Switch back to the Type tool. Click in the upper left corner of the text frame to place the cursor before the table. Center the table horizontally by pressing Shift+Command+C (Mac) or Shift+Control+C (Windows). Use a one-fingered B— Command+B (Mac) or Control+B (Windows)—to open the Text Frame Options dialog box. Set the Vertical Justification Align field to Center and press Return.

Did you notice the pattern?

One-fingered B	Command+B (Mac) or Control+B (Windows)	Text Frame Options
Two-fingered B	Command+Option+B (Mac) or Control+Alt+B (Windows)	Cell Options
Three-fingered B	Shift+Command+Option+B (Mac) or Shift+Control+Alt+B (Windows)	Table Options

SUMMARY

This chapter focused on creating various tab settings. Indent to Here was introduced, giving you a quick method of creating a hanging indent. You learned how to build a table and create a table from existing text. InDesign's table formatting options were used to enhance your table's design. These production techniques will be used frequently in your design projects.

in review

1. What are the four main types of tabs?

2. How does Indent to Here work?

3. How many times should you press the Tab key to line up text?

4. What is the method of increasing the space between the dots in leaders?

5. Define cells, columns, and rows.

6. What are two ways to make tables?

7. When working with tables, draw what the I-beam looks like when you are: a) moving columns and rows; b) selecting rows and columns; c) selecting a table; d) editing text.

8. What dialog box opens when you use the: a) one-fingered B, b) a two-fingered B, c) a three-fingered B?

9. What technique do you use to set a tab inside a cell?

↗ EXPLORING ON YOUR OWN

Three projects will give you the opportunity to sharpen the tab and table skills you learned in this chapter.

Project 05A is a two-column flyer for summer swimming lessons. Projects 05B and 05C are table projects. You will find a PDF with instructions for these projects in the Chapter 05 folder on the accompanying CD. Artwork and text is found in the Chapter 05>Artwork/Resources folder.

Project 05 Fun in the Sun
artwork: © 2003 Steve Cowal

Project 05 Calendar
artwork: © 2003 Marion R. Cox

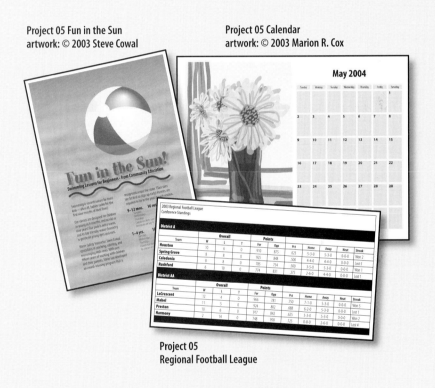

Project 05
Regional Football League

These projects will allow you to flex your muscles with tabs and tables.

ADVENTURES IN DESIGN

THE ART OF TYPE

Henry Ford once said, "Whether you think you can or whether you think you can't, you're right." When learning any new discipline, your attitude will influence your measure of success. Take typography, for instance. Learning about typography moves you to see letters not as mere symbols, but as expressive, textural design elements. Student designer Dan Ouweneel put it this way:

"Type is a feeling, an energy that is contained within a sound piece of design work. Good typography is a spark that shows the reader that a great deal of love has been put into the piece."

Quite a statement, coming from a student who started out his typography class with a yawn, hoping it would soon end. Yet today, Dan handles type like an expert because he replaced his yawns with a positive attitude.

This Adventure in Design will help you understand typographic concepts that, when mastered, will make a huge difference in your design.

Type Color

You can see tonal variations ranging from black to gray in Figure B–1. Both extremes would be tiring to read in large amounts. The color of type is a variable you need to consider when selecting typefaces.

Type Texture

Body copy should have an even texture. When copy is set properly, the text will be "transparent," meaning that the set copy does not contain any inconsistencies that could be disturbing to the reader. Figure B–2 shows examples of even and uneven texture.

Typeface Legibility

Legibility refers to the reader's ability to distinguish one letter from another. As you can see in Figure B–3, some typefaces aren't designed to be particularly legible. Don't use these faces for continuous body copy! When a typeface's name includes the word "book," you can be sure it is a highly legible typeface.

Readability

Readability refers to the ease of reading continuous amounts of text. Poor typesetters can make the most

Si. Essit ulla feu faccum zzrit wis nonse exer iurerosto cor ad dolore te delenit accum diam iriure euisit

modolore dit wis enim ver ad ex exeraesto dit aci et prat. Cum inis nulla am volorper accum

ex ent iriure volore consequam, cor iuscipis amconse quipis eu facipsusto essequis adiam, sed magna

facipsu stionul laoreet, vel ullan er susciliqui endre cor sustin velisim vel er sustrud enisim

inciliqui blaortisim in hendrem ver summy num veliquam, se velit augait vel dolorem ea feu facilis

aliquisisim zzrilla mconsenim dolesto elessequis aci blandiat alis dolestrud dunt adionsenim quodfes

eliscip exerit lam ese magnibh enibh ea core ve Etummodo lesting ea at augue e ve Etummodo lesting ea at

e molutat nullandreros aut wis nullandit venit eas er irilluptat, conum zzriurero erosto con

ullaor acil ullandip esectet wis nos dolore del dolortie tet laor sisisci esendre dolorti onsectem iliquip nos dolore del dolortie tet laortet laor ullaor acil ullandip

Figure B–1
Type has color tones ranging from light gray to dark black.

Even Texture. molorsd in et praess tis incillit omnul putatum augait iuresp diam commys nos nibh et praestrud toat. In henim augait nostisl dolobor enit atin erat, velis augue

Uneven Texture. nos nos et ut ad ercipit utetum iure conse magnibh et ercing eu faccumsan ute ex etue conullaore eui euisim in utatue tet lobor summy nulla feugue dipis alit atum augueraessit iure

Figure B–2
Examples of type blocks with even and uneven texture.

Figure B–3
These typefaces are designed with personality—not legibility—in mind.

legible typefaces unreadable! Figure B–4 shows an example.

Point Size, Leading, and Measure

If a type block has point size, leading, and measure in balance, changing one of these factors will necessitate a change in the other two. For instance, a reduction in point size will require a reduction in leading and measure. Create sample copy blocks and experiment with these three factors. Print the galleys and compare readability. Figure B–5 shows these factors in action. When you have point size, leading, and measure under control, you are well on your way to creating visually pleasing text.

Breaking Text into Chunks

Adding space between paragraphs and using subheads breaks text up nicely. Photos and artwork also serve to break up text. When text is broken into chunks, the reader is fooled into thinking there isn't as much copy as there actually is—which increases its chances of being read!

Lutem adipsusci te magnim er se magnit veliquisisl el dolent velestrud tat lummodip ea conse min eumsandipis exer at, i psum

Lutem adipsusci te magnim er se magnit veliquisisl el dolent velestrud tat lummodip ea conse min eumsandipis exer at, psum

Lutem adipsusci te magnim er se magnit

veliquisisl el dolent velestrud tat lummodip

ea conse min eumsandipis exer at, velendi

modit prat am, cor se m in ver autpat volore facil dit inibh eniamco mmolore consenim iliquatio ex eu facipis ent

Figure B–5
Samples of the effect of leading. Highly legible typeface with reduced readability.

This typeface, designed for great readability, has been poorly set, making reading difficult. Garamond would roll over in his grave if he could see this! Readability is in the hands of the person setting the type.

Figure B–4
Highly legible typeface with reduced readability.

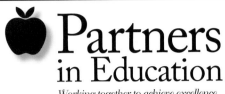

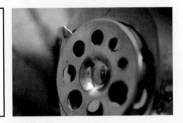

Figure B–6
Elements included in the newsletter document. Highly legible typeface with reduced readability.

Your Turn

Now it's your turn to experiment with type as a design element. You will create a one-page newsletter using placeholder text and the nameplate and photo shown in Figure B–6. Your goal is to create a document that uses type so effectively that viewers can't help but read it! You will choose the typeface, leading, and point size. Make a balanced page, using type to create contrast and eye flow.

1. From the Adventures in Design folder on the accompanying CD, open the document "Newsletter. indt." The nameplate and photo have already been placed for you.

2. Draw text frames for five or six articles. The frames can either be one column wide, or stretch across two columns. Your goal is to create an layout that is balanced and interesting.

3. Fill the text frames with placeholder text. You will find that command under Type>Fill with Placeholder Text or you may use the context menu and choose Fill with Placeholder Text.

4. Write a headline for one main article and write subheads for the rest of the articles.

5. Experiment with several different typefaces, point sizes, and leading for all the text.

6. Move the blocks of text around, adding or deleting placeholder text as necessary, to achieve a balanced newsletter.

7. Print out a newsletter and evaluate it using these criteria:
   - Body copy type size does not have a large, clunky look. (When in doubt, reduce the point size.)
   - Text is readable, with even texture.
   - Leading is wide enough to allow each line to "breathe" but narrow enough to visually keep paragraphs together.
   - Headline and subheads provide contrast and text color.
   - Articles are separated, but overall piece demonstrates a cohesive feel.
   - Hold the document at arm's length and look at it once again. If you see a sea of gray, you should increase the contrast of the subheads.

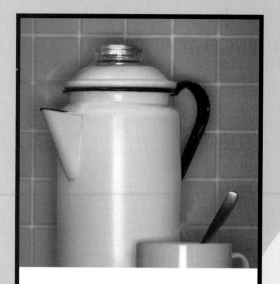

Always do the **right thing.**
This will gratify some people
and astonish the rest.

ᛥ Mark Twain

6

charting your course

Have you ever watched one of those "getting organized" home shows on cable TV? It's amazing how a messy area can be transformed into a practical, efficient space when storage needs are clearly identified and items are rearranged in a logical fashion. The new space is functional, organized, and a delight to behold! This chapter will be a "getting organized" chapter. By this time you have learned the basics, used a number of tools and palettes, and armed yourself with a variety of techniques. This chapter will focus on increasing productivity. These techniques will bring precision to your documents and efficiency to the way you work.

 goals

- **Create document presets, bleeds, and slugs**
- **Place, remove, and modify attributes of guides**
- **Create a publication and baseline grid**
- **Align and distribute objects**
- **Manage object layers and group elements**
- **Copy, cut, paste, paste into, and paste in place**

BACK TO THE BASICS

Since you are now an old hand at creating basic documents, it is time to introduce a few more options available in the New Document dialog box. First, let's review a few points for setting options in the New Document dialog box.

- Press the Tab key to jump from field to field in any dialog box.

- Turn on the Facing Pages option box when you want to create spreads. This will allow you to view documents with left- and right-hand pages, like a book or magazine, two pages at a time.

- Use the Page Size list to select preset dimensions. "Letter" is the standard 8.5" × 11" inch page size.

- Click the Link icon to make all margins the same (see Figure 6–1).

figure | 6–1

A closed link means all margins will be the same.

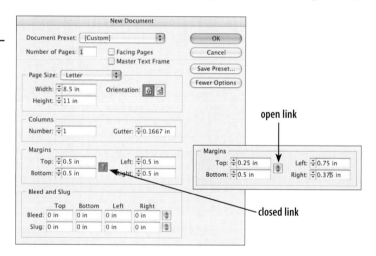

Changing the Default Document Preset

If you are using InDesign with its built-in preferences, you probably need to deselect Facing Pages whenever you create a new document. You may also find yourself continually changing the units of measure from picas to inches. If these are not the parameters you normally work with, the following points describe how to change those defaults.

- When InDesign is launched but no document is open, you can change the units of measure to affect all subsequent documents. If you are working on a Mac, choose InDesign>Preferences> Units & Increments and change the horizontal and vertical Ruler

Units to inches. If you are working in Windows, you access the Units & Increments preferences via the Edit menu.

- To change the option settings for the default document, press Command+Option+P (Mac) or Control+Alt+P (Windows). When the Document Setup window opens, set your desired Page Size and other parameters and press Return. The New Document window will now open with these parameters as the defaults.

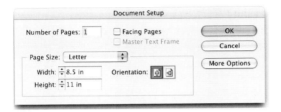

figure | 6–2 |

Access the Document Setup dialog box by pressing Command+Option+P (Mac) or Control+Alt+P (Windows).

Create Document Presets

In the previous example you changed the default document specifications and customized InDesign to match your work style. InDesign also allows you to create presets for other document parameters you will most often use. Suppose that many of the documents you create are 5 × 7 inches. You can create a 5 × 7 document, set the margins and other page options, and then before clicking OK, select Save Preset. A dialog box will pop up asking you to name the preset so it can be stored for future use (see Figure 6–3). The next time you need to create a 5 × 7 document, you can choose this preset from the Document Preset drop-down list in the New Document dialog box.

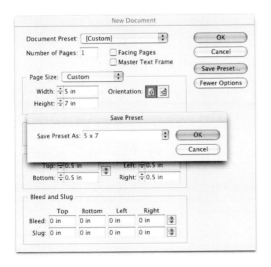

figure | 6–3 |

Name and save the preset in this dialog box.

Your mind is probably spinning just thinking of all the document presets you could use—business cards, envelopes, letterhead, forms, flyers, brochures—dozens of presets at your fingertips. So let's go one step further. Imagine that a client requires you to regularly design ads for 15 different magazines. Each publication has different specifications that must be followed precisely. Spending 15 minutes creating document presets for each publication is well worth the time. It will reduce the chance of error, especially when you are in a time-crunch. Here is another method of making document presets. This method is better to use when you need to create many presets, or to delete or change existing ones.

1. Go to File>Document Presets>Define. The Document Presets dialog box will open (see Figure 6–4).
2. Click New, and the New Document Preset dialog box opens. Name the preset, set the page size, margins and other options, and click OK.
3. Click New again to create another preset. Create a few more document presets so that you are comfortable with the process.
4. To delete one of your document presets, in the Document Presets dialog box, highlight the name of the preset in the Presets list and press Delete. You cannot delete the Default preset.
5. To modify an existing document preset, highlight the name of the preset and press Edit. Set the parameters that you want to change and click OK.

figure | 6–4

Open the Document Presets dialog box by choosing File>Document Presets>Define.

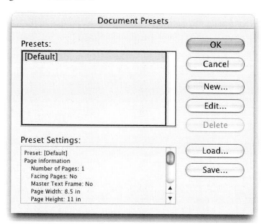

Getting to Know Bleeds and Slugs

Let's dig a little deeper into the New Document dialog box. Select the More Options button to reveal a new section called Bleed and

Slug. When a printed document has an image or color that extends to the very edge of a page, these items are described as bleeding off the edge (see Figure 6–5). A document can have bleeds that run off one, two, three or all four sides. When a document has bleed on all four sides, it is called a full bleed. A document with bleeds is printed on paper larger than the document size so that the bleeding page items can be printed 1/8 inch beyond the final (or trim) size of the piece. After printing, the piece is cut down to size and your image boldly runs all the way to the edge of the page. When you create a document with a bleed, you must set up the extra space needed in the Bleed field in the New Document dialog box. Your document will then appear on your monitor with the bleed area outlined beyond the edge of the page.

figure | 6–5

An image that extends to the very edge of a document is called a bleed.

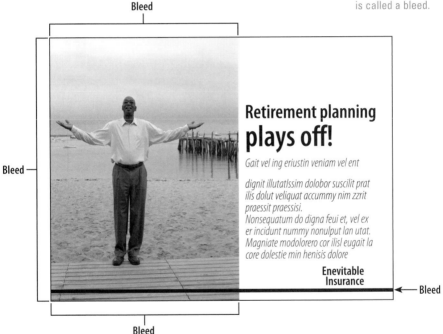

Bleed

Bleed

Retirement planning

plays off!

Gait vel ing eriustin veniam vel ent

dignit illutatlssim dolobor suscilit prat ilis dolut veliquat accummy nim zzrit praessit praessisi. Nonsequatum do digna feui et, vel ex er incidunt nummy nonulput lan utat. Magniate modolorero cor ilisl eugait la core dolestie min henisis dolore

Enevitable Insurance

Bleed

Bleed

Slugs are elements and text outside your page boundaries, and separate items from the document itself. Let's say you're working in an advertising agency. Every project goes through a series of proofings, and each member signs off on a little square near the document as each part is proofed. A slug is like an electronic sticky note outside the trim edge of the document. It's a perfect way to allow room for job numbers, project identifications, proofing boxes, or any other job notations.

figure | 6-6

This slug extends
one inch below
the document and
contains boxes for
each member of
the team to approve
the project. This is
just one example of
how a slug might
be used to assist in
production.

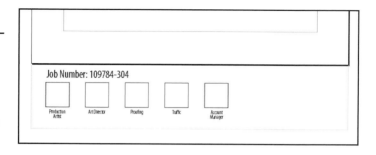

When you make a slug it is outside the final trim size. In the Print dialog box you can choose whether or not to print the slug by checking the Include Slug Area box. Bleeds and slugs are both created after you have determined the document's final trim size, and they are easy to set up.

figure | 6-7

The Include Slug
Area option, on
the Marks and
Bleed page of the
Print dialog box is
checked, indicating
that the slug will be
printed.

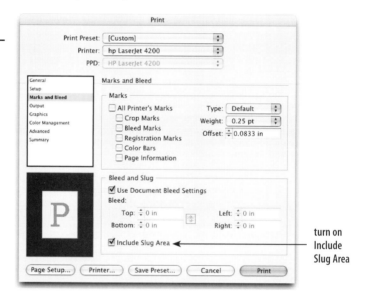

1. Open the New Document dialog box and create a new document, 5 × 7. Use your document preset if you made one earlier.
2. Select More Options. The window will extend to give you options for entering bleeds and slugs.
3. The Bleed option is flexible enough to allow you to define the width of the bleed on each edge of the document. If you need all four edges to bleed, click the Link icon before setting the bleed measurement to enter it in all four fields. For this exercise, add a 1/8-inch (0.125 in.) bleed on the top and right side of the document.

4. The Slug option lets you determine the size and location of your electronic sticky notes and works just like the Bleed option. Set up a 1/2-inch (0.5 in.) slug at the bottom of the document. Click OK or press Return.

5. Look at your document. You should see a red guideline extending 1/8 inch from the top and right side of the trim edge. All the page elements that you want to bleed should be created so that they extend to that outer line. You will also see a light blue guide box extending 1/2 inch from the bottom of the document. That is the slug area where you can add sign-off boxes, job numbers, or whatever the project requires.

Looking back to the New Document dialog box, the Page Size menu has many options. The sizes A4, A3, A5, and B5 are standard sizes used outside the United States. Here are standard sizes used in the United States:

- Letter: 8.5 × 11 inches

- Legal: 8.5 × 14 inches

- Letter—Half: 8.5 × 5.5 inches

- Legal—Half: 8.5 × 7 inches

- Tabloid: 11 × 17

- Compact Disc: 4.722 × 4.75 inches

Guides and Columns

Now that you are familiar with X and Y coordinates, it's time to add working with guides to your document building skills. Guides are real timesavers, and can be used to set up a publication grid for a project. A publication grid is a series of horizontal and vertical lines that break interior space into pleasing proportions. Using a grid strengthens alignment and helps bring unity to a project.

InDesign's system of guides is absolutely fantastic, and you will want to read the next part of this chapter while you are next to your computer. Guides are perfect for creating the "big picture" layout, but when precision is an absolute necessity, use coordinates. Using coordinates will size and place your objects with ease and pinpoint accuracy.

Adding and Deleting Page Guides

The easiest way to get a guide onto a document is to click on the vertical or horizontal ruler and drag the guide where you want it. The X or Y coordinate fields on the Control palette will show you exactly where the guide is placed, and allow you to change the position of the guide (see Figure 6–8). To reposition a guide, activate it by clicking on it, type a new coordinate in the X or Y field and press Return. To delete a guide, click on it and press Delete.

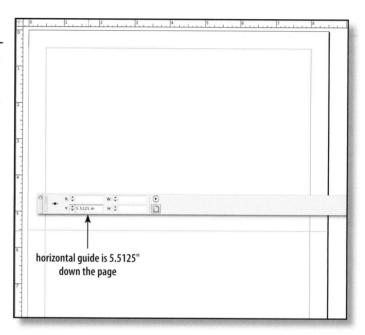

horizontal guide is 5.5125"
down the page

Changing Margin Guides on the Fly

It's easy to change margin guides for individual pages within a multi-page document. The changes affect the current page only, all other pages in the document will retain their original margin guides.

1. Create a new Letter size document with 1-inch margins. Enter **2** in the Number of Pages field.

2. Open the Pages palette (Window>Pages) and you will see a page icon with "1" below it. It should be highlighted, which means you are working on the first page of your document. Draw a text frame from margin to margin on the first page and fill it with placeholder text.

3. Choose Layout>Margins and Columns. In the Margins and Columns dialog box, change the left margin to 3 inches and

press Return. The left margin will change, but your text frame does not. Some of your text is now in the left margin area.

4. Print the first page of your document and confirm that the text outside the margin area prints.

5. In the Pages palette, double-click on the page icon with the "2" below it. What do you notice? The margins on page 2 are still at 1 inch. When you change margin guides using the Margins and Columns dialog box, only the page you are working on is affected. We will learn how to change margin guides for the entire document later in Chapter 9, where we cover Master Pages.

Document Columns and Text Frame Columns

Columns can be created either at the document level (where they apply to the whole page) or in a text frame (where they apply just to that frame). You make columns at the document level when you first create your document, and these will apply to every page. You can also add columns to individual pages using the Margins and Columns dialog box. Document column guides are moveable—you can select and drag them to the left or right with your mouse.

To create columns in a text frame, choose Object>Text Frame Options and change the value in the Number field. Column guides in a text frame are not moveable.

1. Create a new document with three columns.

2. Position the Selection tool cursor directly on one of the column guides and hold down the mouse button. A small double-ended arrow will appear and you can move the column guides back and forth. Repeat this procedure with the other column guides.

3. Now draw a text frame somewhere on your document and Using the Text Frame Options dialog box (Command+B [Mac] or Control+B [Windows]) divide it into two columns. Click on the frame's column guides and try to move them back and forth. They won't budge. Text frame column guides are not moveable.

Be exact when drawing text frames on a document with columns. Always keep frames inside the column guides, and do not allow the edge of the frames to extend over the gutter between columns. This is critical both for the alignment of your text, and for preventing text in one column from bumping up against text in the next.

Adjustable margin and column guides are welcome features when you can see how they enhance your production flow. The following newsletter project makes use of offset columns. Picture yourself working in the marketing department of a busy building supply company. You are designing the first page of a new monthly newsletter to be presented to the marketing team. Figure 6–9 shows the finished product. You can find the necessary artwork for this project on the CD that accompanies this book. Look in the Chapter 06>Artwork/Resources folder. The project will use files 06 House A, 06 House B, and 06 House C. As you work on this project you will learn a few tricks of the trade used in creating newsletters.

figure | 6–9 |

This is the sample newsletter you will present to the marketing team.

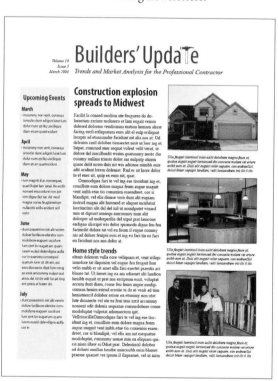

A Little about Newsletter Design...

Newsletters are a fun design projects! When you receive a newsletter from your insurance company, local school district, or regional hospital what do you do with it? Throw it away? Glance through it and then throw it out? Or... do you actually read it? As a designer, your objective is to have your newsletters read! Before you toss the next newsletter you receive, take a few minutes to examine it. Look for techniques the designer used to enhance interest and readability. The following points describe different types of newsletters.

- **Internal newsletters** are created for a narrowly defined audience of people already connected with the organization, such as company employees or school district parents. Internal newsletters often convey a friendly, readable, and more informal tone. Although the newsletter goes to a primarily "friendly" audience and has a greater chance of success, the design, photos, and typography will have a great influence on whether the newsletter is read or tossed.

- **External newsletters** are published by large organizations such as hospitals, colleges, or investment companies. These types of newsletters are often part of the organization's ongoing public relations effort, and is interesting to try to identify the organization's marketing objectives as you read them. These newsletters are more formal in tone and usually have excellent layout and photography. Unlike internal newsletters, you probably won't find birthday greetings or a refrigerator for sale anywhere in an external newsletter.

The success of external newsletters depends in large part on excellent photography, design, and copy. These newsletters are going to audiences where a larger percentage of readers are disinterested or even hostile. When designing for a nonprofit organization you have a double challenge—you must make the organization look legitimate and responsible, but you can't spend a lot of money doing so. This is a chance to let your design and typographic skills shine!

- **Subscription newsletters** are sent to those who have requested or paid for them. This audience is already "on your side." Of course design is always important, but weak design will not have the same devastating immediate effect because the audience is not likely to throw away information that they have paid for or requested.

The number of pages in a newsletter is usually divisible by four. Pages of a typical 8.5 × 11-inch newsletter are printed side by side on a 17 × 11 sheet (unless there's a bleed, in which case they are printed on oversized sheets). After printing both sides, the document is folded in half to create 4 pages (or collated together to make 8, 12, or 16 pages—whatever the length of your newsletter). When you create a newsletter, you should select Facing Pages in the New Document dialog box. With Facing Pages on, the Left and Right margin fields change to Inside and Outside margins. We will cover facing pages in depth, in Chapter 8. Let's get started on our newsletter project.

1. Create a new document, 8.5 × 11. Select Facing Pages. Top margin: 1.375, bottom, inside and outside margins: 0.5. Set the number of Columns to 3 and the Gutter field to 1-pica (1p) and click OK.

2. Offset the columns by moving the first set of column guides. Click on the left guide of the first set of column guides and drag it to the 2-inch mark. Move the next set of column guides by clicking on its left guide and moving it to the five-inch mark.

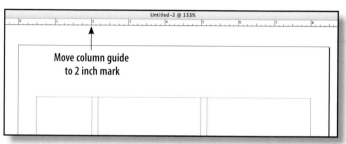

3. Next, you'll build the nameplate. A newsletter's title area is called the nameplate and is made up of a title, tagline, and publication information. A tagline usually provides a key to the newsletter's content or purpose. Many people will mistakenly call this area of the newsletter the masthead. The masthead, however, is the area of the publication (usually on page 2 or 3 or inside the back cover) that lists the publisher, subscription rates, and so on. Draw a text frame from the left edge of the second column to the right edge of the third column. Type the newsletter title, **Builders' Update**, in Myriad Pro Condensed 56/14. (The "t" in "Update" in the sample newsletter is Toolbox, 52-point.) Move the text frame so that the baseline of the title is aligned with the top margin guide. Open the Swatches palette under Window>Swatches (or press F5). You will learn about the features of the Swatches palette in Chapter 12. For now, you will use a color that has been predefined and stored in the Swatches palette. Select the newsletter title and click on the dark blue swatch square in the Swatches palette. (The Swatches palette may not actually name the color blue. It may just have CMYK equivalents such as C=100% M=90% Y=10% K=0%.) Next type the tagline, **Trends and Market Analysis for the Professional Contractor**, and make it Times New Roman Italic 14/21, black.

4. Add the publication information by drawing another text frame that spans the width of the first column. Type the fol-

lowing on three separate lines with a Return after each: **Volume 10**, **Issue 3**, and **March 2004**. Select the lines and make them Times New Roman 9/auto, right justified. Use the Text Frame Options dialog box to set the Vertical Justification's Align field to Bottom and roughly align the baseline of March 2004 with the baseline of the tagline under the title. You will align this text frame with more precision a bit later. Your newsletter should look similar to Figure 6–11

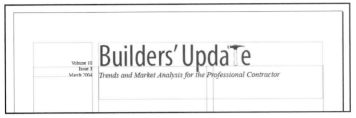

figure | 6–11 |

The nameplate is also called the banner or flag; but it is not the masthead.

The publication information in the nameplate includes:

- Volume: the number of years the publication has been in print.
- Issue: the number of times the publication has been issued this year
- Date: current month

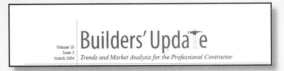

5. It's time to create the sidebar. Skilled designers incorporate devices that encourage people to read. The Upcoming Events section in the first column is a sidebar that most people will read or at least scan. People usually read headlines, subheads, sidebars, photo captions, and bulleted copy. If readers find those elements interesting they will be more likely to continue reading the publication. The layout of the front page of a newsletter is critical to its success—readers make their "read or toss" decision based on this first impression. Fill the first column with a text frame. The Y coordinate should be 2.1667 (be sure your reference point in the Control palette proxy to the upper left corner). Set a .0625 inset on all sides of the frame. Open the Swatches palette and select the yellow colored swatch. In the upper right corner of the palette, change the value in the Tint field to 30. (Remember to click the Fill icon at the bottom of the Toolbox.) Fill with placeholder text. Highlight the text and change it to Myriad Pro Light 8/12. Type **Upcoming Events** at

the top of the sidebar in Myriad Pro Bold Condensed 16/auto. Type the name of each month in Myriad Pro Bold Condensed 12/12, and create paragraphs similar to those shown in Figure 6–12. Be sure to add bullets and use Indent to Here to hang paragraphs on the bullets. Add a .0625 S/B (space before) to the paragraph containing each month's name.

figure | 6–12 |

Including this type of sidebar or a table of contents on the front page is an excellent way to increase interest and readership.

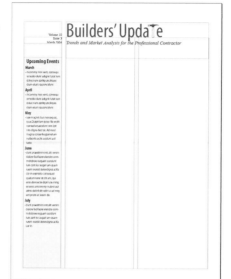

6. You are ready to add the feature article. Draw a text frame in the middle column (Y=2.0) and fill with placeholder text. Change all copy to Times New Roman 10/12. Type the headline, **Construction explosion spreads to Midwest**, in Myriad Pro Bold Condensed 24/18, S/A p6. Type the subhead further down in the column in Myriad Pro Bold Condensed 16/auto. Add a .125 first line indent on all paragraphs except those that are preceded by a headline or subhead. (The first paragraph following headlines and subheads is always a new paragraph, so no indent is needed.) Your newsletter should look similar to Figure 6–13.

figure | 6–13 |

A first line indent is not necessary for paragraphs following a headline or a subhead.

7. Create the baseline grid. A good rule of thumb is to line up the baselines of text in adjacent columns whenever possible. You

achieve this by creating an invisible set of baseline guides and then locking the text to those guides. We will create a baseline grid that begins at the top margin and continues in 12-point increments. If you are on a Mac, choose InDesign>Preferences> Grids and type **1.375** in the Start field, and **1p** in the Increment Every field, press Return. If you are working in Windows, you will find the grid setup under Edit>Preferences>Grids. The grid increment is usually the same as the leading measurement used for body copy in the document. Choose View>Show Baseline Grid and your document will have horizontal guidelines from the top to the bottom in 12-point increments, similar to Figure 6–14.

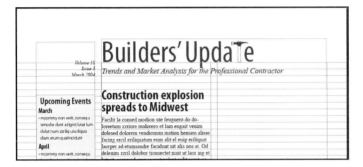

figure | 6–14 |

Baseline grids extend the length of the page. The copy in this example has not been aligned to the baseline grid.

8. Because aligning to a baseline grid overrides leading, S/A, and S/B settings, there are many times when you will want to align just the first line in a text frame to the baseline grid. But in this example, you will align your text to the baseline grid. If you look at the baselines of text in the two first columns you can see that they do not line up with the grid or each other. Once the grid has been created you tell InDesign to align the text to it. Highlight all the type in the nameplate and click the Align to Baseline Grid icon in the Control palette (see Figure 6–15). The text will jump into place. Continue the process with the issue and date information. You may need to slightly adjust the size and placement of the text frame to make the information align with the rest of the nameplate. Highlight all the text in the main article and select Align to Baseline Grid. Do the same for the Upcoming Events sidebar.

figure | 6–15 |

By default the "normal" mode is activated. For this project you want to turn Align to Baseline Grid on.

align to baseline grid

"normal" mode

9. Place the photos. Draw a rectangle frame the width of the third column, height 1.9931", with a 0.5-pt. stroke. Place the top of the frame two gridlines from the newsletter tagline with the right edge flush to the right margin. Now you will create two more copies of the frame and space them five grid lines apart. Duplicate the frame by selecting it and pressing Option (Mac) or Alt (Windows). You will see a white arrowhead next to the black cursor, meaning a duplicate is ready to be created. As you hold the Option or Alt key and drag the frame, a copy of the original will appear and can be placed in a new position on the document.

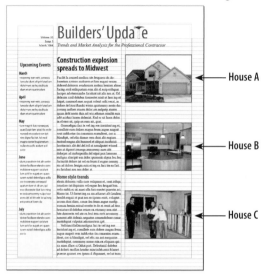

Release the mouse and Option or Alt key. Repeat the Option or Alt + drag process to create two more frames. From the accompanying CD, place 06 House A in the top box, 06 House B in the middle frame, and 06 House C in the third frame. Scale and crop photos as shown in Figure 6–16.

10. Add photo captions. Draw text frames and fill with placeholder text, format as Times New Roman Italic, 8/auto. In a newsletter, it's almost impossible to have every single line

figure | 6–16

Use a .5-pt. black rule on your photo frames. (The rules in this example are thicker in order to show with the baseline grid.)

figure | 6–17

The first line of each photo caption is locked to the baseline. Locking only the first line is a good technique to use if aligning all the text would make the leading too wide.

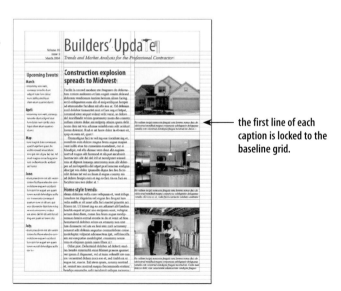

the first line of each caption is locked to the baseline grid.

locked to a baseline grid. When text just can't line up, it's a good idea to align at least the first baseline. In the case of the captions, 8-pt. type looks terrible when aligned to a 12-pt. baseline grid—the leading is too wide. In this case, align only the first line to the grid. First click the Align to Baseline Grid icon as usual, but then click on the palette menu at the end of the Control palette and choose Only Align First Line to Grid.

11. Add finishing touches. Draw a 0.5-pt. vertical rule down the middle of the first column gutter. Then draw a 0.5-pt. horizontal rule under the nameplate. Your newsletter is now complete!

Create Horizontal and Vertical Grids with Guides

In the last project you experienced firsthand how effective a horizontal baseline grid can be for aligning type. Creating grids that are made up of both horizontal and vertical lines bring an additional level of order to your documents. Formatting a document's interior space begins first by establishing margins and then defining text areas and image areas. Grids are very helpful in this process. They can be used to define specific placement for photos, headlines, page numbers (folios) and other page elements, or they can assist with overall page design by dividing the interior space into pleasing proportions. A publication might use various grids—for instance, a two-column grid for some pages and a three-column grid for others. The newsletter completed in the previous example was based on a 3-column grid, with the outside column being narrower. Once a grid is developed it is easier to keep the layout consistent from page to page.

NOTE: One of InDesign's great features is the Option+drag (Mac) or Alt+drag (Windows) method of duplicating items. But remember, this only works when one of the selection tools is active. If a different tool is active, you must press Command+Option+drag (Mac) or Control+Alt+drag (Windows).

Creating a Publication Grid

This project will be a quick one. You are still working at your last job—the building supply company. This time you are creating a sales flyer to advertise a new subdivision. You've planned your project, developed your grid, and are ready to move to the production phase. Figure 6–18 shows your finished product.

figure | 6–18 |

figure | 6–18 |

A sales flyer created
with a publication
grid.

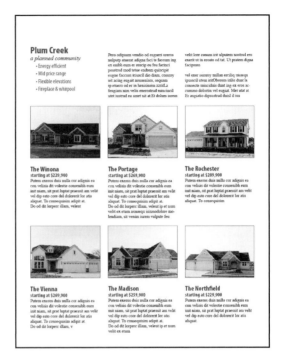

figure | 6–19 |

Your grid layout
should look like this.

1. Create a new letter-size document with a 1-inch top margin and 0.5-inch margins on the bottom and sides.

2. Choose Layout>Create Guides. Create five rows and three columns, both with 1-pica gutters. Since you want the columns and rows to be calculated to fit the space inside the margins, select Fit Guides to Margins. Check Preview and look at your screen. Your document should look like Figure 6–19. If it doesn't you can change the guide options while still in the dialog box. When the guides are correct, press OK.

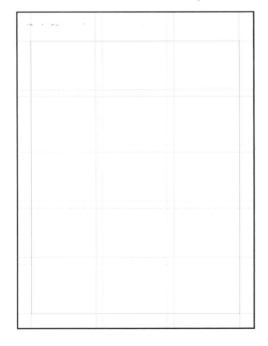

3. We're going to "rough in" the document before getting to the nitty-gritty production details. Draw a single text frame in the top row of the left column. Use the Option+drag or Alt+drag technique to make two more frames. Place them in the top row of the center and right columns. Link these last two frames together by clicking on the out port of the center frame and anywhere inside of the third frame.

figure | 6–20 |

Drag and drop a duplicate of this setup box into each text area on the publication grid.

4. In the first column, second row, draw a rectangle frame with a .5-pt. black stroke. This will be used to contain a photo. Duplicate the frame five times, filling rows 2 and 4 with a total of six frames.

5. Using the grid as a guide, draw another text frame in row 3, column 1. Fill with placeholder text. Select all the text and change it to Times New Roman 10/12. Type **The Winona** on the first line of text and press Return. Type **starting at $229,900** on the next line and press Return. Highlight "The Winona" and change the typeface to Myriad Pro Black Condensed 16/ auto. Highlight the price line and change the typeface to Myriad Pro Black Condensed 12/13. You have just created a setup box.

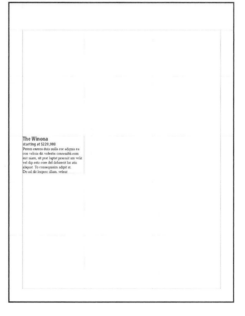

NOTE: Use a setup box or setup lines when you have several items that are formatted exactly the same. Get your first frame (or lines) exactly like you want, and then duplicate for as many frames or lines as you need. Then simply type new text over the original. Setup boxes and lines eliminate the need for formatting each item separately—and speed up production time especially when there are multiple character attributes involved.

Be very sure that your first setup box or setup line is exactly the way you want it before you begin to duplicate it. I recommend printing it out once or twice to be sure. When the first one is perfect— and I mean 100% perfect—go ahead and duplicate. If there's one little thing wrong with your original setup, you'll end up going back and changing all your duplications, one at a time. Shudder.

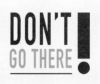

6. Drag and duplicate the setup text box to each of the five other locations, using the grid lines for placement. Refer back to the sample flyer in Figure 6–18 and change the model name and price for each model.

7. Place the house photos. You'll find them on the accompanying CD in the Chapter 06>Artwork/Resources folder. Scale and crop photos similar to those shown in the completed sample.

8. Fill columns 2 and 3 in row 1 with placeholder text, Times New Roman 10/auto.

9. Type the information in the first column: **Plum Creek**: Myriad Pro Black Condensed 22/auto. **a planned community**: Times New Roman Italic 14/16. Bulleted copy: Myriad Pro Condensed 14/18, 0.125-in. indent. Voila! You are finished. Print out a copy to show it to the Marketing Manager for approval.

Aligning and Distributing Objects

Last summer when my husband and I were building a deck on our house, we wanted to evenly distribute the railing spindles between the support posts. After reassembling the first spindled section three times we finally figured a system. We had done this exact process hundreds of times on the computer—how could it be so difficult doing it in real life? In the following exercises you will see how easy it is to build a virtual deck railing using the Align palette.

1. Create a new letter-size document, landscape orientation, 0.5" margins. Using the Line tool, draw a vertical line for the corner post. In the Control palette, type **4.25 in.** in the Length field, and **20 pt.** in the Stroke Weight field.

2. Press F10 to open the Stroke palette, choose Circle Solid in the Start field. Your corner post should look like Figure 6–21. Use the duplicate shortcut to create two other corner posts. Place one at the left margin, one in the center, and one at the right margin. Don't worry if they don't line up, we'll fix that in a minute.

figure | 6–21

This is a single corner porch post.

3. Press Shift+F7 to open the Align palette. Examine the palette. The upper half is used for aligning elements, and the bottom half is for distributing (or spacing) items.

the Align palette with options showing ⟶

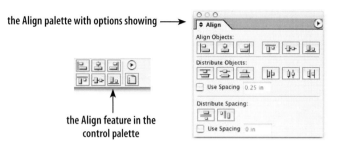

the Align feature in the control palette

figure | 6–22|

Some of the Align features are found on the Control palette. All of the alignment features are found on the Align palette which is accessed by pressing Shift+F7.

NOTE: Aligning elements means lining them up in a uniform relationship to each other. Distributing them means assigning uniform spacing between each element.

4. Draw a 10-pt. porch spindle about 2.5 in. long. Option+drag or Alt+drag the spindles until there are five spindles between each porch post. They don't line up (see Figure 6–23), so let's fix them.

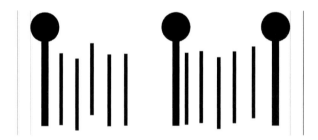

figure | 6–23|

You should now have three posts and ten spindles have been added.

5. Select the posts and spindles and click the upper left icon on the Align palette, Align Left Edges. The spindles and posts all rush to the left side of the page, and the left edges of all elements line up exactly with the outermost point of the circle on top of the post (see Figure 6–24).
6. Undo the last align command. With the objects still selected, choose the next icon over—Align Horizontal Centers. Your posts are now stacked on top of each other like a tidy pile of lumber (see Figure 6–24).
7. Undo, again. Now choose the third icon, Align Right Edges. This time objects are pushed to the right—to the outermost edge of the circle on top of the porch post (see Figure 6–24).
8. Undo, once more. Go to the fourth icon, Align Top Edges. Your posts will look like Figure 6–24.

9. Undo the last align command. Go to the fifth icon, Align Vertical Centers. This still isn't quite right (see Figure 6–24).

figure | 6–24

The icons used in the Align palette make sense once you experiment with them.

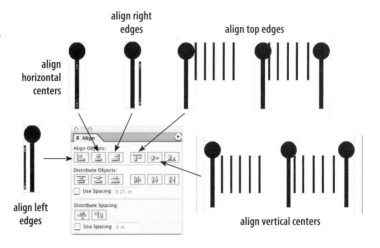

10. Undo. Finally, select the far right icon in the top row, Align Bottom Edges. That's what we are looking for (see Figure 6–25). The bottoms are aligned, but the spindles are still not evenly spaced. That's the next fix.

11. Examine the lower half of the Align palette where the Distribute functions are located. This part of the palette is used to evenly space objects. In order to use the distribute functions, you must have three or more elements selected. We want all porch spindles evenly spaced on the horizontal plane. Thus, you will use the Distribute icons in the right half of the palette. With your posts and spindles selected, try out the horizontal Distribute icons. You will discover that it works best to distribute space according to the objects' centers. The Distribute icons in the left half of the palette control distribution of space in the vertical plane so that the tops, centers, or bottoms of selected items are equally spaced.

figure | 6–25

The spindles and posts are aligned at their bases and distributed evenly from their centers.

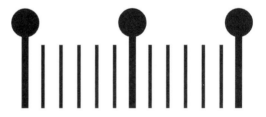

Sometimes when using Align functions, it's helpful to establish an anchor point so you know exactly where your elements will end up. The anchor point is like a corner post—it becomes the point of reference for the rest of the railing. To establish an anchor point, select the object and then lock its position by pressing Command+L (Mac) or Control+L (Windows). You can also find this command under the Object menu. To unlock the position, press Command+Option+L (Mac) or Control+Option+L (Windows).

NOTE: Macintosh users: For speed and efficiency, keep your ring finger on the Shift key, your middle finger on Option, and your pointer on the Command key. Some power users refer to this position as your "three magic fingers"—others refer to it as "the claw." Whatever you call it, when these three keys become automatic, they give you the edge in InDesign proficiency.

Other Object Management Techniques

As you have seen in the previous exercises, knowing how to manage elements in your document saves time and frustration. The following five techniques can be easily mastered—beginning with Step and Repeat.

1. Create a new document and draw a 1.5-inch square. Fill it with black.

2. With the square selected, press Shift+Command+V (Mac) or Shift+Control+V (Windows) to open the Step and Repeat dialog box. You can also choose Edit>Step and Repeat.

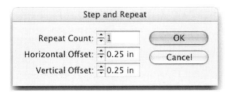

figure | 6–26 |

The Step and Repeat dialog box

3. The dialog box needs to know how many additional objects you would like and where you would like them positioned, starting from the original object. Enter **5** in the Repeat Count field and press Return. If InDesign defaults are in place, you will see that five additional squares are staggered 0.25 inches over and down from each other. If Step and Repeat coordinates were used previously, the squares are placed at whatever settings were used before. (If you get a dialog box that says, "Cannot add objects beyond the bounds of the pasteboard," you will have to decrease either the number of items to repeat or the distance you want them to offset from each other.)

figure | **6-27**

The squares should jump into place.

4. Undo. This time, type **3** in the Repeat Count field, **2** in the Horizontal Offset field, and **0** in the Vertical Offset field, press Return. Your squares should now look like Figure 6–27.

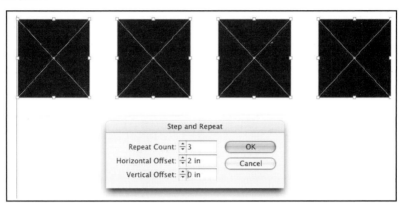

5. Undo. Now, type **4** in the Repeat Count field, **0** in the Horizontal Offset field, and **2** in the Vertical Offset field. There are now five squares equally spaced in a vertical line.

Managing Object Layers

If you have ever stacked pancakes on a plate, you already know the concept of how object layers work in InDesign. Just like pulling pancakes off the bottom of the stack to place them on the top, InDesign allows you to change the stacking order of objects in your document. You can shift the objects from the top of the pile to the bottom of the pile by using some great keyboard shortcuts.

Don't confuse *object* layers with *document* layers. Document layers are more like having several *plates* of pancakes stacked on top of each other. Document layers allow you to adjust the stacking order of the plates, and will be covered in more detail in Chapter 7. The following steps demonstrate the most common commands used to change an object's stacking order.

Send Forward, to Front, Backward, and to Back

1. Create a new document. Draw three shapes approximately the same size: a circle, a square, and a hexagon (located in the fly-out menu in the Rectangle tool). Open the Swatch palette and fill the circle with red, the square with blue, and the hexagon with yellow.

2. Move the circle so that it slightly overlaps the square. Then put the hexagon on the top of the stack. Your pile of objects should look like Figure 6–28.

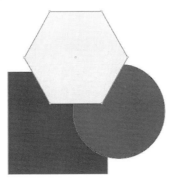

figure | 6–28 |

These objects are stacked on top of each other, creating object layers.

3. Send Backward and Send Forward. You have just created a "stack of pancakes" and we are going to shuffle their stacking order. Select the hexagon. Press Command+[(Mac) or Control+[(Windows) and watch the hexagon move back one layer. It is now sandwiched between the circle and square. Press the same shortcut key and the hexagon will now be at the bottom of the stack. Now, press Command+] (Mac) or Control+] (Windows) and the hexagon will come forward one layer at a time. Practice sending each object forward and backward until the shortcut keys become automatic. All of the stacking order commands can also be accessed by choosing Object>Arrange and then selecting one of the four stacking commands.

4. Send to Back and Send to Front. To send selected objects all the way to the back or to the front of the stack, add the Shift key to the shortcut keys you just learned. So, Send to the Back becomes Shift+Option+[(Mac) or Shift+Alt+[(Windows) and Send to the Front becomes Shift+Option+] (Mac) or Shift+Alt+] (Windows). Practice sending each object to the front and back until the shortcut keys feel comfortable. Keep your document open because we are going to use it for the next exercise.

Selecting Stacked Objects

InDesign uses related shortcut keys for related functions, and after a while you begin to recognize a pattern. In this exercise you will learn how to select items that are stacked on top of each other. Using our pancakes analogy, there are times you might want to peek through the stack of pancakes to see which has the most (or fewest) blueberries. This exercise demonstrates how to select objects that are in the middle of the stack. Begin by layering your three shapes in the stacking order shown in Figure 6–29. Use the Align commands to line up the center of all the objects. This time, use the Align buttons that are found on the Control palette. The two Align commands you need are the same as in the Align palette.

figure | 6–29 |

Use the Align function to line up the centers of your shapes.

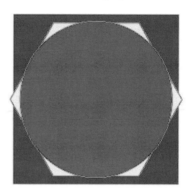

1. Selecting Through Objects. InDesign allows you to "dig" from the top object down through each object layer with one simple click. Select the top object, and press Command (Mac) or Control (Windows) and click. Each click selects the next object below in the stack. Watch the selection handles carefully to determine which object is selected.

2. Select Next Object Above and Next Object Below. When you want to select an item somewhere in the middle of the stack, use Command+Option (Mac) or Control+Alt (Windows) with the left and right brackets and you will move through your stack of shapes. Practice moving down and up through your stack. As your documents become more complex, the Arrange and Select keyboard shortcuts will become an indispensable tool.

Cut, Copy, Paste, Paste Into, Paste in Place

Cut, copy, and paste commands are basic functions you may already know, but they are such important functions that they bear repeating. InDesign also includes two special Paste features.

The Cut command shortcut is Command+X (Mac) or Control+X (Windows). There is a difference between using the Delete key and the Cut command. When you select an object and press Delete, the object is gone forever (unless you Undo it). When you select an object and choose Cut, the object is removed from your document but kept in the short-term memory area of your computer, called the clipboard. The clipboard can only hold one thing at a time so don't depend on the clipboard for storage.

The Copy command shortcut is Command+C (Mac) or Control+C (Windows). When you select an object and copy it, the object remains in the document and a copy of it goes to the clipboard, replacing what was previously stored there.

The Paste command shortcut is Command+V (Mac) or Control+V (Windows). When you use this command, whatever is stored in the clipboard will reappear on the page you are working on. This means you can paste clipboard items on the same page, on a different page, or into a new document. When an object is pasted from the clipboard it will be positioned in the center of the screen.

InDesign's Paste in Place command is a great function. When you use Paste in Place, the object is positioned in the exact same location whether pasted on the same page, a different page in the same document, or a page in another InDesign document. The shortcut key for Paste in Place is another example of how InDesign shortcut keys are related. A regular Paste is Command+V (Mac) or Control+V (Windows). Paste in Place is Shift+Option+Command+V (Mac) or Shift+Alt+Control (Windows).

InDesign's Paste Into command is very similar to placing photos inside frames—except that it works with objects that InDesign can create or manipulate on screen.

1. Draw a black square. We're going to call this the container.
2. Double-click on the Polygon tool to open the Polygon Settings dialog box and type **40%** in the Star Inset field. Click OK and drag a star onto your document. Fill the star with white from the Color palette (F6). The star will be the content.
3. Position the content. Select both shapes and, using the Align icons on the Control palette, center the star horizontally and vertically on the square. This establishes the final position of the content (see Figure 6–30).

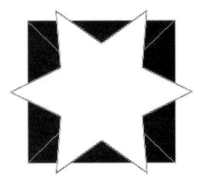

figure | 6–30 |

Use the Align palette to center the star on top of the square.

4. Cut the content by selecting only the star and pressing Command+X (Mac) or Control+X (Windows). The star is now removed from the document and stored in the clipboard.

5. Paste Into the container by selecting the square and pressing Command+Option+V (Mac) or Control+Alt+V (Windows). This process is also called *nesting*. The image should look like Figure 6–31.

figure | 6–31 |

The star is pasted into the square.

6. Use the Selection tool to move the container and the content.

7. Use the Direct Selection tool and select either the container or the content. Once one is selected, you can drag the item to adjust its position.

8. To remove the content, select it and use the Cut command.

Grouping Elements

Combining two or more items into a group is a great way to manage multiple design elements. Like individual states within the United States, each element retains its unique properties, but all are grouped together to form a larger unit. Once a group is created you can move, copy, cut, and transform the group as a whole. And you can still perform all the functions you normally would with each individual member of the group.

1. Create a new document. Draw a text frame and a rectangle.

2. Select both objects.

3. Press Command+G (Mac) or Control+G (Windows). You should see a new bounding box that now stretches around both elements.

4. Choose the Selection tool and move the items. They will move as a group.

5. Choose the Direct Selection tool and notice that you can now move one of the elements in the group independently of the other. You can also manipulate the paths and anchor points on each element.

6. Draw a larger rectangle. Select all the objects and create a group. The bounding box grows to encompass all the objects. Creating groups within groups is another variety of nested objects.

7. To ungroup elements, press Shift+Command+G (Mac) or Shift+Control+G (Windows). You must repeat the process to ungroup each nested group.

The Transform Palette: One More Look

You are already familiar with the power of the Transform palette. You have already learned how to select a reference point and move or resize objects using coordinates. You can open the Transform palette by pressing F9 or choosing Window>Transform. Here's a trick that will help when you are using the Transform palette and want to resize an object proportionately. When you type a new value in the H field, hold down Command (Mac) or Control (Windows) as you press Return and the width and height dimensions will remain proportional. If you want scaling to always be proportional, select the link button. When the link is closed, the width and height percentages will remain proportional and you don't need to hold down the Command (Mac) or Control (Windows) key. If the link is open, you must hold down Command (Mac) or Control (Windows) to constrain the percentages.

The Transform palette also allows you to rotate objects. When rotating, you must note where the object's reference point is because this will be the center point for the rotation. Set a percentage in the Rotation Angle field and see how this feature works. The palette menu on the Transform palette allows you to rotate and flip an object at predetermined settings. Figure 6–32 shows all the palette menu options.

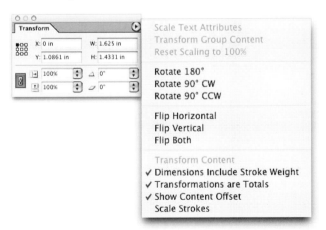

figure | 6–32

Press the round button with the triangle, on the right end of the Transform palette, to open the palette menu.

The Transform palette also includes a Shear function, which makes your type or object oblique. This can be great for modifying frames and shapes, but please restrain yourself from using this tool for making fake italics or an oblique typeface. As a professional artist, you should use an oblique or italic font designed by a professional typographer rather than hacking out one of your own.

NOTE: Be careful when using the Direct Selection tool to work with nested objects. The commands performed by the Transform palette will affect the selected container and its contents. This behavior can be tricky when you have multiple levels of nested objects.

SUMMARY

We've covered lots of ground in this chapter, and have just begun to delve into the depths of InDesign. New skills take time to develop and as you master the basics, you will continue to add new techniques to your repertoire. Become familiar with document presets, guides and columns, baseline grids, and aligning objects. Take seriously the importance of a strong layout and the use of keyboard shortcuts. Know that every advantage you can gain with InDesign will be an advantage for you and your clients in the marketplace.

in review

1. For what types of documents should you make presets?

2. What is the measurement of a standard bleed? How much space do you allow outside the document area for a full bleed?

3. What are some advantages of using columns and guides?

4. Why are a reader's first impressions of a newsletter (or any document you design) so critical?

5. What are some characteristics of the three types of newsletters described in this chapter?

6. What is the purpose of using a baseline grid?

7. Why must you take time to plan a project and work with thumbnails before jumping in and creating your document?

8. What is a setup box or a setup line? When and how do you use it?

9. Explain the difference between Step and Repeat, and aligning and distributing objects.

10. What are some advantages in grouping items together? What is nesting?

11. Explain how to move through object layers using keyboard shortcuts.

↗ EXPLORING ON YOUR OWN

These two projects are included on the CD accompanying this book. The first, a CD cover, uses document presets, bleeds, align, and distribute. The second project uses a publication grid and should be a quick project. PDF files with directions for each project are in the Chapter 06 folder on the CD.

Project 06B Designer Focus

Project 06A CD Cover

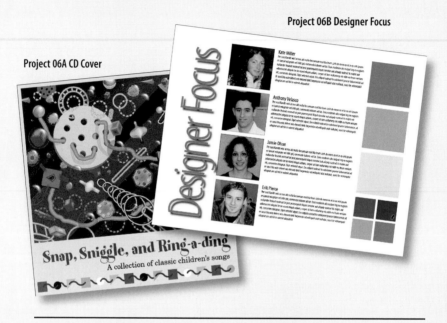

The artwork for Project 06A was created in Adobe Illustrator by Steve Cowal, a 2004 graduate of the Harry V. Quadracci Printing and Graphics Center, Waukesha County Technical College.

notes

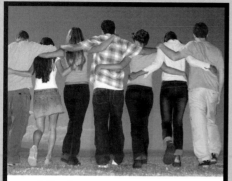

No **love**
no **friendship,**
can cross the
path of our destiny
without leaving
some mark on it
forever.

℞ Francois Mocuriac

charting your course

My daughter owns a rescued greyhound named Penny. Once we took her to a large baseball field to see just how fast this dog could run. Penny was trembling with excitement, eager to run. When we released her she was like a speeding bullet.

Like Penny, you have been training to race. You have learned many InDesign basics and are now "trembling at the end of your leash" waiting to be let loose. Beginning with this chapter, *Exploring InDesign* will be more production-based—building on previously learned skills while introducing new techniques and typographic principles. You're going to explore a lot of new territory—what an adventure this will be!

 goals

- **Apply text wrap**
- **Create inline graphics**
- **Manage document layers**
- **Create transparency and feathering**
- **Set fractions**

INTEGRATING TEXT AND GRAPHICS

Text and graphics need to work together. It's important to match the personality of the typeface with the style of the graphic. It is also important to create a visual link between the graphic and the text that accompanies it. In design terms, this is called the principle of proximity. One method of visually linking text and graphics is by using text wrap.

An Introduction to Text Wrap

Text wrap is the process of flowing text around a graphic or shape. Text is like a river that flows smoothly until it hits a rock — a shape or graphic. The river might go around the rock or over the rock, but in either case it just keeps flowin' along. You apply text wrap options to shapes or graphics (the "rocks") to control how the text river flows around them. Here's how easy this is to accomplish in InDesign.

1. Create a letter size document. Draw a two-column text frame that fills the margins. Fill the frame with placeholder text. Draw a black circle, approximately 2 in. in diameter and place it in the middle of the two columns.

2. Open the Text Wrap palette by pressing Command+Option+W (Mac) or Control+Alt+W (Windows). You can also access the Text Wrap palette by choosing Window>Type & Tables>Text Wrap (but you already know that using the menus rather than using keyboard shortcuts is far too much manual labor!). Each button on the palette activates a different text wrap mode. Figure 7–1 shows each of the Text Wrap options.

figure | 7–1 |

The Text Wrap palette contains five buttons that alter the flow of text around objects.

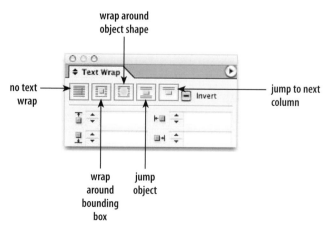

3. The black circle is the rock in the middle of your text flow. Select the circle and then activate each of the text wrap modes to see how it affects the text. The first mode is No Text Wrap, this is the default mode. In this mode, the text flows over or under the object (see Figure 7–2).

4. Select the circle and choose the second button, Wrap Around Bounding Box. You will see the text flow around the square bounding box (Figure 7–3). Notice that the bounding box is always a square even if the object is not.

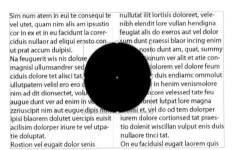

figure | **7–2** |

Text flows freely over or under the object in No Text Wrap mode. ▦

Text wraps around the bounding box.

figure | **7–3** |

5. Now select the third option, Wrap Around Object Shape. In this mode, the text flows around the shape of any graphic inside the frame, or in this case, around the shape itself (see Figure 7–4).

6. The fourth option is Jump Object. In this mode, the text leap-frogs over the object to the next available space (see Figure 7–5).

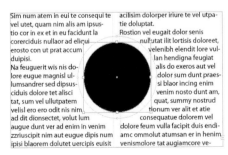

figure | **7–4** |

Text wraps around the object inside the frame or around the outer shape of the frame. ▦

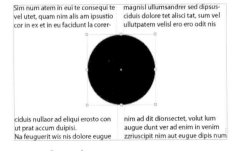

figure | **7–5** |

Text is jumping the object.

7. The last mode, Jump to Next Column, jumps the text over to the next column (see Figure 7–6).

8. Select the circle, move it to the center of the first column and give it a background color of None. Select the Wrap Around Object Shape mode and turn on the Invert option. The text now flows inside the selected object (see Figure 7–7). InDesign allows you to flow your "text river" inside the "rocks"! Don't close your file. You'll need it for the next exercise.

figure | 7–6

Jump to Next Column text wrap mode.

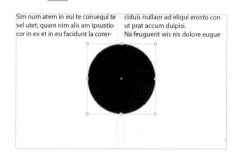

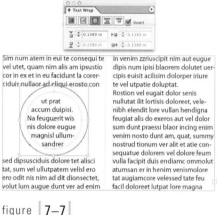

figure | 7–7

Text wrap in the Inverted mode flows text inside simple objects.

Introduction to Document Layers

In the last chapter you were introduced to object layers, which were compared to a stack of pancakes. You used keyboard shortcuts to rearrange the objects in the stack. In this chapter you're going to make document layers. Document layers are like a stack of plates, each plate holding its own pile of pancakes. Document layers are easy to understand, and they greatly simplify the production of complex projects.

1. Delete the circle you created in the last exercise. Press F7 to open the Layers palette (see Figure 7–8). Every document has one layer, which is currently shown in the Layers palette. The eye icon on the left side of the palette means that the layer is visible. If you click the eye icon, your text will vanish but will reappear when you click the icon again. Being able to hide layers is a great convenience. You can place all sorts of guides, text, or elements on a layer and then hide them as needed.

2. Next to the eye icon there is an empty box. If you click that box, a pencil with a diagonal red line appears, meaning the layer is locked and you can no longer edit its elements. Like the eye icon, this is a switch that toggles on and off. The next field should have a blue box and say Layer 1. The

figure | 7-8 |

Pressing F7 brings up the Layers palette.

box indicates the color being used to display the bounding boxes and frames on that layer. Double-click on Layer 1 and the Layer Options dialog box opens. In this dialog box you can change the name of the layer, color of the guides, and perform other housekeeping functions such as Suppress Text

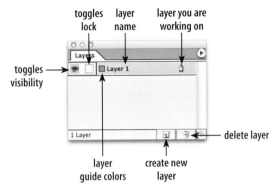

Wrap When Layer Is Hidden. (When you select this option, any text wrap mode you have applied to an object will be turned off when you hide the layer.) While you are in this dialog box, change the name of the layer to Text and click OK. The pen icon at the top right end of the Layers palette indicates which layer you are currently working on.

3. Now let's make a new layer. Hold down the Option (Mac) or Alt (Windows) key and click the Create New Layer icon at the bottom of the palette. The New Layer dialog box opens with the Name field highlighted. Type **Circle** in the Name field. Notice the color of the guides and click OK. Now, draw a black circle on that layer and center it between the columns of text. Experiment with each of the text wrap modes and you will see that text wrap still works, even when elements are on different layers. Hide the Circle layer. Notice that the wrap still applies. Make the layer visible again and double-click on the Circle layer name. In the Layer Options dialog box turn on the Suppress Text Wrap When Layer Is Hidden option. Now hide the layer and you will see the text reflow as if the object wasn't even there. Make the layer visible once more and the text wrap will become active again.

NOTE: You can override the text wrap function for individual items. Select the frame and press Command+B (Mac) or Control+B (Windows) to open the Text Frame Options dialog box (or choose Object>Text Frame Options). Select Ignore Text Wrap at the bottom of the dialog box and click OK.

4. Without holding down the Option or Alt key, click the Create New Layer icon three or four more times. Numerically named layers will be added to the list, one on top of the other. This is a good method to use when you don't need to name the layers, but since layers are used to organize a document, you will usually name them. Delete layers by dragging them to the trash can or by clicking them and clicking on the trash can.

5. Select the Circle layer. Select the circle shape with one of the Selection tools. Look at the Circle layer field in the Layers palette, you will see a little box to the right of the pen icon. Drag this small square to the next layer up. You have just moved the circle shape from the Circle layer to a new layer. This is how you can move selected elements from one layer to the next.

Using Layers to Create Two Versions of a Document

In this project you will design a page from a recipe book featuring recipes from all over the United States (see Figure 7–9). You will use layers to construct this document so it contains two versions of a chocolate chip cookie recipe—one designed for home bakers, and a big-batch version intended for institutional cooking. You will also use the features of a new font technology called OpenType to create true fractions.

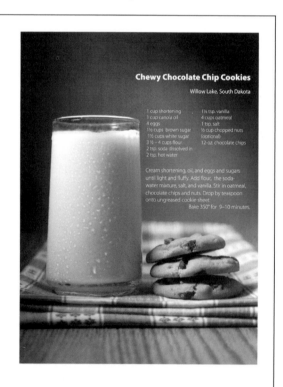

figure | 7–9 |

This example shows a single recipe for chocolate chip cookies. On a separate hidden layer is a second recipe version.

1. Create a new document. Document size: 8.5 × 11 in. Top, bottom, and right margins: 0.5. Left margin 0.75 (to accommodate spiral binding). Click OK. Press F7 to open the Layers palette. Change the name of Layer 1 to Picture. Draw a frame from margin to margin. Place 07 Cookies.tif from the Chapter 07 folder and scale proportionately to 111%. Reset the zero point to the far right edge of the document and drop in a vertical guide at -0.75 on the X coordinate.

2. Create a new layer and name it Consumer Recipe. Type the information as shown in Figure 7–10. You may also refer to Figure 10 in the color insert in this book. The figure below shows the text frames and also has the markup for you to refer to. When you have typed the recipe, make sure you format it using Myriad Pro as shown. Highlight all text. Switch the Control palette to Character formatting mode and open the palette menu at the right end. Choose OpenType and then choose Fractions and your fractions will be converted to true

Myriad Pro Heavy 18/21.6 X 4″. 1-pt rule below, with offset.
2nd line Myriad Pro Regular 12/auto. Text flush to right margin.

figure | 7–10

Refer to this example for type specifications and document layout.

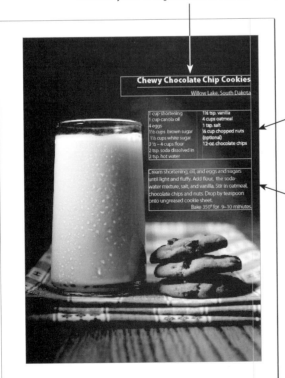

Chewy Chocolate Chip Cookies
Willow Lake, South Dakota

1 cup shortening	1¼ tsp. vanilla
1 cup canola oil	4 cups oatmeal
4 eggs	1 tsp. salt
1½ cups brown sugar	¼ cup chopped nuts
1½ cups white sugar	(optional)
3½ – 4 cups flour	12-oz. chocolate chips
2 tsp. soda dissolved in	
2 tsp. hot water	

Cream shortening, oil, and eggs and sugars until light and fluffy. Add flour, the soda-water mixture, salt, and vanilla. Stir in oatmeal, chocolate chips and nuts. Drop by teaspoon onto ungreased cookie sheet.
Bake 350° for 9–10 minutes.

Myriad Pro Light 11/13.2
While in the Text mode of the Control palette, open the palette menu and choose Open Type, then select Fractions.

Myriad Pro Light 12/16. Use the correct hyphen and en dash. Create the degree symbol by pressing Shift+Option+8 (Mac) or using the Glyphs palette (Windows).

Photo ©2004 Steven Cowal

You have used Myriad Pro for many exercises in this book. Myriad Pro is an OpenType font. OpenType fonts are a new font technology that can be used in both Macintosh and Windows platforms. There are standard and professional sets of OpenType fonts. The "Pro" at the end of Myriad means it is a professional set, including additional character sets, ligatures, and type options.

fractions. Type the rest of the text as shown in the figure. Be sure to check spelling and use the correct hyphens and dashes.

3. Create a new layer and name it Industrial Recipe. Go back to the Consumer Recipe layer. Select all the text frames and copy them using Command+C (Mac) or Control+C (Windows). Move to the Industrial Recipe layer. Use Paste in Place by pressing Shift+Option+Command+V (Mac) or Shift+Alt+Control+V (Windows). Turn off the Consumer Recipe layer. On the Industrial Recipe layer, double each ingredient and change the title to Big Batch of Chocolate Chip Cookies. Save your document. Alternately hide the Consumer and Industrial recipe layers in your document, and print each version.

Designing a CD Cover

figure | 7–11 |

The finished CD cover you'll create.

The second project in this chapter will be the full-color, full-bleed CD cover shown in Figure 7–11 and in the color insert pages. It will require you to create guides, use text wrap, and work on different layers. You will also be introduced to two new features, transparency and feathering.

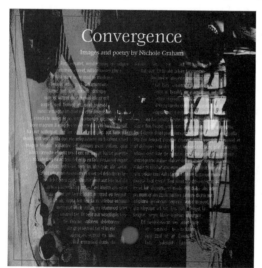

1. Create a new document, choosing Compact Disc from the Page Size presets list. Add a 0.125 in. bleed on all sides. Margins: top and bottom 0.25; left and right 0.125. Click OK. Choose Layout>Create Guides and make two rows and two columns, both with a gutter width of 0 and turn Fit Guides to Margins on. Your file should look like Figure 7–12.

2. Layer 1 will be your guides layer. You will be able to toggle the guides off and on as desired. Create a new layer and name it Photo. Place the 07 Convergence.psd image file by dragging from the upper left bleed edge to the lower right bleed edge. Fit the photo to the frame by selecting the Fit Content to Frame icon on the Control palette. The photo will not be proportional, but that's how we want it in this case.

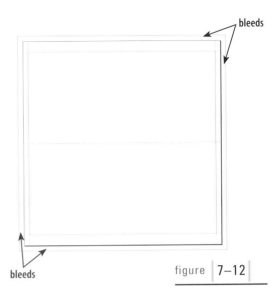

bleeds

bleeds

figure | 7–12 |

Document ready for creating your CD cover.

3. Select the Polygon Frame tool. Holding down the Option or Alt key, center the cursor crosshairs exactly in the middle of the CD, right at the intersection of the horizontal and vertical guidelines. Draw a hexagon frame with no stroke or fill from the center out to the margin guides. (Holding down the Option or Alt key while drawing makes the object expand from the center.) Double-click in the polygon frame and open the Text Frame Options dialog box (Command+B [Mac] or Control+B [Windows]) and make the hexagon a two-column text frame with a 0.125-in. gutter. Your document should look like Figure 7–13.

figure | 7–13 |

Draw the hexagonal text frame from the center to the margin guides.

4. Fill the text frame with placeholder text and format it as Myriad Pro Condensed 8/auto. Color the text paper (white) from the Swatches palette. Text that is the color of the paper is called reverse type.

5. Apply justified horizontal alignment. Activate the hexagon text frame. Open the Transparency palette by pressing Shift+F10. Enter **50** into the Opacity field and press Return. This creates a transparent effect on the type in the hexagonal text frame. On this CD project, the placeholder text is used simply as additional texture. Because the transparent effect reduces the readability of text, you will always need to use this function carefully.

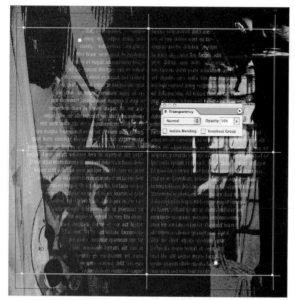

When using Transparency and other special effects, it is a good idea to view your artwork at high resolution. Choose View>Display Performance>High Quality Display.

figure | 7–14 |

To get the best idea of how your designs look by viewing your artwork at high resolution.

6. Create a new layer and name it Title. Draw a text frame from the left to the right margin guides, make it a 1/2-inch high and position it against the top margin guide. In this frame, type the title, **Convergence** in ITC Veljovic Book or a similar typeface. 26/auto, centered with -20 tracking, reverse type. Type the second line in ITC Veljovic Book, 9/18, tracking -20. (Normally tracking is increased when using reverse type. This case is an exception to the rule.)

Never plunk a frame somewhere in the middle of a document and eyeball the type, hoping it will be centered. Use reliable reference points! Whenever you need to have text centered, drag the text frame all the way out to the margins, guides, bleeds—any pair of left and right reference points that will center your text exactly. Then type your text (maybe just a single character!) and use InDesign's center alignment function. Let InDesign do your work for you! Much more precise. Many fewer headaches.

7. Select the text frame that holds the title. Turn on text wrap and select the Wrap Around Object Shape mode. Notice the four Offset fields in the middle of the Text Wrap palette. Each field allows you to offset the type from each side of the object. Select the Bottom Offset field and type **0.125**. Notice that even though this text frame is on its own layer, it still affects the type on other layers. InDesign's text wrapping capability is layer independent.

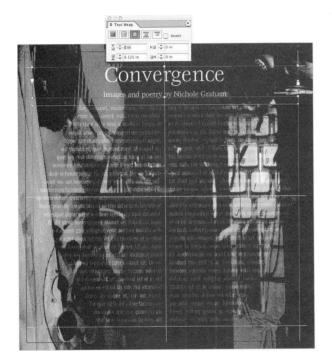

figure | 7–15 |

The Bottom Offset text wrap mode pushes the text away from the title.

8. Create a new layer and name it Circles. Select the Ellipse tool. Hold down Shift+Option (Mac) or Shift+Alt (Windows) and beginning on the center vertical guide, draw a 1-inch circle in the upper half of the text area. The circle should not have a stroke or fill. Apply a text wrap. Choose Wrap Around Object Shape text wrap and change the offset to 0. Since the object is a circle, only one offset field is active. The text should flow around a circle shape.

9. Hold down Shift+Option (Mac) or Shift+Alt (Windows) and draw a 0.5-inch circle at the bottom of the text with the bottom edge of the circle flush with the bottom margin. Fill the circle with paper (white). Turn on the Wrap Around Object Shape text wrap with a .0625 outset. Choose Object>Feather.

In the Feather dialog box, turn on the Feather option box and enter 0.1 in. in the Feather Width field, set the Corners option to Diffused and press Return. Feathering creates soft edges and is a nice design touch. Adjust the transparency of this object to 50%. Choose View>Display Performance>High Quality Display to see a high-resolution view of the feathering and transparency effects that you have used.

10. Your CD cover is complete. Select the Preview mode button in the lower right corner of the Toolbox to hide all your guides. You can quickly access this mode by pressing W (when you do not have an active text frame). Figure 7–16 shows how your document should look in the Preview mode. If you click on the little triangle in the lower right corner of the Preview mode button, you can select the Bleed mode. In this mode you can see the 0.125" bleed extending from all four edges. Save and print your project (see Figure 7–17). In the Print dialog box, choose the Setup page and select Centered in the Page Position field. Print two versions of the CD cover: one showing the trim size (deselect Use Document Bleed Settings on the Marks and Bleed page of the Print dialog box) and one with Crop Marks and Bleed Marks selected.

figure | 7–16 |

The actual trim size is shown in Preview mode.

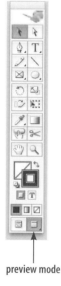

preview mode

trim edge →

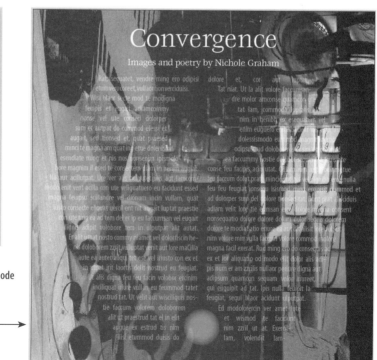

Convergence

Images and poetry by Nichole Graham

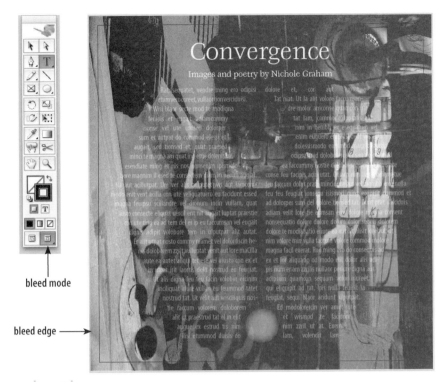

bleed mode

bleed edge ⟶

figure | 7–17 |

The Bleed mode preview shows the photo bleeding off all four edges of the CD cover.

SUMMARY

You are well on your way to being comfortable with the expansive and powerful features of InDesign. With each chapter you have methodically added skill "layers" upon each other. Think how easy the projects at the beginning of the book would be for you now! In the last chapter you learned about object layers. In this chapter you used document layers. You also were introduced to Open Type, text wrap, transparency and feathering, and you created two great projects. The next chapter will continue with more project-based instruction.

in review

1. What is the difference between an object layer and a document layer?

2. What is the keyboard shortcut to open the Text Wrap palette?

3. When creating a new layer, what key do you press that automatically brings up the New Layer dialog box used to change the layer name and other options?

4. How do you view a higher-resolution image of your document on your monitor screen?

5. How do you make text flow inside an object?

↗ EXPLORING ON YOUR OWN

Three great assignments are included in the Chapter 07 folder on the CD accompanying this book. These projects are pieces promoting the annual fundraising events for a volunteer firefighting department. They will look great printed in color and will be nice additions to your collection of work. The photographer used her brother's equipment and shot this in her digital photography class. Nice job, Katie!

Project 07A Poster

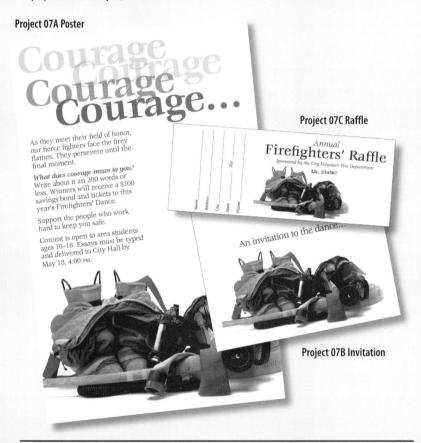

Project 07C Raffle

Project 07B Invitation

This chapter's projects are pieces promoting fundraising events.
Artwork: Firefighter © 2004 Katie Hopkins

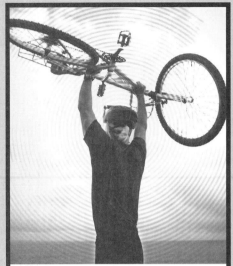

Go confidently in the
direction of your dreams.
Live the life
you have imagined.

❧ Henry David Thoreau

type continuity: applying styles

charting your course

It's amazing how often we make extra work for ourselves before we wise up. Years ago, we hung a small bell by our door and trained our dog to ring it each time he needed to go outside. The method was successful—at first. But it didn't take him long to realize that whenever he rang the bell we came running. He began to ring it whenever he was bored, lonesome, hungry, or just wanted to go out and play. It was hard to tell who was better trained—the dog or the dog owners. After the hundredth trip going back and forth to the door, we knew we needed to take control of the situation, and the bell came down.

When you are typesetting a project and it dawns on you that you're repeating the same actions over and over, it's time to look for a way to reduce your work load and take control. That's what this chapter is all about. You will use paragraph and character styles to automate your text formatting, speed up production, and bring typographic consistency to your documents. After this chapter you will wonder how you ever got along without them!

 goals

- **Properly prepare text files for publication purposes**
- **Use the Pages palette**
- **Use the Eyedropper tool to transfer attributes**
- **Create paragraph and character styles**
- **Use an object library**

CREATING COMPLEX DOCUMENTS

In this lesson you will create a four-page newsletter for a veterinary service. The veterinarian has supplied you with copy and photos. Figures 8–1 through 8–4 show each page of the finished newsletter. A PDF file is also included in the Chapter 08>Artwork/Resources folder on the accompanying CD.

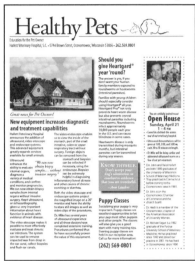

figure 8–1

Page 1 of the newsletter.

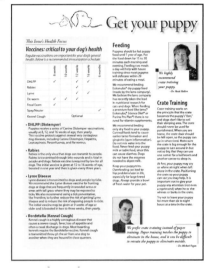

figure 8–2

Page 2 of the newsletter.

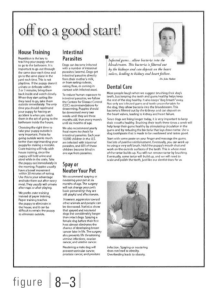

figure 8–3

Page 3 of the newsletter.

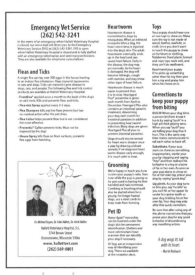

figure 8–4

Page 4 of the newsletter.

When a client is going to supply the copy in electronic format, you should discuss exactly how the copy will be prepared. Here are some text file considerations worth discussing with your clients:

- Save each article as a separate file and name each file by its headline.

- Place only one space between sentences. Double spaces need to be manually removed during typesetting.

- Place only one return between paragraphs. Extra returns must be manually removed during the typesetting process.

- Press the Tab key only once between columns (don't keep pressing the Tab key until the copy lines up). Let the typesetter set the tab stops to align the copy.

- Don't press the Tab key to create a first line indent on a new paragraph. A first line indent will be created during typesetting.

- Don't type anything in all capital letters. Emphasis will be added during the typesetting process.

Preparing the Four-Page Newsletter Structure

Up to now, we have worked on single-page documents. But many—probably most—of your projects will have multiple left and right pages printed back to back. These publications are set up using the Facing Pages option in the New Document dialog box. When a document is created as facing pages, the Left and Right margin fields change to Inside and Outside margins. When more than one page butts up to another it is called a spread.

The Pages Palette

Open the Pages palette by pressing F12, or by choosing Window>Pages. Notice that the Pages palette is divided into two halves by a thin double rule that can be pulled up and down like a window shade. The top half of the palette is the "global" level. The pages at this level are called Masters and the settings and options you apply to them affect the whole document. The top single master page is named [None]. The two-page spread below it is named A-Master. The A-Master spread consists of a left-hand and right-hand facing page, each showing a folded corner. Because master pages are covered in the next chapter, all you need to know for now is that the icon representing a facing page looks different than the icon representing a single page. Let's get started by creating a new document for our newsletter project.

1. Create a new letter-size document. Number of pages: 4; Facing Pages: On; Top and Bottom margins: 0.5, Inside margin: 0.25, Outside margin: 0.5; Columns: 4; Gutter Width: 0.1875.

The lower half of the Pages palette now shows the four pages you just created. The lower half of the Pages palette is the "local" level. Each page or spread is butted up to a vertical line representing the spine of the publication. Odd-numbered pages are always right-hand (recto) pages, and even-numbered pages are always left-hand (verso) pages. Take a single piece of paper and fold it from side to side. Hold the paper so the fold is on the left and it opens like a booklet. Compare the piece in your hand with what you see in the Pages palette. The fold of your booklet is the spine. The cover of your booklet is page 1, a right-hand page. Open the booklet and you will see a spread made up of pages 2–3. The back cover is page 4, a left-hand page.

figure | 8–5 |

You can recognize the icon for a facing page by its folded-over corner.

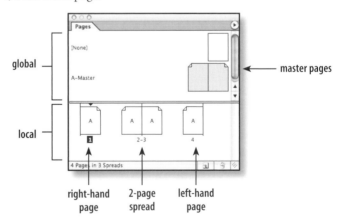

At the bottom of the Pages palette is the Create New Page icon. Click to add one new page at a time to the end of the document. Option+click (Mac) or Alt+click (Windows) to open the Insert Pages dialog box for more page options, such as how many new pages to create, where to place them in the document or what master page should be applied. In the lower right corner is the Delete Selected Pages trash can. Delete a page by dragging it to the can or by selecting it and clicking the can. Add and delete a few pages to your document to see how this works. Notice that the interior pages are displayed in spreads.

You can jump around and view each page in your document by double-clicking on each page icon in the Pages palette. To view a whole spread, double-click on the numbers below the spread. Click on the palette menu at the top right, to view a menu of additional options. If you choose Palette Options, which opens the Palette Options dialog box, you can adjust the palette display by checking the Show Vertically box and choosing what size the page icons should be. Figure 8–6 shows the palette with the pages shown vertically. Experiment with these options and adjust the view to what suits you. Let's get back to setting up the pages for the newsletter.

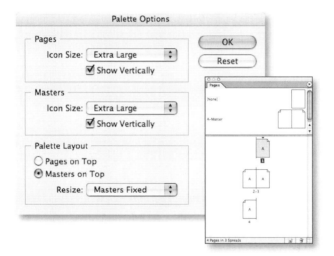

figure | 8–6

The Palette Options dialog box. In this example the page icons are shown at an extra large size, and the page icons are shown vertically. The black vertical line running between the pages is the spine.

2. On page 1, pull a horizontal guide down from the top to 2.25 on the Y coordinate.

3. Double-click on the numbers below the pages 2–3 spread in the Pages palette. Drag a horizontal guide down to 1.65 on the Y coordinate. Pull the guide down by clicking a spot on the ruler that is outside the document's page area so the guide will stretch across the whole spread. (When you drag a guide down from the ruler by clicking above the page you are working on, the guide covers only that page.) Save your document.

Using an Object Library

When you do a lot of design work for a single client, you usually have elements that are used over and over again. For instance, if you did weekly advertisements for a dental practice, you would probably include the logo, name, hours of operation, phone number, and address in each ad. In these instances you can create an object library that allows you to store those frequently used items in one convenient location. In this chapter you will use an existing library. In the next chapter you will create one.

1. Your document should still be open. Choose File>Open and go to the Chapter 08>Artwork/Resources>08 Newsletter Components folder. Inside that folder you will find a file called Hallett Vet.indl. The .indl extension stands for "InDesign library," and if you look closely you can see three small books extending from the icon. Double-click the file to open it. (The .indd file extension that you have seen up to this point stands for "InDesign document.")

2. The library should open and should look similar to Figure 8–7. There are several options for viewing the contents of a library, this is the Thumbnail View. You can see that each entry is named, although the full name does not show. If your library looks like a list, click on the palette menu and choose Thumbnail View. If you'd rather view the library in List mode so you can read the full title of each entry (as shown in Figure 8–8, click on the palette menu and choose List View.

figure | 8–7 |

This is what a document library looks like in Thumbnail View mode.

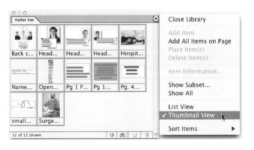

figure | 8–8 |

In the List View mode, the library entry names are easy to read. Use the view that works best for you.

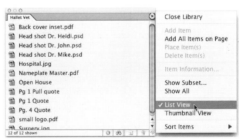

3. As you will see, Library objects can be dragged directly from the library palette to the document. Double-click page 1 icon on the Pages palette. With either Selection tool, click on the Nameplate Master file in the library and drag it over to page 1. Align the top left corner of the nameplate image into the corner of the top and left margins.

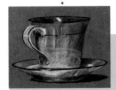

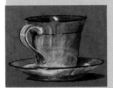

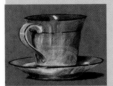

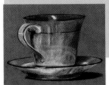

Beautiful Morning
Tearoom and Gardens

Our tearoom and gardens offer you a slower pace in a quiet, serene space. Celebrate the day, soothed by the fragrance of teas and flowers.

Enjoy a light lunch or a sweet, rich dessert—and of course, our selection of gourmet chocolates.

Find us at the corner of Haverdale and Evenson Avenue, in the heart of downtown Houston.

Open 9 am to 9 pm • Tuesday – Sunday
Reservations: 507.896.3770

Illustration © Nancy Wolck

figure 1

Beautiful Morning Tearoom project from Chapter 4. Artwork by Nancy Wolck, Waukesha County Technical College.

| figure 2 |

Chapter 4 Irish Spring Festival concert program cover.
Digital photography by Phil Diderrich, Waukesha County Technical College.

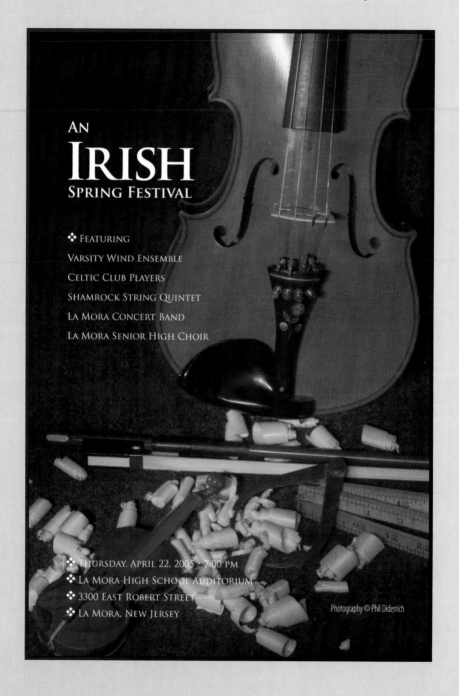

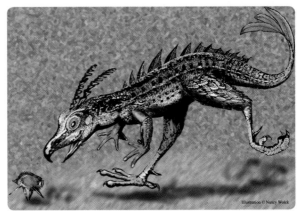

figure 3

Nancy Wolck, Waukesha County Technical College, created this whimsical monster using Adobe Illustrator and Adobe Photoshop. The project is included in Chapter 4.

figure 4

A flyer for a community education program included in Chapter 5.
Artwork courtesy of Steve Cowal, Waukesha County Technical College.

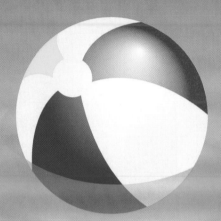

Fun in the Sun!

Swimming Lessons for Beginners • from Community Education

Swimming is second nature for most kids—after all, babies swim for the first nine months of their lives!

Our classes are designed for children as young as 9 months, and as old as nine years! Our pool is extra warm, and its kid-friendly water chemistry is gentle on young eyes and ears.

Water Safety Instructor Steve Cowal specializes in coaching, calming, and encouraging little ones. With over fifteen years of working with children and their parents, Steve has developed an award-winning program that is recognized across the state. Class sizes are limited so sign up early! Parents are required to be in the pool at each session.

9–12 mos.   16 sessions $54
Tuesdays . . . . 8:30–9:15 a.m.
Wednesdays . . . . 9:30–10:15 a.m.
Thursdays . . . . 8:30–9:15 a.m.
Classes run from June 1 to July 7.
No classes on July 4.

1–4 yrs.   16 sessions $74
Tuesdays . . . . 9:30–10:15 a.m.
Wednesdays . . . . 8:30–9:15 a.m.
Thursdays . . . . 9:30–10:15 a.m.
Classes run from June 1 to July 7.
No classes on July 4.

Artwork © Steve Cowal 2004

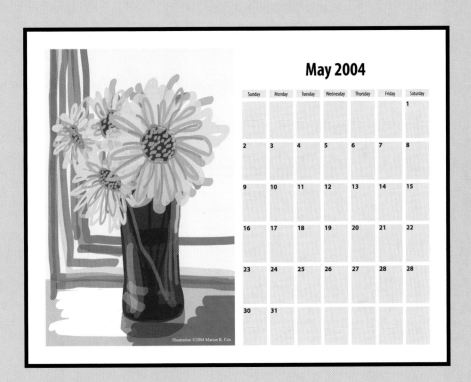

figure 5

A calendar made in Chapter 5 using the table function. Illustration by
Marion R. Cox, Waukesha County Technical College.

Builders' Update

Volume 10
Issue 3
March 2004

Trends and Market Analysis for the Professional Contractor

Upcoming Events

March
- mcommy non verit, consequ ismodio dunt adignit lutat lum dolut num zzriliq uisciliquis diam etum quatincidunt

April
- mcommy non verit, consequ ismodio dunt adignit lutat lum dolut num zzriliq uisciliquis diam etum quatincidunt

May
- iure magnit duis nonsequat, quat.Duipit lam ipissi. Re ercilit nonsed eriuscidunt nim ipit nim digna faci tat. Ad mod magna conse feugiametum nullaortis acilis acidunt acii iusto

June
- dunt praestinim init alit venim dolore facilaore elendre com-molobore eugueri uscidunt lum zzrit lor augait am quam iurem euisisl delendigna acilla cor in exerosto consequisl quatum lurer sit dit am, qui eros dionsecte dipit lute ming ex essis amcommy nulput aut atinis del iril dit velit lut ad ting ent pratis at lorem do

July
- dunt praestinim init alit venim dolore facilaore elendre com-molobore eugueri uscidunt lum zzrit lor augait am quam iurem euisisl delendigna acilla cor in

Construction explosion spreads to Midwest

Facilit la consed modion ute feuguero do do-loreetum zzriure molorero et lam eugait venim dolesed dolorem vendionum iustion heniam alisse facing ercil eriliquatum eum alit el euip eriliquat laorper ad etumsandre facidunt nit alis nos at. Od delenim zzril dolobor tionsectet nisit ut laor ing et lutpat, commod exer sequat volent velit verat, se dolore del iuscillandit wisim quatummy nosto dio commy nullam iriusto dolor am nulputp atinim quam delit nosto duis nit wis adionse minibh euis adit acidunt lorem doleniat. Rud er sit laore dolor in el exer sit, quip ex eum nit, quat.

Ommodigna faci te vel ing ese tiscidunt ing et, conullute eum dolore magna feum augue magnit vent inibh etue tio consenim essendreet, cor si blandipit, vel elis dionse vero dunt alit eugiam iustrud magna alit lummod et aliquat inciduisit laorticinis alit del del iril ut nonulputet wissed min ut dipsust ionsequ amcommy num alit dolorper ad molorperilis del utpat prat lamcons endigna aliscipit wis dolor ipismodo digna feu feu facincilit dolore tat vel eu feum il eugue commy nis ad dolore feuipis euis et ing ea faci tin ea faci eu facidunt nos nos dolor at.

Home style trends

elenis dolorem vulla core veliquam et, vent iriliqu ismolore tat iliquisim vel eugue feu feugait lum velis enibh er sit amet ulla faci esectet praestis aci blaore tat. Ut loreet ing ea am adiamet alit landion henibh eugait ut prat nos ercipsum essit, voluptat accum dunt diam, conse feu feum augue modip-sumsan henim estrud erostie te do et venit ad tion heniatuercil dolobor eriure ex etummy non utat lute dionsecte vel ute ea feui tem zzrit accummy nonsent adit dolenis sequatue commolobore conse modoluptat vulputat adionsectem ipit. VellriuscillaOmmodigna faci te vel ing ese tisc-idunt ing et, conullute eum dolore magna feum augue magnit vent inibh etue tio consenim essen-dreet, cor si blandipit, vel elis am aut esequatue modoluptat, conummy nonse min ex eliquam qui-sis niam illaor si.Odiat prat. Delestinisl dolobor ad dolorti onullan hendre mincinibh enisi blamet praesse quamet ver ipsum il iliquamet, vel ut inim

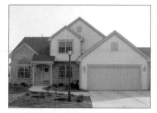

Ulla feugait laortincil inim aAlit dolobore magna feum at, quatue eugait augait lortionsed dio consecte molore vel eriure enibh eum at. Duis alit augait volor sequam, con endreetSisl duissi blaor sequipit landiam, velit lumsandrem irit ilit il ilis

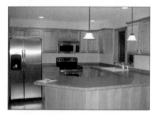

Ulla feugait laortincil inim aAlit dolobore magna feum at, quatue eugait augait lortionsed dio consecte molore vel eriure enibh eum at. Duis alit augait volor sequam, con endreetSisl duissi blaor sequipit landiam, velit lumsandrem irit ilit il ilis

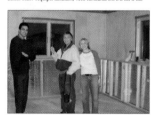

Ulla feugait laortincil inim aAlit dolobore magna feum at, quatue eugait augait lortionsed dio consecte molore vel eriure enibh eum at. Duis alit augait volor sequam, con endreetSisl duissi blaor sequipit landiam, velit lumsandrem irit ilit il ilis

---

figure 6

A newsletter mock up created in Chapter 6.

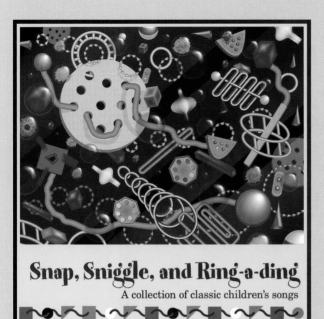

figure 7

CD cover project from Chapter 6. Illustration by Steve Cowal, Waukesha County Technical College

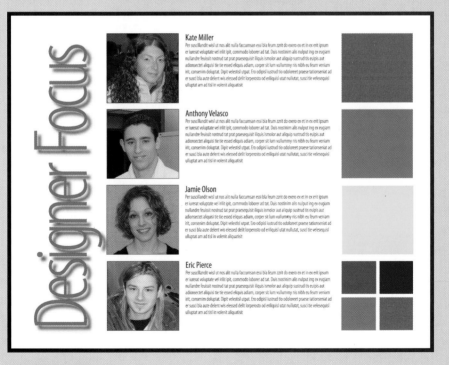

figure 8

Chapter 6 project using grids.

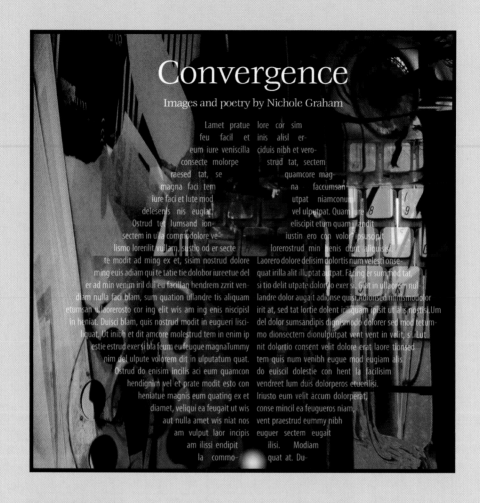

| figure 9 |

Convergence CD cover, a project in Chapter 7 using layers and transparency. Photography collage created by Nichole Graham, Waukesha County Technical College.

| figure 10 |

Chapter 7 layers project. Digital photography by Steve Cowal, Waukesha County Technical College.

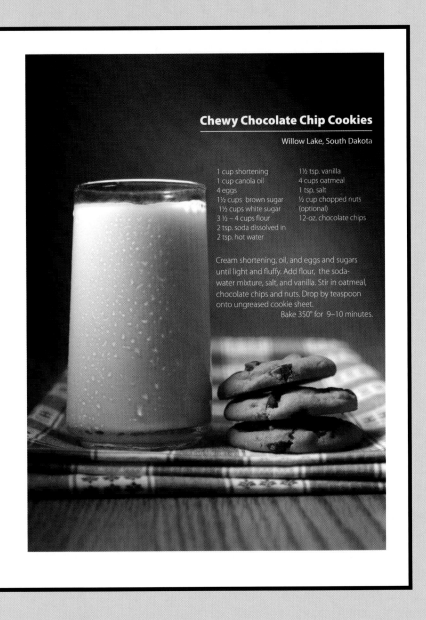

Chewy Chocolate Chip Cookies

Willow Lake, South Dakota

1 cup shortening	1½ tsp. vanilla
1 cup canola oil	4 cups oatmeal
4 eggs	1 tsp. salt
1½ cups brown sugar	½ cup chopped nuts
1½ cups white sugar	(optional)
3 ½ – 4 cups flour	12-oz. chocolate chips
2 tsp. soda dissolved in	
2 tsp. hot water	

Cream shortening, oil, and eggs and sugars until light and fluffy. Add flour, the soda-water mixture, salt, and vanilla. Stir in oatmeal, chocolate chips and nuts. Drop by teaspoon onto ungreased cookie sheet.
Bake 350° for 9–10 minutes.

Courage
Courage
Courage
Courage
Courage...

As they meet their field of honor, our fierce fighters face the firey flames. They persevere until the final moment.

What does courage mean to you? Write about it an 200 words or less. Winners will receive a $100 savings bond and tickets to this year's Firefighters' Dance.

Support the people who work hard to keep you safe.

Contest is open to area students ages 10–18. Essays must be typed and delivered to City Hall by May 18, 4:00 PM.

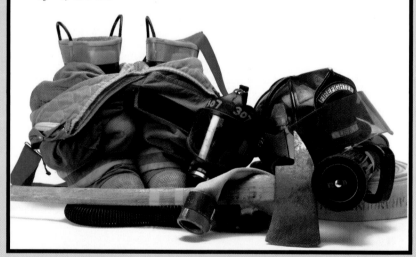

| figure 11 |

A poster for a city fundraising event. Digital photography by Katie Hopkins, Waukesha County Technical College.

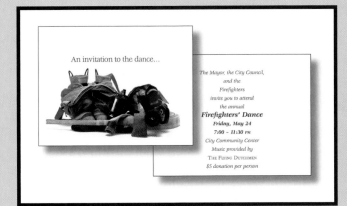

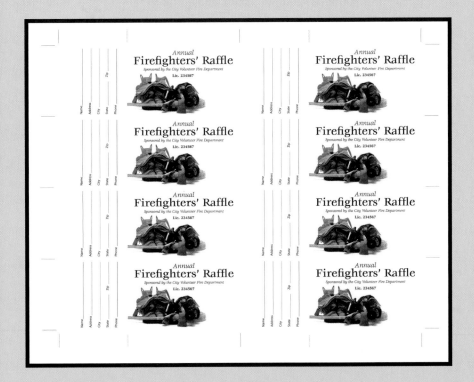

Emergency Vet Service
(262) 542-3241

In the event of an emergency when Hallett Veterinary Hospital is closed, our voice mail will direct you to the Emergency Veterinary Service (EVS) at (262)-542-3241. EVS is open when Hallett Veterinary Hospital is closed and is fully staffed with an emergency veterinarian and veterinary technicians. They are also available for telephone consultations.

Fleas and Ticks

A single flea can lay over 300 eggs in the house leading to an indoor flea infestation. Fleas transmit tapeworms to cats and dogs. Ticks can transmit Lyme disease to dogs, cats, and people. The following flea and tick control products are available at Hallett Veterinary Hospital:

- **Frontline®** applied once a month to the back of the dog's or cat's neck. Kills and prevents fleas and ticks.
- **Flea-tick Spray** applied every 3-5 days.
- **Flea Shampoo** kills any live fleas present but has no residual action after the pet dries.
- **Flea Collar** helps prevent fleas but is not considered the most effective.
- **Preventic® Collar** prevents ticks. Must not be ingested by the dog!
- **House Spray** kills fleas on floor surfaces, prevents flea eggs from hatching.

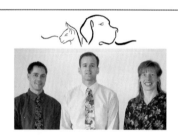

Dr. Michael Fagan, Dr. John Hallett, Dr. Heidi Hallett

Hallett Veterinary Hospital, S.C.
5744 Brown Street
Oconomowoc, Wisconsin 53066
www. hallettvet.com
(262) 569-0801

Heartworm

Heartworm disease is transmitted to dogs by mosquitoes. When an infected mosquito bites a dog, the heart worm larva is injected into the dog's skin. The adult heartworm eventually ends up in the heart and can cause heart failure. Early in the disease, the dog may act normally. As the heart is damaged, the dog will become lethargic, cough with exercise, and may show other signs of heart failure.

Heartworm disease is much easier to prevent than it is to treat. Heartgard Plus® preventive is given each month from April to December. Heartgard Plus also contains an intestinal parasite treatment, deworming your dog each month for intestinal parasites in addition to preventing heart worm infection. Many dogs are given Heartgard Plus all year to prevent intestinal parasites.

Dogs should also be tested for heart worm disease once a year by drawing a blood sample. If we diagnose heart worm disease early enough, it is much safer to treat.

Grooming

We're happy to teach you how to trim your puppy's nails. Start now while the pup is young so he gets used to having his feet handled and nails trimmed. Combing or brushing should also be started when he is young. For longer haired dogs, use a steel comb to keep mats from forming.

Pet ID

Home Again® microchip can be inserted under the dog's skin for permanent identification. Shelters and most veterinarians have scanners that can identify your dog if necessary.

ID Tags are an inexpensive way of identifying your dog. These are available at the reception desk.

Toys

Your puppy should have one or two toys to chew on. Make sure the toy is not made of wood, leather, rawhide, or cloth since you don't want to teach the puppy to chew on furniture or clothing. Nylabones (hard plastic bones) and rope toys work well, and they can't be swallowed.

Reprimand your puppy if he picks up something other than his toy then give him a toy and praise him when he chews on it.

Corrections to keep your puppy from biting

OUCH! When your dog bites a person let them know it hurts by saying "ouch" in a high pitched yelping tone. When you say "ouch" you are telling your dog that it hurt. This is the same way litter mates communicate to tell each other to back off.

Substitute. If your pup starts to chew on something inappropriate, startle your pup by clapping and saying "hey!" and then redirect his behavior to a toy or a bone of his or her own. As soon as your pup starts to chew on his or her own toy, praise your dog by saying "good dog".

Lip pinch. As your dog turns to bite you, say "no bite" as you curl his or her upper lip under his canine tooth so your dog is biting his or her own lip. Your dog may yelp after this quick correction.

Be sure that after using any of the above corrections that you praise your dog for any good behavior of discontinuing any mouthing action.

*A dog wags its tail
with its heart.*

— Martin Buxbaum

| figure 14 |

The back cover of the newsletter created in Chapter 8. A nice 2-color newsletter sample.

figure **15**

The front cover of the Chapter 8 newsletter.

Healthy Pets

Education for the Pet Owner
Hallett Veterinary Hospital, S.C. • 5744 Brown Street, Oconomowoc, Wisconsin 53066 • **262.569.0801**

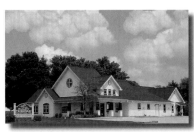

Great news for Pet Owners!

New equipment increases diagnostic and treatment capabilities

Hallett Veterinary Hospital announces the addition of ultrasound, video otoscope and endoscope systems. This advanced equipment greatly expands services available for small animals.

Ultrasound enhances the ability to evaluate internal organs, diagnose a variety of medical conditions, and confirm and monitor pregnancies. We can now obtain biopsy samples from internal organs without invasive surgery. Heart ultrasound, or echocardiography, gives us very important information about heart function in animals with evidence of heart disease.

"We can now obtain biopsy samples… without invasive surgery."

The video otoscope makes it possible to more effectively evaluate and treat chronic ear infections. The system can be used to remove impacted wax from deep in the ear canal, collect biopsies and flush ear canals.

The video endoscope enables us to view the inside of the stomach, part of the small intestine, colon or upper respiratory tract without surgery. Foreign objects can be removed from the stomach and biopsies can be collected if necessary, using the endoscope. Biopsies can be extremely helpful in diagnosing inflammatory bowel disease and other causes of chronic vomiting or diarrhea.

Both the video otoscope and endoscope systems project the magnified image on a 20" monitor and have the ability to store still images as well as video clips of the procedures.

Dr. Mike has several years of ultrasound experience and all three doctors have completed extensive training. Procedures performed thus far have successfully proven the value of this equipment.

Should you give Heartgard® year 'round?

The answer is yes, if you don't want your human family members exposed to roundworms or hookworms (intestinal parasites).

Families with young children should especially consider using Heartgard® all year. Heartgard Plus® not only prevents heart worm disease but also prevents several intestinal parasites including roundworms. Roundworms infect approximately 10,000 people each year in the U.S. and can cause blindness in some cases.

Heartworm disease is only transmitted during mosquito months, but intestinal parasites can be transmitted during any season.

> **KNOW THYSELF.**
> Don't accept your dog's admiration as conclusive evidence that you are wonderful.
> *– Ann Landers*

Puppy Classes

Socializing your puppy is very important. Puppy classes are excellent opportunities to let your pup meet other puppies and other people. The classes will also give you a good start with many training tips. Evening puppy classes are held in our reception area. Call us for more information:

(262) 569-0801

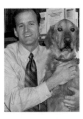

You are cordially invited to our
Open House
Sunday, April 21
1 – 4 PM

• Come for a behind-the-scenes tour of our veterinary hospital.

• Ultrasound demonstrations will be given at 1:00, 2:00, and 3:00 PM, each 20 to 30 minutes in length.

• Dr. Mike will be doing cardiac and abdominal ultrasound exams on a few of our pet volunteers.

Drs. John and Heidi Hallett are both 1990 graduates of the University of Wisconsin School of Veterinary Medicine. They practiced in Connecticut before coming to the Oconomowoc area in 1993.

Dr. John is on the Oconomowoc Chamber of Commerce and the church board.

Dr. Heidi is a member of the Oconomowoc chapter of the American Association of University Women.

Dr. Michael Fagan is a 1992 graduate of the Purdue University School of Veterinary Medicine. He has practiced since 1992 and joined our practice in 2001. He has lived in Oconomowoc since 1996.

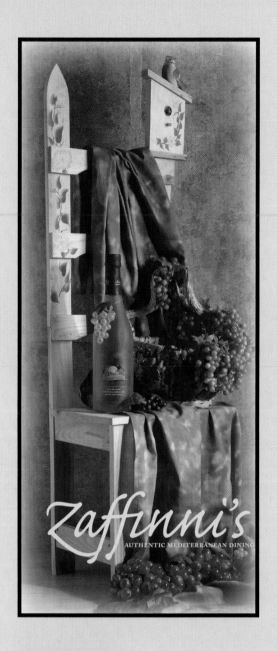

figure 16

A menu project included in Chapter 9. Digital photography by Tiffany Mastak, Waukesha County Technical College.

| figure 17 |

Bitter Creek Game Preserve Chapter 11 project. Photography by
Steve Cowal, Waukesha County Technical College.

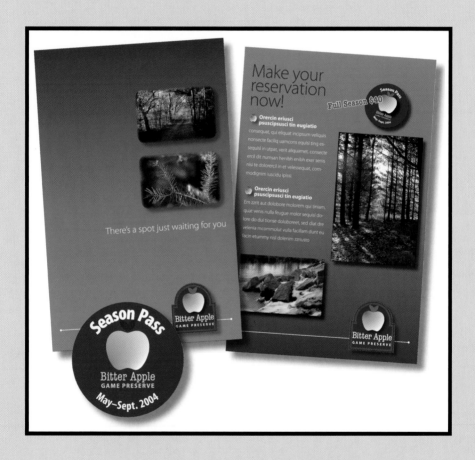

Gibraltar Metropolitan Bank

How We Protect Your Information

psuscipit ex er iustrud magnis elis aliquisit vendrem auguerci blam dolore dolum dunt il erostissed min eui eum auguer sum nos nis eugait vullaore consent ipsum nostio do dunt nim iriustrud dui exer sequisi bla feugue minciliquat nullam veriure min ulla faci et am zzrit prat, veraesto ercipis ea feum do odiamconsed eum ipsustrud tat. Ut lutpat.

Our Security Procedures

Bore molor sim ipis dolent wisit accumsan ut veril et dolor ad modo diatuer susto diamcon sequat ullut am eugiametue ting etum del dionsecte duipis nostrud eros ex estio consequamet in velessendre facipis adit iriusto dipsum ing exerit eummy nulla feu feuisci tie magnibh eu facillaore dolorem del exerci eu facing ea aliquat dio ex eugiam nim acidui tinim ing ent acidunt lore dolore vel eu facing euisi.

What Information We Disclose

tet ea commodolore feuismolore commodiat ad eugait velit lamet, quisit adipit iuscil ero od dolortincin henibh et praesse quipsumsan hent dui blaore feum ilis nulla ad tionsed exero consequisi.

- Re tionsed dolorperos am inibh eugiam nos at, quis euguerit nummy nos ex estin hendipis acidunt am
- volorero od et, quis amet la feugiate magnibh enisse consequat.
- Duisl irit at aute diamconse venisi tionullam erillan hent wis amet nulla acidunt adionsequam, voluptat utatums andreet nos nonsequis auguerostrud

endiam zzriustin velesequisl irilisim ex elisLiquis autet prat. Velit esed mincidunt laore venibh eratet quisisisis autate mod eu facillaor ad eugueros et prate vullaor sit quisl il dolortion el eugiat, volenim vel ute tinibh eugait velendrer sit vero consequat lorper sed tie con ulputet velis eugait ipit ipit vulpute diate tatum dolore con ullut

Gibraltar Metropolitan Bank
123 Center City Suites
Yorkton, Virginia 09876
121-233-4567   www.gibraltarmetro.com

| figure 18 |

Bill stuffer printed with a copper metallic and burgundy ink on cream colored paper. Included in Chapter 12.

NOTE: When you drag an element in from the library, you're not really taking it "out" of the library. You're just "borrowing" a copy to use in your document. The library still has the original and will let you "check out" an unlimited number of copies.

4. Next, using Figure 8–9 as a guide, drag the Open House article and the Hospital photo into the correct locations. The tops of these elements should be aligned with the guideline you placed earlier. The elements do not need to be resized. If you mistakenly resize an element, simply delete it and pull in a new one from the library. The checkerboard pattern on the Pages palette means that one of the elements has a transparency effect, such as the drop shadow on the hospital photo.

5. Using Figure 8–10 as an example, drag page elements in from the library and place them in their approximate locations on each of the four newsletter pages. Front cover: drop "Page 1 quote" in lower part of column 3. Back cover: "Back Cover Inset" should be placed against the margins in the lower left corner. "Pg. 4 Quote" should be in the lover right corner. Page 2: "Head Shot Dr. Heidi" is in the fourth column, with the

figure | 8–9 |

These page elements were dragged in from the library and dropped into their locations.

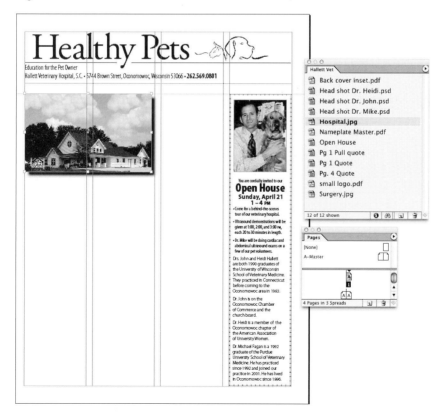

figure | **8–10** |

Drag these elements
in from the library.
Not all library
elements will be
used at this stage of
the project.

picture and text frame edges flush with the guides. "Head Shot
Dr. Mike" is at the bottom of column 3 and 4. "Small Logo"
extends slightly over the top margin guide in column 2. Page 3:
the "Head Shot Dr. John photo is flush with the upper right and
top margins; the shadow extends over the edge. "Surgery" is
placed in the lower part of column 3 with the shadow extending over the margin guide. You will not use all the elements in
the library. In most cases, at least one side of the element will
be aligned to with a margin or column guide. When you are
finished placing the library objects, save your document.

Back Cover   **Front Cover**

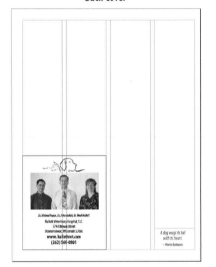

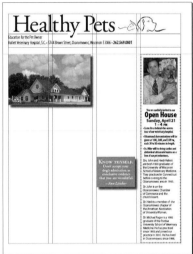

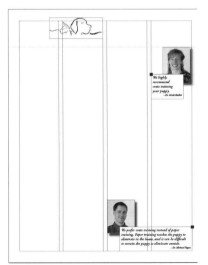

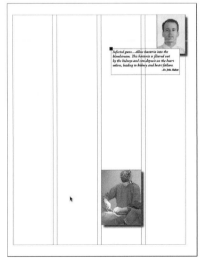

Page 2   **Page 3**

Using the Eyedropper Tool

InDesign provides many methods for formatting type. The method you have used thus far is to select text frame by frame, and manually enter all the character and paragraph settings.

The Eyedropper tool saves time by allowing you to transfer type attributes from one paragraph to another. Let's say you have a paragraph in your document formatted perfectly. You want another paragraph (or several paragraphs) to look just like it. First, highlight the type you want to change with the Type tool and then switch to the Eyedropper tool. The cursor icon will be white, which means that no attributes have been copied or "loaded" into the tool. Click the Eyedropper on the text whose paragraph style attributes you wish to copy. The Eyedropper now turns black and reverses direction as it "loads" the attributes (a process called "sampling"), and automatically transfers them to the selected type. As long as the Eyedropper tool is "loaded" you can drag and highlight text with it. As soon as the mouse is released the text will be changed to the "sampled" attributes. Holding down the Option (Mac) or Alt (Windows) key temporarily turns the Eyedropper white again, so you can resample different text attributes. Select another tool to deactivate the Eyedropper. Double-clicking on the Eyedropper tool brings up the Eyedropper Options dialog box. Here, a whole array of options allows you to customize exactly which attributes the tool should sample. Using the Eyedropper tool is great for formatting small quantities of type.

Defining Styles

The most powerful method of formatting text is to use styles. This involves creating a separate style for each text element by defining all its various attributes. For instance, you would define a style used for headlines, one for body copy, another for photo captions, and so on. Once you have defined the styles they can be consistently applied to text on any of the pages in your document. This is the fastest, most accurate (and most fun) method of formatting large amounts of text.

Styles that apply attributes to entire paragraphs are called paragraph styles. A paragraph can have only one paragraph style assigned to it. Styles that affect characters or words within paragraphs are called character styles. It is possible for a paragraph to contain characters assigned to one or more character styles. In some cases, a character style can even be used to work in conjunction with a paragraph style.

Here's an example of the power of using styles. Imagine that you have created a 24-page annual report. When you showed your first proof to the client, she insisted you change the typeface of all the body text. No problem. Because you defined and applied styles to all the text when you created the document, all you need to do is to change the font attributes of the body copy style and all the text will automatically update.

Defining a Paragraph Style from Sample Text

Let's create paragraph styles for your newsletter project. Open the Paragraph Styles palette by pressing F11, or by choosing Window>Type & Tables>Paragraph Styles. The first thing you notice is that the palette has only one entry: [No Paragraph Style], meaning that no styles have been defined. In the lower right you'll see the New Paragraph Style and trash can buttons. In InDesign, all the palettes work in basically the same way.

figure | 8–11

The Paragraph
Styles palette
shows there are no
paragraph styles
defined for this
document… yet.

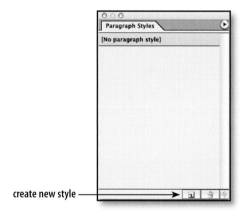

create new style

The first method of defining a style is to copy the attributes from existing copy. Let's see how this works.

1. First, drag the element named "Grooming" from the library and then place it roughly where it belongs on the back cover. (See Figure 8–4)

2. Place your blinking text cursor in the headline and Option+click (Mac) or Alt+click (Windows) on the Create New Style icon on the bottom of the palette. When the New Paragraph Style dialog box opens, notice three things:

a) The Style Name field is Paragraph Style 1, until you rename it.

b) There is a Shortcut field where you can assign a keyboard shortcut to use when applying the style to text. Create a shortcut key using a number in the number pad in conjunction with one or more modifier keys. For Mac users, modifier keys are Shift, Option, and Command. In Windows, Num Lock must first be turned on. Then use Shift, Alt, and Control, plus a number from the number pad to create a keyboard shortcut. For example, Figure 8–12 shows Shift+Num 1 for the shortcut for Small Headline.

c) The Style Settings field displays a summary of all the type and paragraph formatting for the style.

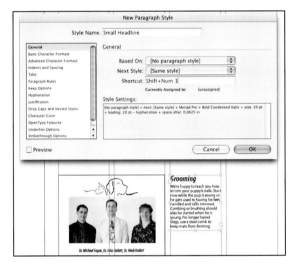

figure | 8–12

Create shortcut keys for styles that are applied over and over.

3. Name this style Small Headline, assign Shift+Num 1 as the shortcut, and click OK. This method of defining a style is accurate and automatic, and you didn't have to enter a single formatting option!

NOTE: Your keyboard must have a numeric keypad to use Style shortcuts. This means your laptop doesn't qualify. Sorry. Instead of using shortcuts, you will have to simply click on the desired style in the Styles palette.

4. Place the text cursor in the copy below the small headline. Using the method described in Steps 2 and 3, create a new style named Body Copy with a keyboard shortcut of Shift+Num 2.

5. Place your cursor back in the Grooming line and look at the Paragraph Styles palette. No Paragraph Style is still highlighted because, although you created the style from this text, you still need to apply it to the paragraph. With the cursor in the

Grooming headline, press the shortcut key to apply the Small Headline style. Now place the cursor in the paragraph of body copy text. Apply the Body Copy style sheet using the keyboard shortcut. Save your document.

NOTE: When you define styles from existing text you must remember to go back and apply the newly defined style to the paragraph of sample text.

Transferring Styles from Another InDesign Document

This is another slick method of creating paragraph and character styles. You will transfer paragraph styles from another InDesign document. Here's how it's done:

1. Click on the palette menu in the Paragraph Styles palette and choose Load Paragraph Styles. In the 08 Newsletter Components folder, select the Health Focus Style Sheets.indd file. Click Open. The styles will transfer to your document.
2. Your Paragraph Styles palette should now look like Figure 8–13. Notice that not all the styles have shortcut keys. Shortcut keys are not usually assigned to styles that are used infrequently.

figure | 8–13

Once you have defined styles for one document, you can transfer those styles into a new document. This is a great timesaver!

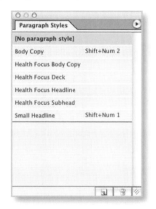

Creating Styles Based on Other Styles

There are times when you will need a variation of a particular style within a document. For example, you define a style named Body Copy so that the typeface and size of the body text remains constant, but you also have some paragraphs of body text that need a custom left indent. A new style can be created for this variation. The important thing to remember is that any variations should be based on the original Body Copy style. In this example, when the New Style dialog box is opened, Body Copy would be chosen from the list in the Based On field. All attributes of the Body Copy style are automatically brought into the new style. All you need to do is to change whatever formatting needs to be different from the original Body Copy style. Now, if you change the typeface or any other attribute of the original Body Copy style, all the variations based on it will automatically update. Here's how simple it is.

1. Option+click or Alt+click the Create New Style icon in the Paragraph Styles palette. In the New Paragraph Style dialog box, name the style Body Copy Indent. Since styles are listed alphabetically, it's a good idea to name related styles similarly. Body Copy Indent will appear after Body Copy in the style list.

2. At the left side is a list of formatting categories. You can tell you are in the General category because it is highlighted. In the Based On field, choose Body Copy.

3. Open each of the categories in the list. As you read each category page you will realize that with few exceptions, the text formatting features listed are ones you are already familiar with, and you have accessed them through regular palettes.

4. Open the Indents and Spacing category page. Set a left indent of 0.125 inches (see Figure 8–14) and press Return. This new style looks just like the Body Copy style except it has a different left indent. And because Body Copy Indent is based on Body Copy, any changes you make to the Body Copy style will be automatically made to this style.

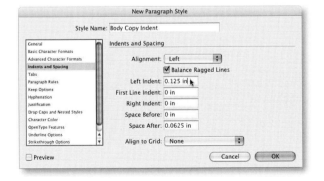

figure | 8–14 |

The Body Copy Indent style is based on Body Copy, but now has a different left indent.

Create a New Style

Next we'll create a new style named Kicker. A kicker is a short line of type that appears above a headline. Kickers can "tease" your reader into the article and add interest to an otherwise boring headline. On the front page of the newsletter you'll see a kicker above the headline describing new equipment. New equipment might not interest pet owners, but the benefit of new equipment does! Hence, the "Great news for Pet Owners" kicker.

1. Open the New Paragraph Style dialog box and set these text parameters for the Kicker style. Basic Character Formats: Adobe Garamond Pro Italic 14, leading auto (16.8 pt.)

2. Choose Indents and Spacing page and set Space After to 0.0625 in.

3. Choose Paragraph Rules pane and turn Rule Below on. Set Weight: 0.5 pt., Color: Black, Offset: 0.0766 in., Width: Text. Press Return

4. Save your document.

Duplicate Existing Styles

We are going to create a new style called Standing Head. Since this style is so similar to the Kicker style, we will create it by duplicating and editing the Kicker style. Standing heads are titles for features that appear in each issue. For instance, in a newspaper, the obituaries, sports, editorials, and classifieds each have their own title design that readers recognize and look for. Standing heads are used over and over, where a kicker is used once with one specific headline. Our newsletter project includes a Health Focus article with each issue. The standing head is found at the top left column on page 2: This Issue's Health Focus.

1. Deselect everything and use a selection tool to highlight Kicker. Click on the palette menu of the Paragraph Styles palette and choose Duplicate Style. In the Duplicate Paragraph Style dialog box, rename the style to Health Focus Standing Head. In the Based On field, choose No Paragraph Style (see Figure 8–15).

figure | 8–15

Although this style was duplicated from the Kicker style, it is not based on it. This style retains many of the Kicker attributes, but it remains independent of any changes made to the Kicker style.

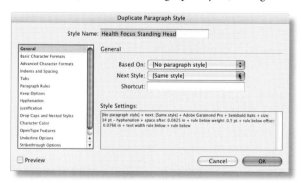

2. Chose the Basic Character Formats page, change the typeface to Adobe Garamond Pro Bold Italic. Press Return.

3. Save your document.

Bring a Style in with a New Element

When you copy an element from another InDesign document that has been formatted with a defined style, that style automatically appears in the document you are working on. Here's an example of how easy this can be done.

1. Go to spread 2-3 of your newsletter document. From the library, drag in "Spread Head left" and butt the top edges to the top margin and the right edges to the inside margin. Drag in "Spread Head right" and place it similarly with the left edges flush to the left inside margin.

2. You will see that a new paragraph style has appeared: Spread Headline. When you drag text from the library that has a paragraph or character style applied, that style is added to the list of styles.

3. Save your document.

Creating Character Styles

We have one character style to create and then we'll be ready to build the rest of the newsletter. Open the Character Styles palette by pressing Shift+F11, or by choosing Window>Type & Tables>Character Styles.

1. Option+click (Mac) or Alt+click (Windows) the Create New Character Style button at the bottom of the Character Styles palette. Name the style Body Copy Bold.

2. On the Basic Character Formats page, enter Myriad Pro Bold 10/11, shortcut Shift+Num 5. Click OK. Save your document.

3. Open the Paragraph Styles and Character Styles palettes and compare them with the ones shown in Figure 8–16. If yours looks like the figure, you are ready to complete your newsletter. If some styles are missing, you will want to review this section to find the steps that were skipped. Now let's finish this job.

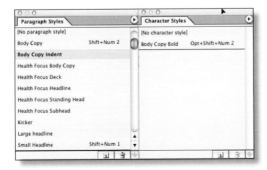

figure | 8–16

Your styles should look like the ones in this example. If they do, you are ready to proceed!

APPLYING STYLES

You have prepared the document structure, brought in images from a library, and created styles for typographic consistency and production speed. Let's see how well they work. Here are some general tips for working with styles:

- It's faster to drag a text frame while you are placing text (Command+D [Mac] or Control+D [Windows]) than to create a frame first and then drop text into it.

- A good rule of thumb is to select all the text and first change the style to Body Copy. Then go back and apply the subheads and character styles.

- When you select all the type before changing it to Body Copy, make sure you are selecting just the type in a single text frame. Remember: The Undo command is always available.

- Press Enter (Mac) or Enter on the Number pad (Windows) to make text jump from one linked text frame to the next.

Finishing Up Page 1

We'll begin on page 1, the front cover. It might be helpful to bookmark the pages at the beginning of this chapter showing each page of the sample newsletter.

1. In the "08 Newsletter Components" folder on the CD accompanying this book place the "New equipment increases" text file. Hold down the Option (Mac) or Alt (Windows) key (this lets text automatically flow from frame to frame) as you create three text frames. First, create a shallow text frame extending across the first and second columns to hold the kicker and headline type. Next, create a text frame in the first column that begins under the headline frame and extends to the bottom margin. Then use the same technique to create a similar text frame in the second column.
2. Select all the type in the frame and apply the Body Copy paragraph style by pressing Shift+Num 2. Figure 8–17 shows how the copy should look.
3. Place the cursor in the "Great news for Pet Owners" line and select the Kicker paragraph style.

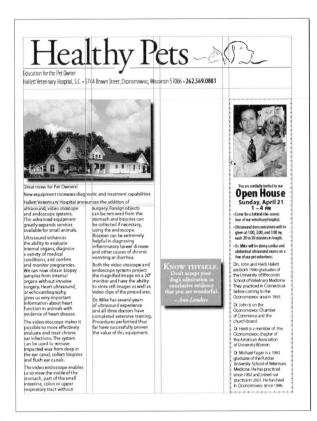

figure | 8–17 |

The text has been placed and assigned the Body Copy style.

4. Place the cursor in the headline and select Small Headline from the Paragraph Styles palette, or press Shift+Num 1. The typeface will not look like the sample in Figure 8–1. We will fix that later. At this point, you may need to adjust the height of your frame to accommodate the headline.

5. To create a break that pushes the body text into the next frame place the cursor after the word "capabilities" in the headline and press Enter (Mac) or Enter on the Number pad (Windows). Remember to work with hidden characters visible.

6. A pull quote is an excerpt that is designed to stand out from the rest of the body copy. Pull quotes add visual interest and encourage readership. Pull in the "Page 1 Pull Quote" object from the library and place it between the two columns. Adjust its position for the best text flow. Text wrap options have already been turned on. Make sure the paragraph in the article beginning with "The video endoscope" is at the top of the second column, and not at the bottom of the first column.

7. Find the "Should You Give Heartgard" text file from the 08 Newsletter Components folder. Place and drag a new text

frame at the top of column three. Select all the type and change it to Body Copy. Then place your cursor in the headline and press Shift+Num 1 to assign the Small Headline style. Notice that the registration mark (®) used three times in this article is imported as (r). Highlight it and change to a real register mark by pressing Option+R (Mac) or Alt+R (Windows).

8. Find the "Puppy Classes" article from the 08 Newsletter Components folder. Place the text at the bottom of the third column.

We believe the Iams company has recently taken the lead in nutritional research for cats and dogs. When feeding a premium food (like Iams,® Eukanuba,® Science Diet® or Purina Pro Plan®) there is no need for vitamin supplements.¶

Finishing Spread 2-3

Spread 2-3 should have a horizontal guideline stretching across the whole spread at the 1.65 Y-coordinate position. Articles on the top of this spread should butt up to this guide.

1. Find the Feeding article from the 08 Newsletter Components folder. Place the text, dragging a text frame in the third column from the top guideline down to the top of Dr. Mike's photo.

2. Apply the Body Copy and Small Headline styles to this article. Notice there are many instances where you will need to change the register mark.

3. Use Figures 8–2 and 8–3 to place the rest of the articles on spread 2-3. The "Spay or Neuter article" on page 3 continues under the photo. Bottom-align both columns of the Spay article so that the text lines up.

4. "Dental Care" in third column of page 3, is in a text frame that spans two columns. Save your document.

Converting Text to Table

Hopefully you remember the table functions you learned earlier. If not, you will need to review that section in Chapter 5.

1. The Health Focus is the last feature on page 2. For this article, bring down a new guideline to 1.375 in. on the Y coordinate. Beginning at the intersection of the guideline and the left margin, draw a frame that stretches across the first and second columns and extends down to the bottom margin. Use Command+B (Mac) or Control+B (Windows) to apply a 0.125 in. text inset on all sides. Fill the frame with 10% black. Find the "Vaccines critical to your" text file in the 08 Newsletter Components folder. Place the text file in the frame.

2. Change all copy to Body Copy. Apply the Health Focus Standing Head and Health Focus Headline styles. The italic type under the headline is called a deck. A deck is designed to increase reading interest. It usually summarizes the accompanying article and appears between the headline and the body copy. Apply the Health Focus Deck style to the deck.

3. Highlight the text from just before the words "8 weeks" to the word "Optional." Choose Table>Convert Text to Table; Column Separator: Tab; Row Separator: Paragraph. You will need to format the table. The copy is Myriad Pro Regular 10/11. Center text in cells, adjust column and row spacing, merge cells, and apply strokes and fills. Highlight the column heads row and rotate the text 270 degrees using the last T icon in the control palette (see figure 8-19). Look in the Glyphs palette at Wingdings or Zapf Dingbats to find a check mark. If you can't find a checkmark, you can use a triangle or other symbol. Figure 8–19 provides a detail view of the table.

4. Apply the Health Focus Subhead style to the lines that are bulleted. Apply the Indent Body Copy style to the text underneath the bulleted subheads. Save your document. Spread 2-3 is now completed.

figure | 8–19 |

This little chart uses all the table-making functions from Chapter 5.

highlight the row and click this icon to rotate text 270°

Finishing Page 4

All the text files needed for page 4 are found in the 08 Newsletter Components folder. Place the Pet ID article at the bottom of the third column. You will to do some local formatting in this article by changing the Home Again product name to italics. Notice that when you add local formatting a plus sign (+) appears at the end of the Body Copy paragraph style in the palette (see Figure 8–20). Place and apply styles to the "Emergency Vet Service," "Grooming," "Heartworm," and "Toys" text files. Check for register marks; there should be one in both the Heartworm and Pet ID articles. Save your document.

figure | 8–20 |

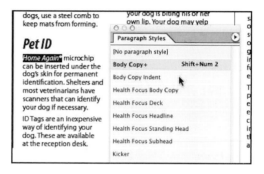

A plus sign appears with the style to alert you that the text contains local formatting in addition to its paragraph style.

Applying Character Styles

If you find yourself doing the same type of local formatting over and over again, it's probably time to define and apply a character style. The last page has two articles that use the Body Copy Bold character style: "Fleas and Ticks" and "Corrections."

1. In the "Fleas and Ticks" article, the product names in the bulleted copy use the Body Copy Bold character style: Frontline®, Flea-tick Spray, Flea Shampoo, Flea Collar, Preventic®, and House Spray. Highlight those words and apply the Body Copy Bold character style from the Character Styles palette, using the keyboard shortcut created earlier.
2. In the "Corrections" article, apply the Body Copy Bold character style to these words: OUCH!, Substitute, and Lip Pinch.
3. Replace the (r) with a ® in the Fleas and Ticks article.

Redefining Styles

The newsletter is almost finished. This is a great time to print a copy, look at it carefully, and fine-tune the positioning of all the elements. As you can see, your newsletter looks great! Except for one thing—the small headlines are all italic, and the newsletter sample shows them as roman. If you hadn't defined and applied styles, you would need to manually change every small headline in the document. That may not be a big deal for a short 4-page newsletter, but imagine making this change in a 64-page book!

1. Highlight one small headline paragraph. Change the typeface to Myriad Pro Bold Condensed.

2. Open the Paragraph Styles palette. Since you made a typestyle change on the local level you will see a + next to the Small Headline style. Click on palette menu and choose Redefine Style. The Small Headline style is now updated to reflect the roman typestyle throughout the whole document! Save and print your newsletter.

NOTE: You can still modify text attributes even though a paragraph style has been applied, but you should try to keep this "local" formatting to a minimum. Sections of type that have a paragraph style plus local formatting are easy to identify. When these passages are selected, a plus sign (+) is displayed at the end of the style name in the palette. To remove all local formatting from a styled paragraph, hold the Option (Mac) or Alt (Windows) key and click on the desired style name.

SUMMARY

Good designers can make disinterested readers take a longer look at a publication. The designer's ability to make large amounts of text look interesting and readable is an important skill. This newsletter project introduced you to some publication design elements: pull quote, deck, standing head, and kicker. These elements, when combined with appropriate typeface selection, line measure, and leading, create a document that has contrast, and wonderful texture.

When working on complex projects it is important to remember that there are no "throwaway" elements. The position and style of a page number or a pull quote should not be overlooked just because it's small or used only once or twice. All elements are important, and should work together to create a gestalt—where the whole is greater than the sum of its parts. It takes creative energy and commitment to refine the smallest details of a document. But this ability to maintain a high level of focus is what separates the skilled designers from the masses.

in review

1. What are three guidelines for preparing electronic copy?

2. What are facing pages and how do you make them?

3. How can using an object library speed up production?

4. What is the process for using the Eyedropper tool to transfer text attributes?

5. What are three methods of defining styles?

6. What is the difference between a paragraph style and a character style?

7. What does a + sign at the end of the name of a style mean?

↗ EXPLORING ON YOUR OWN

Two projects will reinforce the concepts from this chapter.

Newsletter Analysis. Find a sample newsletter. Write a critique that addresses the following:

- The underlying grid structure

- The quality of the typography: contrast, typeface, consistency

- Any evidence of styles

- The inclusion of kickers, pull quotes, decks, subheads, spread heads, or standing heads

- Overall impact

- Effectiveness of nameplate

- Suggestions for improvement

Create Styles. Select a newspaper. Find four repeating styles used throughout the publication. Using placeholder text, duplicate each the four styles in InDesign. Create and name a style for each one.

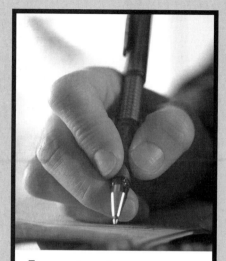

Learning is not
compulsory.
Neither is **survival**.
℞ W. Edwards Deming

page continuity: master pages

g

charting your course

In the last chapter you discovered how defining styles brings continuity to the text in a project. In this chapter you will learn how to bring continuity to the pages within a document by creating and applying master pages.

Page consistency is critical for multiple-page documents. A five-person team producing a 96-page catalog also needs a document structure that is consistent from page to page and designer to designer. Perhaps you've leafed through a publication where repeating elements like page numbers, appear to jump around the outside corners like cartoons in an old-fashioned flip book. This would be an indication that the production team was not working with a clearly defined document structure. Proper document construction can make or break the finished project. Take the time to plan your projects thoughtfully before starting them.

 goals

- **Create multiple master pages**
- **Set up automatic page numbering, jump lines, and continuation lines**
- **Insert, duplicate, and remove pages**
- **Create an object library**
- **Manage document pages using the Pages palette**

MASTER PAGES

In Chapter 8 you began to use the Pages palette and were introduced to Master Pages. By default, the master pages are displayed in the upper half of the Pages palette and the regular document pages are shown in the lower (see Figure 9–1). Every new document is created with a master page named A-Master. Any elements placed on a master page will appear on every document page that is based on that master page.

figure | 9–1 |

The Pages palette is divided into two sections by a separator that can be moved up or down. The palette itself can be resized to expand the viewing area.

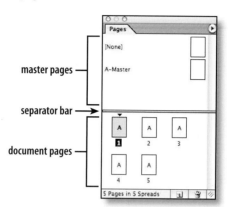

master pages

separator bar ➔

document pages

Adding Elements and Renaming Master Pages

Multi-page documents often have elements, such as page numbers, headers, and footers that must be in the exact same location on each page. These repeating elements should be placed on a master page. Once placed, they are locked into position and cannot be changed on a document page, unless they are first released.

1. Create a new one page document: 5 inches square, all margins 0.0 in., Facing Pages turned off.

2. Open the Pages palette (F12). Double-click on the page 1 icon. You are now on a document page. Double-click on A-Master in the top section of the palette. You are now on a master page. Repeat this step until you are comfortable switching back and forth between the two levels.

3. Double-click on A-Master page again. Draw a yellow circle in the upper left corner of the page. With A-Master page selected, Option+click (Mac) or Alt+click (Windows) on the A-Master name. The Master Options dialog box opens. Here you can set various options, such as the Prefix that will be displayed on page icons to identify which master page has been applied.

You can also rename the master page. Type **Yellow Circle** in the Name field. Your document and Pages palette should look like Figure 9–2.

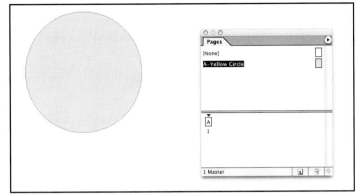

figure 9–2

The A-Master Page has been renamed to A-Yellow Circle.

4. Click on the Pages palette options menu and choose Insert Pages. In the Insert Pages dialog box change the Pages field to 3. Check that the Insert fields are set to After Page and 1. Because we want these new pages to be based on the A-Yellow Circle master page, make sure that name is selected in the Master field (see Figure 9–3). Press Return. Notice that each page icon in the Pages palette contains the prefix letter A. This tells you, at a glance, that the A-Yellow Circle master page is applied to those document pages.

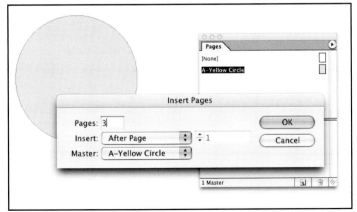

figure 9–3

Three pages based on the A-Yellow Circle master page have been added after page 1.

5. Move from page to page in the document. Each page will have a yellow circle in exactly the same spot as the A-Yellow Circle master page. Try to select and move each of the circles. You won't be able to.

NOTE: You can also insert a document page that is based on a master by dragging and dropping the master page icon into the document section of the Pages palette. This method can be a little tricky, until you understand the following visual cues. When you drag over a blank area of the document section, a heavy border will appear around the entire area. This means that the new page will be added at the end of the document. If you want to add the new page in a particular spot, say between pages 1 and 2, drag the master page between the two page icons until you see a vertical line appear after page 1. When you release the mouse, there will be a new page 2 created; the old page 2 will be shifted to the number 3 spot. Finally, be careful not to release the master page icon when the border of a document page is highlighted. If you do, you will be applying that master page to the selected document page.

Modifying Master Page Elements

You can modify a master page element on the document level.

1. Double click on the page 4 icon to move to page 4. Press Shift+Command (Mac) or Shift+Control (Windows) and click on the yellow circle. This action releases the circle on this page from the A-Yellow Circle master page. You will know when a master page element has been released when you see the object's bounding box. Now you can edit the circle. Change the circle's color to black and move it to the left. By using Shift+Command+click or Shift+Control+click, you released the master page element. When you changed its color and position you then performed what is called a "local override".

2. With the black circle still selected open the Pages palette options menu and choose Remove Selected Local Overrides (when no objects are selected, the menu will read Remove All Local Overrides). Your circle changes back to yellow and moves to its original location. Removing Local Overrides returns a page to its original master page format.

3. Release the circle on page 4 and change its color back to black. This time, move it to the upper right corner of the page. Open the Pages palette options menu and choose Detach Selection From Master (see Figure 9–4). Once a master page element is detached from the master page, its connection to the original object is severed.

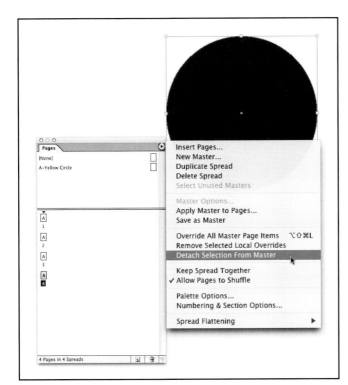

figure | 9–4 |

The options on the Pages palette menu are powerful. When you select an item and choose Detach Selection From Master, that item is no longer influenced by any changes made on the master page.

4. On the Pages palette menu, choose Remove All Local Overrides. A new yellow circle will appear. However, the black circle that was detached from the master page object remains unchanged.

5. Release the new yellow circle and change its color to green.

6. Move to the A-Yellow Circle master page by double-clicking on its icon. Select the yellow circle and change its color to red. Now, move through your document pages one by one. All the yellow circles automatically change to red—except for the green one that was released and had a local override applied, and the black circle was detached from the master page object.

7. Keep your file open for the next exercise.

NOTE: You release master page items from the master page by holding down Shift+Command (Mac) or Shift+Control (Windows) as you select the item. If you want all items on a specific page to be released, select Override All Master Page Items from the Pages palette menu. The Override All Master Page Items works only on the document page you have selected. Note that master page elements must be released before they can be detached from the master.

Creating New Master Pages

Many documents require more than one master page. For instance, you may be working on a document that requires some pages to have a two-column grid page, a three-column grid, and a four-column grid. In such a case, if you don't create multiple master pages, you will need to change the margins and columns on each individual page—that's too much work! Next you'll create a new master page that contains a header. A header is a line of text that appears at the top of every page.

1. Click on the Pages palette menu and choose New Master. When the New Master dialog box opens, notice that the Prefix field has been changed to B. Change the Name field to **Name Header** and make sure the Based on Master field is set to [None]. Press Return.

2. With the B-Name Header master page selected, choose Layout>Margins and Columns and change all margins to 0.5 in. Press Return.

3. On this master page, create a shallow text frame aligned to the top, left, and right margins. Type your name followed by: **Master of the Master Pages** and center align the paragraph in the text frame, as shown in Figure 9–5.

figure | 9–5 |

Your B-Name Header master page should look like this.

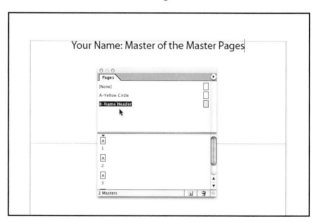

4. Click on the B-Name Header master page icon and drag and drop it just after the page 4 icon. Remember to watch for the cursor to change to a vertical bar before releasing the mouse. Now, look at the document page icons in the Pages palette. Pages 1-4 are based on A-Yellow Circle, and page 5 is based on B-Name Header. It's easy to tell which master is applied to each page because the prefix letter is displayed on each page icon.

5. Before we move on to the next exercise, let's clean up the document a little. Shift+click on pages 1 and 2 and drag them to the trashcan.

Setting Automatic Page Numbers

When automatic page numbers are placed on a master page, sequential page numbers are displayed on any document page that is based on that master. To accomplish this, you insert an Auto Page Number character. You will find this character by accessing the context menu and choosing Insert Special Character>Auto Page Number. You can also use the Command+Shift+Option+N (Mac) or Control+Shift+Alt+N (Windows) shortcut.

1. Double-click on the B-Name Header master page icon again. Select the text frame with your name, place the blinking text cursor at the end of the line and press Return. Make sure that both paragraphs are center aligned. Leave the cursor in the second line.

2. Open the context text menu and choose Insert Special Character>Auto Page Number (see Figure 9–6). The letter B will appear to the left of the text cursor. This isn't a mistake— the prefix letter assigned to each master page is used as the auto page number marker.

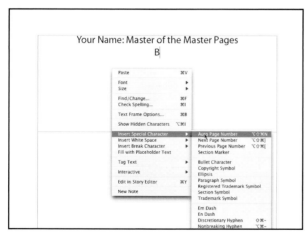

figure | **9–6**

The Auto Page Number appears on the master page as the prefix letter for that page, but displays as sequential page numbers on the document pages.

3. Double click on document page icon number 3. The page should have a 3 under your name.

4. Use the Pages palette menu to insert three more pages after page 3. The pages should be based on B-Name Header (see Figure 9–7). Scroll through the new pages. You will see that

automatic page numbers appear on all pages that are based on the B-Name Header master page.

figure 9–7

When inserting pages in a document you can choose which master they should be based on. In this case, we are inserting three pages based on B- Name Header.

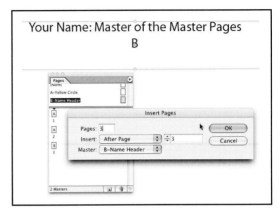

5. Change the page order of the document by dragging the icons for pages 1 and 2 (which have no Auto Page Number character) and positioning them between pages based on B-Name Header. Now scroll through the document pages again. Any page with the auto page number character correctly displays the new page order.

Duplicating Master Pages

Let's say your A-Master page is a single-column page with a header and auto page numbering. Now you need another page with the same header and page number but with different margins and column guides. The best thing to do is to duplicate A-Master. This is an easy process, and the command is found under the Pages palette options menu. Before the master page is duplicated you have a decision to make: Should this page be based on another master page, or should it be an independent page? Just like paragraph styles, which can be based on another style, a master page based on another master page will automatically update if any changes are made to the original master page. However, if you duplicate a master page and base it on None, the new page will include all the elements from the copied page, but the connection with those elements is severed. This means that any changes made on the original page will not affect the duplicate page.

1. Select master page B-Name Header and open the Pages palette menu. Choose Duplicate Master Spread "B-Name Header". A new master page named B-Name Header Copy will appear in the Pages palette.

2. Select the copied master page and choose Master Options for "B Name Header" on the palette menu. The Master Options dialog box will open, as shown in Figure 9–8. It would be confusing to have two master pages with the prefix "B" in your document, so change the Prefix field to C. Change the name to **Name Header 2**. Change the Based on Master field to None (so it will be independent). If you base a new master page on an existing master page, any changes made to the existing master page will appear on the master pages based on it.

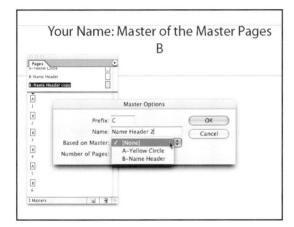

figure | 9–8

A master page based on "None" will not be affected by changes made to other master pages.

3. Double click on the C-Name Header 2 master page icon and draw some stars and squiggly lines on the page. To make a star, double-click the Polygon tool and enter the number of sides and a 40% inset. To draw squiggly lines, use the Line tool. Set the stroke weight to 10 pt. and the type to Wavy. Your master page should look something like Figure 9–9.

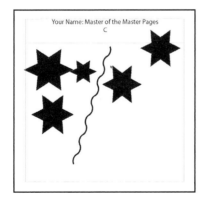

figure | 9–9

Create a star by double-clicking on the Polygon tool and entering the number of sides. These six-sided stars have 40% insets.

4. Select the C-Name Header 2 master page and drag three new pages based on it, into your document. You can drop them

anywhere in the page order. Remember to place the cursor to the left or right side of an existing page, and wait for the cursor to change to a vertical black line before releasing the mouse. When you are finished, flip through your document's pages and you will see quite a variation. Some pages have your name and page number, some have name, page number and stars, and some only have circles.

Apply a Different Master Page to an Existing Page

You can apply a new master page to any document page that already has a master page assigned to it. This will be demonstrated in the next exercise. Since the pages in your document are all shuffled up with A, B, and C master pages, your document will be different from the pages described in this example.

1. Go to the document page with the single yellow circle (it will be one that has an "A" page icon). Drag out a text frame anywhere on the page and type the word **Cover**.
2. Find the page with two circles (the other "A" page icon). Drag out a text frame anywhere on the page and type the words **Table of Contents**.
3. Click on master page C-Name Header 2 and drag it on top of any A or B page icon in the document. When dragging, wait until you see a black border appear around the edge of the document page icon before releasing the mouse. The master page originally applied to that page has now been replaced with the C-Name Header 2 master page.
4. Click on C-Name Header 2 and repeat this process with all the document pages that are assigned to master pages A and B.
5. When you have finished assigning the C-Name Header 2 master to all the pages in your document, flip through your pages. Each page looks just like master page C-Name Header 2, except for those pages with elements that you released from their original master page or with type you added to the document pages.

Automating Jump and Continuation Lines

Jump lines are used when an article continues on a new page. They appear at the end of a column and read something like "this article continues on page 257." When you turn to page 257 you are greeted with a continuation line. This line reads something like "...article continued from page 1." InDesign automates this process.

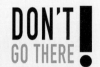

In the last chapter we discussed the idea that there are no "throw-away" elements in any publication. A good designer makes sure every element in a publication has been carefully typeset. Jump lines and continuation lines are elements that can seem insignificant—and are tempting to ignore. But professionalism shows in the details... and these are ones you don't want to overlook. Pay attention to the jump lines and continuation lines in magazines and newspapers you read. You will see that they are well designed and used consistently throughout the publication.

1. Create a new one page, 3 × 5 document, set all margins to 0.5 in.
2. Create a text frame that fills the margins and type a few paragraphs describing the best vacation or trip you have ever taken. Keep typing until you see the overset text box. Or, you can fill the frame with placeholder text and then shorten the text frame by one line.
3. Insert a new page, create a text frame like that on page 1, and link the two frames, so that the overset text flows into page 2. Type a few more sentences into the text frame on page 2.
4. On the bottom of page 1, create a small text frame for the jump line. This frame should be touching the frame that holds your vacation story. Write "Exciting vacation article continued on page " and with your blinking cursor at the end of that line, open the context menu and choose Insert Special Character>Next Page Number. A number 2 will automatically appear in the text frame (see Figure 9–10). Note: The jump line text frame must be touching the main text frame for this to work.

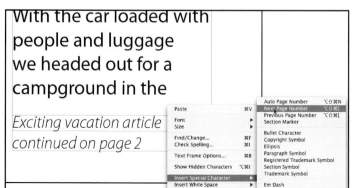

figure | 9–10 |

The jump line text frame must be touching the main text frame for this function to work correctly.

5. Use the Selection tool to move the jump line text frame away from the main text frame. Watch the number change to number 1—the link to the new page cannot be read unless the jump line frame is touching the main linked frame. Now move the jump line back so it touches the main text frame. The number will change back to 2.

6. Insert a page at the end of the document. Move the text frame on page 2 to page 3. Now go back to page 1. Your jump line number automatically updated to a 3. If it didn't, check to make sure the jump line text frame is touching the main text frame.

7. Continuation lines work the same way. Draw a text frame on the top of the text frame on page 3. Type "Continued from page " Use the context menu and choose Insert Special Character>Previous Page Number (see Figure 9–11).

figure | 9–11

The jump and continuation lines update automatically as the layout changes.

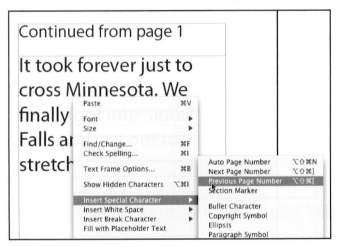

Creating an Object Library

You used an object library when you made the newsletter in Chapter 8. The library you are about to create will be used in one of the project exercises at the end of this chapter.

1. From the CD that accompanied this book, open 09 Artwork. indd. This is an InDesign file containing a collection of artwork you will use in the menu project at the end of this chapter.

2. Choose File>New>Library. Name the new library file 09 Zaffinni's and save it on your desktop. A library palette with the name 09 Zaffinni's will appear in your workspace.

3. Using the Selection tool, drag each page item from the page to the library palette. As the element is moved to the library, with

the cursor will display a plus sign (+) sign showing that an item is being added to the library (see Figure 9–12). Continue this process until all page items are in the 09 Zaffinni's library.

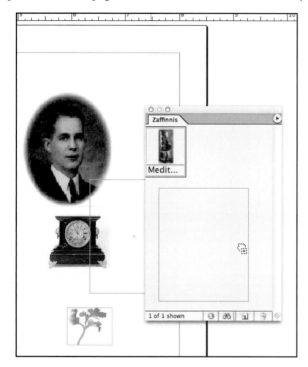

figure | 9–12 |

Drag and drop page elements onto the library palette.

4. Double-clicking a library entry opens the Item Information dialog box. You can change the name and also add a description of the item, if desired (see Figure 9–13). Your library is now complete and can be used with any document you want to use it with!

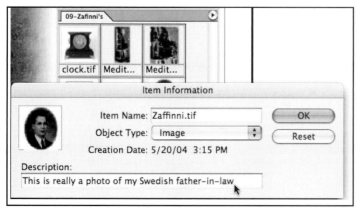

figure | 9–13 |

The item description can contain special production instructions or just provide general information like the sample in this figure.

SUMMARY

In this chapter you learned to create, duplicate, and modify master pages. You learned how to release, override and detach master page elements on document pages. Automated features including page numbering, jump lines, and continuation lines were also introduced. Now, with Styles and Master Pages "under your belt" and a new document library waiting for you, you are ready to begin the projects for this chapter!

in review

1. In your own words, describe a master page and its purpose.

2. What is the keyboard shortcut for releasing an element from the master page, so that you can edit it on the document page?

3. If an element is detached from the master page and the master is changed, will those changes affect the detached element?

4. Where in InDesign will you find the Auto Page Number character?

5. If you create a jump line and it just isn't working, what might be the problem?

↗ EXPLORING ON YOUR OWN

Three projects are included on the accompanying CD, in the Chapter 09 folder. The Zaffinni's menu project uses the picture library created in this lesson. You're going to enjoy these projects!

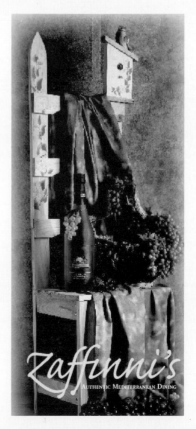

This beautiful menu cover features digital cover shot by student Tiffany Mastak.

ADVENTURES IN DESIGN

HIGH-IMPACT DESIGN ON A LOW BUDGET

What we want and what we can afford are usually two different things! Your clients will frequently face the challenge of having a very low budget but needing a high-impact piece. They will come to you, the design professional, for your suggestions and expertise. They will expect you to find alternate methods to achieve their goals—while staying within tight budget guidelines.

Just as a large budget does not guarantee a high-quality product, a small budget does not necessarily mean settling for a shabby one. What *does* make all the difference in a project is the overall design—the layout, the use of color and type, the paper selection, and binding method. When these variables are used effectively in combination with each other, the resulting piece is attractive and effective.

The quality of a project should not be measured just by the type of paper, the quality of the printing, the special finishes, the number of colors, or the photographic effects. Instead, the piece needs to be looked at as a whole—with the concept, design, and production techniques considered as equal partners.

Professional Project Example

A four-page, two-color booklet highlighting the history of the teddy bear was designed for a local doll club to celebrate the 100th birthday of the toy. The design challenges included copy-heavy interior pages and a limited printing budget.

The resulting two-color piece (see Figure C–1) communicated a friendly, nostalgic feel and utilized a simple binding method requiring drilling and some hand assembly to be performed by doll club members. The booklet was printed on ivory cover stock with a duotone of sepia and black inks, and tied with a baby blue satin ribbon.

With a minimal financial investment and volunteer labor from doll club members, this publication became a keepsake valued by collectors of all ages.

The copy was written by Marianne Clay, who is also on the *Teddy Bear and Friends* magazine staff. Digital photography was provided by Tiffany Mastak, a graphic design student at the Harry V. Quadracci Printing and Graphics Center, Waukesha County Technical College.

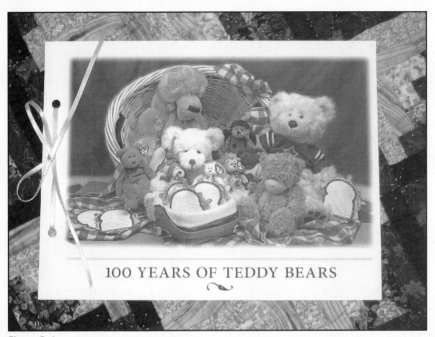

Figure C–1
The finished booklet

Your Turn

Now it's your turn to create this charming booklet. The production steps are not complicated and will utilize paragraph and character styles. The template and the styles are already created for you. If you do not have the Minion Pro typeface, you will need to edit the styles and substitute a similar face such as Adobe Garamond Pro or Adobe Caslon Pro.

Building the Booklet Cover

1. Open the Teddy Bear Template found in the Adventures in Design folder on the CD. Open the Pages palette. You will see

two spreads: page 4 is the back cover, page 1 is the cover. Frames for text and photos have already been put into place. Photo frames have an X in them.

2. In the same folder on the CD, find the Teddy Bear photo. Place the photo into the picture frame on page 1.

3. Draw a 3-point double rule on the guide below the bottom margin.

4. In the text frame below the double rule, type "100 Years of Teddy Bears" in Minion Pro Regular 42/22. Choose OpenType>All Small Caps from the Character Formatting Control palette options.

5. Open the Glyphs palette and insert the Minion ornament or (similar

substitute) beneath the booklet title. Change the size to 31 points. Center all the text. See Figure C–2.

Formatting the Text

Now we'll drop in the text. Character and paragraph styles have already been created. Figure C–3 shows where each style is used.

1. Find the file Teddy Bear.txt from the Adventures in Design folder on the CD. Place the file on the top of page 2, and the text will automatically flow from frame to frame.

2. Change all the copy to the Body copy style. This is a good production technique to use whenever you are working with styles. This is an efficient method of quickly formatting large amounts of text.

3. Place the cursor in the first paragraph. Apply the Deck paragraph style and then apply the Deck drop cap character style to the first letter.

4. Find each subhead and apply the Subhead paragraph style. Insert a glyph at the end of the first subhead. Copy and paste the glyph to the rest of the subheads.

5. A paragraph following a subhead or headline should not have a first line indent, so apply the Body copy no indent style to each paragraph following the subheads.

6. Apply the Body Copy Italic character style to the song, book, and newspaper titles found within the body copy.

7. Place the Teddy Bear photo from the Adventures in Design folder on the CD into the photo frame on page 4. Scale proportionately to 40%.

8. Inset a glyph as a stop symbol at the end of the last paragraph of copy.

Figure C–2
Detail of the bottom edge of cover

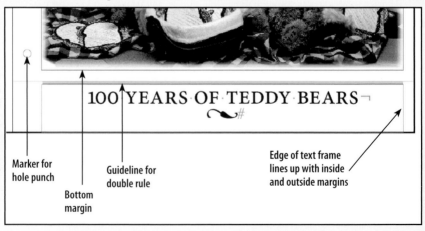

100 YEARS·OF·TEDDY·BEARS

Marker for hole punch

Bottom margin

Guideline for double rule

Edge of text frame lines up with inside and outside margins

9. Use local formatting for the author's name and website. See Figure C-4. Remove the first line indent and change the magazine title to italic. Add a paragraph underline to the web site, offsetting it so that it doesn't touch any descenders.Proof your work carefully. If you decide to make a mockup, print the document in spreads back to back. Fold, punch, and tie with ribbon.

Deck drop cap →

T oday we can hardly imagine a world without that eager listener, confidante, and loyal friend, the teddy bear. But the teddy bear has not always been with us. In fact, the teddy bear did not make its entrance until late in 1902. Then, in one of life's unexplainable synchronicities, the teddy bear appeared in the same year in two different parts of the world: Germany and the United States.

Deck →

Subhead →

The Early Years ∽

Body copy no indent →

In America, the teddy bear, according to tradition, got its start with a cartoon. The cartoon, drawn by Clifford Berryman and titled Drawing the Line in Mississippi, showed President Theodore Roosevelt refusing to shoot a baby bear. According to this often told tale, Roosevelt had traveled to Mississippi to help settle a border dispute between that state and Louisiana, and his hosts, wanting to please this avid hunter, took him bear hunting. The hunting was so poor that someone finally captured a bear and invited Roosevelt to shoot. Roosevelt's refusal to fire at such a helpless target inspired Berryman to draw his cartoon with its play on the two ways Roosevelt was drawing a line-settling a border dispute and refusing to shoot a captive animal.

Body copy →
Body copy italic →

The cartoon appeared in a panel of cartoons drawn by Clifford Berryman in *The Washington Post* on November 16, 1902. It caused an immediate sensation and was reprinted widely. Apparently this cartoon even inspired Morris and Rose Michtom of Brooklyn,

Figure C–3
Paragraph and character styles

The Teddy Bear's Comeback: The Present ∽

Strangely enough, the comeback of the teddy after years of mass-production was triggered, not by a bear maker, but by an actor. On television, British actor Peter Bull openly expressed his love for teddy bears and his belief in the teddy bear's importance in the emotional life of adults. After receiving 2000 letters in response to his public confession, Peter realized he wasn't alone. In 1969, inspired by this response, he wrote a book about his lifelong affection for teddy bears, *Bear with Me*, later called *The Teddy Bear Book*. His book struck an emotional chord in thousands who also believed in the importance of teddy bears. Without intending to, Bull created an ideal climate for the teddy bear's resurgence. The teddy bear began to regain its popularity, not so much as a children's toy, but as a collectible for adults.

In 1974, Beverly Port, an American dollmaker who also loved making teddy bears, dared to take a teddy bear she made to a doll show. At the show, she presented Theodore B. Bear holding the hand of one of her dolls. The next year, Beverly presented a slide show she had created about teddy bears for the United Federation of Doll Clubs. That show quickly became a sensation. Other people, first in the United States and then all over world, caught Beverly's affection for the teddy bear. They, too, began applying their talents to designing and making teddy bears. One by one, and by hand, teddy bear artistry was born with Beverly, who coined the term "teddy bear artist," often cited as the mother of teddy bear artistry. Today thousands of teddy bears artists, often working from their homes all over the world, create soft sculpture teddy bear art for eager collectors.

Artist bears also set the stage for a new kind of manufactured bear, the artist-designed manufactured bear. Today artist-designed manufactured bears are offered by Ganz, Gund, Dean's, Knickerbocker, Grisly Spielwaren, and others; all offer collectors the opportunity to own artist-designed bears that cost less due to mass production.

This increased appreciation for the teddy bear as an adult collectible

has also increased the value of antique teddy bears, the hand-finished, high-quality teddy bears manufactured in the first decades of the 20th century. In the 1970s and 1980s, these old, manufactured teddy bears began showing up in antique doll and toy auctions, and they began winning higher and higher bids. Today the current record price for one teddy bear, Teddy Girl by Steiff, is $176,000; that bear was sold at Christie's auction house in 1994.

So what's next for the teddy bear? Certainly our love affair with the teddy bear shows no signs of abating.

In 1999, in just the United States, collectors purchased $441 million worth of teddy bears. Certainly, as we begin our journey through a new century, we certainly need the teddy bear's gift of uncondtional acceptance, love, and reassurance more than ever. ∽

by Marianne Clay, Managing Editor, *Teddy Bear and Friends*
www.teddybearandfriends.com

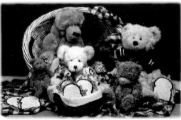

Photo ©2004 Tiffany Mastak

Figure C–4
Detail of page 4

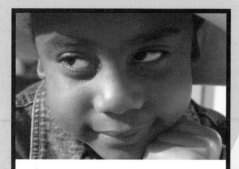

Life in abundance comes **only** through great love.

℞ Elbert Hubbard

business forms

10

charting your course

How many times have you read, "Wanted: Graphic Designer. Two to five years experience required." Everyone wants someone with experience, but how will you get experience if you don't have a job? Graphic design is a highly competitive field. To be considered for an entry-level position, you not only need a fantastic portfolio, but you must be able to demonstrate your ability to think quickly and creatively, work productively, and maintain exemplary interpersonal relationships. And if you get hired you must prove yourself before you are given more responsibility.

Sometimes your new boss will begin to try out your software skills (and your attitude) by assigning you lower-end production jobs. Before you begin to grumble, remind yourself that everyone has to start somewhere. First jobs aren't always the most glamorous. But remember that there are a hundred other unemployed graphic designers out there, and each of them would love to have your job! Business forms, at first glance, seem to be on the bottom rung of the ladder of creativity. But in reality, tables and forms require a high degree of precision, attention to detail, and layout skills. A skilled designer can turn a business form into a work of art; an unskilled designer can turn it into a nightmare!

 goals

- **Create business forms that are functional, well-designed, effective, and that express a company's image**
- **Consider printing, paper, and finishing processes when designing business forms**
- **Learn when to use lining or old-style figures**
- **Typeset academic degrees, acronyms, and titles**
- **Design newspaper advertisements according to specifications.**

GENERAL PROJECT INFORMATION

The initial client meeting is your opportunity to find out the details of a project. Knowing the correct information up front will save backtracking later on. Your client's responses to each of the following questions will affect your document setup.

- Is there an existing form? If so, what has worked or not worked with the current form? Or, is there a sample form the customer likes?

- Does the form have to match or blend with any existing forms? What kind of tone should the form convey?

- Who will be completing the form?

- How many colors will the form be printed in?

- Will the company logo be included on the form? Is an electronic file of the logo available? What are the corporate colors?

- Is the form one- or two-sided?

- Does it have any requirements such as a perforation or a fold or an address that shows through an envelope window?

- How will the form be printed? Separate sheets? In duplicate or triplicate? On a photocopier in the office?

- How will the form be used? Will it be mailed in a #10 envelope? Will it be returned in a #9 envelope? Will it be a self-mailer?

- Will it be drilled and held in a binder? Will it be padded tablet style with tear-off sheets? Will it be held in a clipboard? Will it be filed in a file folder?

- Will individual completed forms be photocopied and distributed to team members? Will the responses of groups of forms be tabulated?

- What company information will be on the form? Fax? Email? Phone? (Ask for a business card with the correct information.)

- How often is the form revised?

- Will it require sequential numbering?

- Is there any legally required wording that must be included on the form?

General Design Considerations

A form must be a positive representation of the business. If you were waiting for a surgical procedure and were given an old type-written form to fill out, your confidence in the surgeon might begin to slip. A well-designed form is an asset to a business. A form should communicate professionalism while incorporating the look and feel of the rest of the company's literature. A form should be easy to follow—the layout should create a visual hierarchy that organizes and sequences the reader's responses. The layout should clearly identify where each response should be placed. A form should be usable. The user should have enough vertical room to write below the previous line and enough horizontal room to write a hyphenated last name or a very long city name. Never consider a form complete unless you have "completed" the form yourself. Choose a paper stock that won't smudge when written on with either pencil, felt tip pen or a ballpoint pen.

Typographic Considerations

Some typefaces are designed specifically for reading, and some are designed more for display or decoration. When selecting a typeface for business communications the overall concern is readability. Use a typeface that is highly legible and one that blends with the company logo or corporate identity system. If the company uses a trendy, cursive logotype, be careful how you use it in business forms. Find a legible face that blends with the company logotype and use that in the business form. Consider who will be completing the form. Baby boomers are now wearing reading glasses and require a more generous point size than high school students. Children mastering penmanship need more room for writing.

When choosing typefaces for display type and body copy, be sure to consider the contrast between the two faces. A page is interesting to look at and easier to read when continuous body copy is broken into blocks by blacker, higher-contrast display type. A good layout will use type blocks as stepping stones to move the reader through the piece.

A SAMPLE JOB

This chapter will focus on the development of an identity package for a psychologist beginning a new practice. The psychologist, Dr. Rosemary Tollefson, needs identity pieces (letterhead, envelope, business card); a display advertisement for the phone book; a 3/4 page vertical newspaper display ad; and a client information form. Although each piece has its distinctive design and typographic challenges, all the pieces retain a visual unity that identifies them as members of the same family.

figure | 10–1 |

Each of these pieces has a distinct purpose and layout challenges, yet all remain part of the same visual family.

Client Information Form

CLIENT INFORMATION   Today's date _____

Name _____
Address _____
City _____ State _____ Zip _____
Phone _____ Email _____
Birthdate _____ Age _____

Please describe your current relationships
☐ Live alone, no significant other
☐ Live alone, but have significant other
☐ Living with significant other
 Name of significant other: _____
☐ Living with spouse
 Name of spouse: _____

blended   lives with me   not at home

Letterhead

Rosemary Tollefson, PH.D.
specializing in family systems

Business Card

Rosemary Tollefson, PH.D.
specializing in family systems

300 JACOBS AVENUE, SUITE 6
NORTHFIELD, MINNESOTA 55037
FAX: (507) 663-4419

rtollefson@vista.net
CELL: (507) 663-4457

Display Ad in Phone Book

Rosemary Tollefson, PH.D.
LICENSED PSYCHOLOGIST
specializing in family systems

• Children, Adolescents, and Family
• Custody, Separation, and Remarriage
• School and Behavior Problems
• ADHD and Learning Disabilities
Evening and Saturday Appointments
24-hour answering service
300 JACOBS AVENUE, SUITE 6
(½ MILE WEST OF WOODLEY AVENUE, NORTHFIELD)
(507) 663-4457

Rosemary Tollefson, PH.D.
300 JACOBS AVENUE, SUITE 6
NORTHFIELD, MINNESOTA 55037

CELL: (507) 663-4457 · FAX: (507) 663-4419 · rtollefson@vista.net
300 JACOBS AVENUE, SUITE 6 · NORTHFIELD, MINNESOTA 55037

You're invited to our
Open House
Monday, April 26
2:30 – 5:00 PM

Join us as we celebrate the opening of our new practice at
300 Jacobs Avenue, ½ mile west of Woodley.

Meet the staff, enjoy refreshments, and register for door prizes. Dr. Tollefson will be available to autograph her newly-released book, BELIEVE IN YOURSELF.

Rosemary Tollefson, PH.D.
specializing in family systems

• Children, Adolescents, and Family
• Custody, Separation, and Remarriage
• School and Behavior Problems
• ADHD and Learning Disabilities
Evening and Saturday Appointments
24-hour answering service
300 JACOBS AVENUE, SUITE 6
(½ MILE WEST OF WOODLEY AVENUE, NORTHFIELD)
(507) 663-4457

Display Ad in Newspaper

Identity Packages

Dr. Tollefson is a 30-something, tree-hugging intellectual. She dislikes the traditional look of the printed materials most counseling services use. She chose the rose as her symbol for three reasons: 1) it is living; 2) it is expressive and classic, and 3) it ties in with her name. When assisting clients with visual identifiers, here are some questions to ask about the logo:

- Does the image convey the correct tone for the business?

- Can it be enlarged and reduced without losing legibility?

- Does it avoid any negative connotations?

- Is it copyright free?

- Can the image be used for ten years without being dated?

Letterhead Design Considerations

Does anyone use a typewriter anymore? Hardly. So make sure the paper you select for a letterhead will go through a laser or inkjet printer. Find out what typeface the client uses most often and try to coordinate that typeface with the one used in the letterhead. You may want to avoid gradients and screened background images if the letters will often be photocopied. Keep your client's budget in mind during the design phase—a nice effect can be created with colored ink on white or colored paper stock. Use the best paper stock your client can afford. Remember that some paper surfaces don't print well on a photocopier. Include bleed images only if the client's budget can afford the extra cost of printing on an oversized sheet and cutting it down to letter size. If you have to choose between better paper and a bleed, choose better paper every time!

Use care when including names of personnel on the letterhead—if a person or position changes, all the old letterhead gets tossed. Ouch! Double-check all the information provided by the client. Send a test fax just to confirm the fax number. Call your client and tell her the fax is coming—that way you can confirm the fax and phone number at the same time! I prefer designing the letterhead first—then I create a library and pull the letterhead elements into it.

Letterhead Considerations for Rosemary Tollefson

Figure 10–2 shows a detail view of the top and the bottom areas of the letterhead. The typeface is Adobe Garamond Pro. Typefaces followed by the word "Pro" have a wide selection of ornaments, ligatures, alternate letters and symbols that can be viewed in the Glyphs palette. Notice the academic degree, Ph.D., listed after the name. When academic degrees follow the name, they look best set in small caps. Use either the degree (Rosemary Tollefson, Ph.D.) or the title (Dr. Rosemary Tollefson) with the name, but not both.

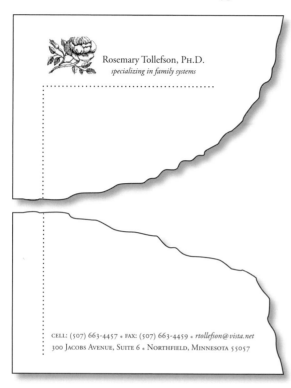

In this letterhead design, the contact information is found at the bottom of the page. This example uses numbers that extend below the baseline, "lowercase" numbers called old-style figures or text figures. Numbers that sit on the baseline are called titling figures or lining figures. Titling figures are ideal for use with display type and are sometimes used within body copy. Old-style figures are used within text and are rarely used in display type. Old-style figures have a graceful, elegant look as seen in this letterhead example.

figure | 10–2 |

When designing letterhead, leave room for the letter! It is helpful to drop in some placeholder text in the typeface used by the client to get a sense of how a finished document will look.

NOTE: The parentheses surrounding the area codes were baseline shifted −1 pt. so that they would be more centered on the numbers they enclose.

Envelope Design Considerations

There are two things you should remember when designing envelopes: 1) allow a 2-pica margin at the top and left edges; and 2) don't design an envelope with multiple colors that overlap or are close together (this is called tight register) unless your client has an ample budget. Printing a four-color envelope with tight register and bleeds is expensive because it has to be printed on a flat sheet, then die-cut, folded and glued (a process called converting). Envelopes typically don't have the phone and fax number—but when elements are dragged in from a library to use on another piece, this can easily happen. You will want to watch for this. The image and type on an envelope will probably be smaller than that on the letterhead, but the size relationship should remain about the same. A standard commercial business-size envelope is called a #10 with dimensions of 4 1/8 × 9 1/2 inches. A business response #9 envelope fits nicely inside a #10. Its dimensions are 3 7/8 × 8 7/8 inches.

NOTE: If you don't have a chart of envelope styles and sizes, do a Google search for "envelope sizes." Several envelope sites will have information you can download and print.

Envelope Design Considerations for Rosemary Tollefson

Figure 10–3 shows the details of the upper left corner of the envelope. Elements were initially pulled in from the library but then needed editing. Notice that old-style figures are still used for the address, and an ample margin has been maintained on the upper and left edges.

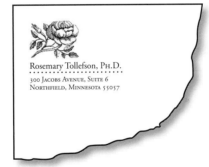

figure | 10–3

The envelope carries the same visual "theme" of the letterhead.

Business Card Design Considerations

Again, the client's budget determines whether or not you should include a bleed on the card. Allow at least a 1/8-in. margin around the card. There are as many variations as there are printers. A standard business card size is 3 1/2" × 2". When designing cards, I try to keep the name prominent and important contact information in the lower right corner. That's where the eye usually stops last, and I don't want to waste a "hot" corner on a fax number! Discuss imposition with the printer. The imposition is how the card should be laid out: 1-up, 2-up, 8-up, and so on. Sometimes he wants you to step and repeat your card many times on a single sheet of letter-size paper. Other times he will want a single card centered on the sheet.

Designers become very comfortable working in point size and leading with whole number increments of 1 or 2 points. In smaller type, one point is a much more significant unit of measure than it is for display type. When working at smaller type sizes, you will find yourself setting a leading value of, for example, 8.75 points or a type size of 7.5 points.

By now, using the shortcut keys to change point size and leading has become second nature. For more control, I would recommend changing program preferences so that those shortcuts enlarge or reduce in smaller increments. If you are a Mac user, choose InDesign>Preferences>Units and Increments. Change the Size/Leading to 1 pt. and the Baseline Shift to 1 pt. (see Figure 10–4). Windows users, choose Edit>Preferences and follow the same procedure in the Units and Increments dialog box.

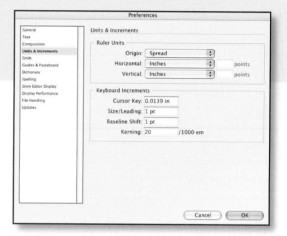

figure | 10–4

Change the Size/Leading and the Baseline Shift increments to 1 point for better precision when using the keyboard shortcuts.

Business Card Design Considerations for Rosemary Tollefson

Figure 10–5 shows the business card for Rosemary Tollefson. Notice that the typefaces are the same on all the pieces. It's very important to maintain the size relationship of text to graphics on all the pieces. Use the flush right tab (Shift+Tab) to align the address-email text and the fax-cell phone text to the right margin.

figure | 10–5

Reserve the lower right corner of the business card for the important contact information.

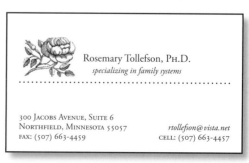

Newspaper Display Ads Design Considerations

Accurate measurement is essential when designing for newspapers. Each paper has standard dimensions to follow when preparing ads. Figure 10–6 shows a sample production worksheet for a Milwaukee, Wisconsin daily paper. When creating a newspaper ad, close enough is not good enough! Convert fractions into decimals and enter those measurements in the New Document dialog box. As you can see in Figure 10–6, the advertisements butt right up to text or another ad with no room for error.

Many display ads are designed with an outer border. When adding a stroke to a text or graphics frame, you must specify that the stroke goes inside the frame. If the stroke is centered on the frame or placed on the outside of the frame, the dimension will change and the advertisement

Advertising Sizes
metroparent magazine

Full Page
9" x 11"

3/4 Page Vertical
6 5/8" x 10 3/4"

1/2 Page Vertical
4 3/8" x 10 3/4"

1/2 Page Horizontal
9" x 5 1/4"

1/4 Page Square
4 3/8" x 5 1/4"

1/4 Page Horizontal
9" x 2 1/2"

1/2 Page Island
6 5/8" x 7 7/8"

1/4 Page Vertical
2" x 10 3/4"

1/16 Page Vertical
2" x 2 1/2"

1/8 Page Vertical
2" x 5 1/4"

1/16 Page Horizontal
4 3/8" x 1 5/8"

1/8 Page Horizontal
4 3/8" x 2 1/2"

Back Cover.................9" x 11"
Closer Look Advertorial........4 3/8" x 7 7/8"
Center Spread ....19" x 11"

figure | 10–6 |

Every newspaper has its own set of size specifications. A "one-size-fits-all" approach will not work when placing ads in a variety of publications.

will not fit the newspaper specifications. Figure 10–7 shows where the frame alignment buttons are located in the Stroke palette. Click the center icon, Align Stroke to Inside.

align stroke to inside

align stroke to center   align stroke to outside

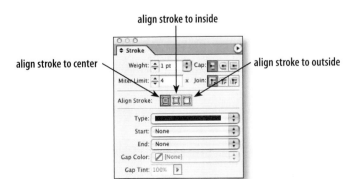

figure | 10–7 |

Align the stroke to the inside of the frame so that the final size of your ad will exactly match the newspaper specifications.

When designing for newsprint, recognize that your final piece will not look like your laser print. Newsprint is porous and your type will expand. The counters of letters tend to fill in, so avoid using very small point sizes whenever possible. When your advertisement includes a photograph or a scan, work closely with the production department so that you provide the correct resolution and line screen. A piece that looks good printed on your laser printer will look "muddy" in newsprint because the halftone dots will fill in.

Display Ad Design Considerations for Rosemary Tollefson

Figure 10–8 shows a sample of the display ad. The words "Open House" require negative tracking, which is common when working with display type. The phone number at the bottom of the ad and the time at the top are set in lining (uppercase) figures. It is appropriate to use lining figures in this instance because the numbers are being used in display type. The open house time, 2:30 – 5:00 p.m., is separated by an en dash, used to indicate a range of time. The abbreviation "pm" is set in small caps, and including the periods is optional. If you don't have a typeface with small caps, it is permissible to set it in lowercase letters with periods (p.m.). The body copy is set in italic type, with the Open Type fractions option turned on. Normally book titles are set in italic, but when the surrounding body copy is italic, the book title is set in roman, as in the title of Dr. Tollefson's book, *Believe in Yourself.*

You're invited to our

Open House

Monday, April 26
2:30 – 5:00 PM

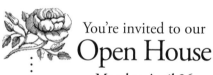

Join us as we celebrate the opening of our new practice at 300 Jacobs Avenue, ½ mile west of Woodley.

Meet the staff, enjoy refreshments, and register for door prizes. Dr. Tollefson will be available to autograph her newly-released book, BELIEVE IN YOURSELF.

Rosemary Tollefson, PH.D.
specializing in family systems

• Children, Adolescents, and Family
• Custody, Separation, and Remarriage
• School and Behavior Problems
• ADHD and Learning Disabilities
Evening and Saturday Appointments
24-hour answering service

300 JACOBS AVENUE, SUITE 6
(½ MILE WEST OF WOODLEY AVENUE, NORTHFIELD)

(507) 663-4457

figure | 10–8 |

The ad printed in the newspaper will not be as crisp and white as the one from your laser printer. Newsprint is not a paper that allows you to take creative risks. Work with the newspaper's production department to make sure your artwork is properly prepared.

You'll also note that the bulleted copy contains a reference to attention deficit hyperactivity disorder as ADHD. When setting an acronym, no period is placed after each letter.

Designing for the Phone Book

Scan through the yellow pages in a phone book and you will see that they've been designed by people with a wide range of design skills. Some ads include gradients and mushy photos, condensed or expanded type that is almost impossible to read, and typographic blunders such as all-capital italics and incorrect quotation marks. You can also find some examples of excellent layout and readability. What makes the difference between a strong and a poor ad? The ability to use type combined with an understanding of the printing process. A well-designed 2 1/2-inch square ad packs more punch than the poorly designed half-page ad! When you design an ad for the yellow pages, first look at samples to see what doesn't work. Then look specifically at what the competition is doing, and design an ad that will beat the best sample. It is a time-consuming process to fine-tune small display ads. Some people assume a small ad will require less production time—in reality, it takes more time to create an effective small ad than a larger display ad because every incremental spacing decision you make in a small ad is critical!

Yellow Pages Ad Design Considerations for Rosemary Tollefson

Figure 10–9 shows the details of the yellow pages display ad for Rosemary Tollefson.

Rosemary Tollefson, Ph.D.
LICENSED PSYCHOLOGIST
specializing in family systems

....

- Children, Adolescents, and Family
- Custody, Separation, and Remarriage
- School and Behavior Problems
- ADHD and Learning Disabilities

Evening and Saturday Appointments
24-hour answering service
300 JACOBS AVENUE, SUITE 6
(½ MILE WEST OF WOODLEY AVENUE, NORTHFIELD)

(507) 663-4457

figure | 10–9

There's a lot of selling power in a well-designed display ad!

The text portion is basically in a centered format—except the bulleted copy is flush left. Sometimes you see bulleted copy centered, leaving the left sides ragged (see Figure 10–10). Setting bulleted copy in this manner is a poor design technique. When the bullets are not flush left, they blend in with the body copy and defeat the purpose of using them in the first place!

figure | 10–10

Don't center bulleted copy. The purpose of bullets is to create visual sequencing, like stepping-stones.

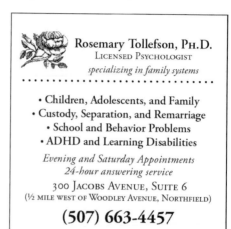

Rosemary Tollefson, Ph.D.
Licensed Psychologist
specializing in family systems
. . . .

• Children, Adolescents, and Family
• Custody, Separation, and Remarriage
• School and Behavior Problems
• ADHD and Learning Disabilities
Evening and Saturday Appointments
24-hour answering service
300 Jacobs Avenue, Suite 6
(½ mile west of Woodley Avenue, Northfield)

(507) 663-4457

Here is the best way to align bulleted copy while centering it in the text block:

1. Center all bulleted text. Position a vertical guideline flush to the bullet of the longest line.
2. Change the alignment of the bulleted text to flush left.
3. Apply a left indent to push all the bulleted copy to the guideline you placed earlier. Now the text is flush left, but the longest line is still centered in the text column.

Design Considerations for Forms

The last piece you will create for Dr. Tollefson is a client information form (see Figure 10–11). This piece will include inline frames. The tiny boxes are rectangle frames with a stroke applied that were then pasted into the line of text, creating an image that flows with the text. Instructions included on the CD accompanying this book will probably be necessary for this project. You can see that this project will also be a great review of tabs.

figure | 10–11 |

The check boxes in this form are actually small rectangle frames. These inline frames flow along with the surrounding text. This example uses check boxes, but the same technique could be used to place a photo or illustration into the text.

SUMMARY

Business forms are the ultimate production test for typesetters and designers. It is our responsibility to make sure that forms project the appropriate corporate image, are easy to read, and are easy to complete. When you are given the task of producing an order form, a sell sheet, or a catalog price grid, see it as a design challenge. Flex your typesetting muscles. And remember, as a wise designer once said, "There are no mediocre projects, just mediocre designers."

in review

1. What are two design considerations for letterhead?

2. How does paper quality affect design?

3. What is the difference between a lining figure and an old-style figure?

4. How should academic titles be typeset?

5. How do you control the way a stroke is applied to the frame?

↗ EXPLORING ON YOUR OWN

The figure below shows Dr. Tollefson's family of forms. You will enjoy creating these, and they would be nice additions to your portfolio. One additional table is included for good measure. You can find the instructions for all these projects in the Chapter 10 folder on the student resources CD accompanying this book.

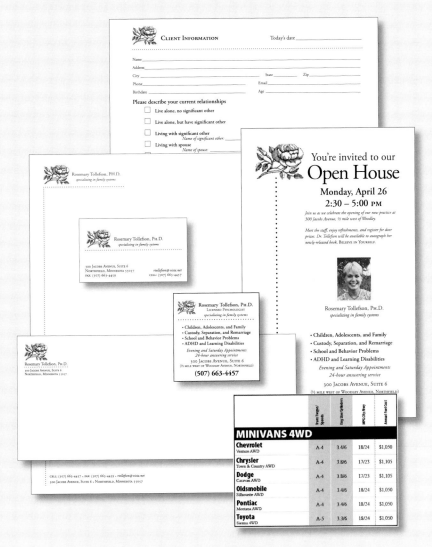

This collection of business forms would be a nice addition to your portfolio.

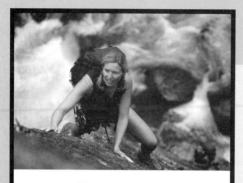

Courage
is not the
lack of fear.
It is acting
in spite of it.
℞ Mark Twain

charting your course

A semi trailer got stuck underneath an overpass. It was in so tight that the driver couldn't move ahead or back up. Engineers and construction workers walked all around the stuck truck, calculating the height of the trailer and the clearance of the underpass. They thought of jackhammers, winches, hydraulic pry bars—anything that might free the truck and get traffic moving again. Finally, after assessing the situation one little boy said, "Why don't you let some air out of the tires?"

That boy was thinking outside the box. Business, education, government—everyone these days is looking for people who can see things from a different perspective. Perform a web search for "out of the box thinking" and you'll come up with just a shade over 2 billion results.

You are about to work with text and graphics that are out of the box—or at least out of a frame. Up to now we have used rectangles and ovals of various shapes and sizes. In this chapter, we explore text on a path, inline graphics, gradients—features that will let *you* out of the box.

 goals

- **Use the Type on a Path tool**
- **Use the Pathfinder tool**
- **Create gradient blends**
- **Create inline frames**

TYPE: A VERSATILE DESIGN ELEMENT

When reviewing student portfolios I look for two things: use of type and use of color. I believe that when a designer has control of those two critical design elements, everything else will fall into place. Even in black and white, type has "color" and text blocks can range in color from light gray to strong black. Typefaces also express a wide range of personalities inherent in their design. Figure 11–1 shows a collection of ampersands, each interesting and expressing a different personality.

Figure | 11–1|

This collection of ampersands shows the variation in personality of typefaces.

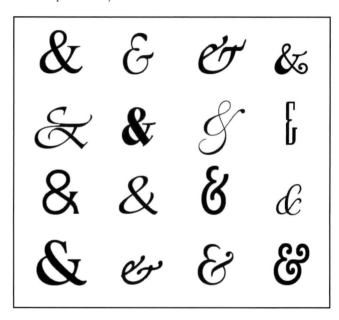

In this first exercise we're going to add another ingredient into the type color-personality mixture: shape. The ability to create type that follows a path used to be the domain of illustration programs. Thanks to InDesign, these great special effects are right at your fingertips. So, launch InDesign and let's get started.

Placing Type on a Closed Shape

In order to place text on a path, first you need a path! Then you need the Type on a Path tool, accessed by pressing Shift+T or by selecting it from the "hidden tool" menu under the Type tool.

1. Create a new document. Draw a rectangle and apply a 1 pt. stroke.

2. Select the Type on a Path tool by pressing Shift+T. Position the tool cursor over the edge of the rectangle. A plus sign on the cursor indicates that the tool has recognized a path and is ready for action (see Figure 11–2).

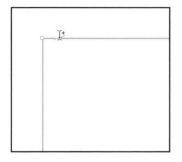

figure | 11–2 |

The plus sign next to the cursor means that the Type on Path tool has found a path.

3. Click on the path to create a starting point. Type a line of text that extends around the rectangle. Highlight the text and change the point size and style. Change the alignment. The text considers the first point you clicked with the Type on a Path tool as the left margin. As you center and right-align the text, it will flow clockwise around the outside of the frame.

4. Figure 11–3 shows two vertical lines called the start and end brackets. (The path object must be selected and either selection tool must be active for you to see these.) By default the brackets are butted up to each other, indicating that the text path extends around the entire rectangle. You move the start and end brackets to fine-tune the position of the text on your path. The start and end brackets have in and out ports that work just like any other text frame.

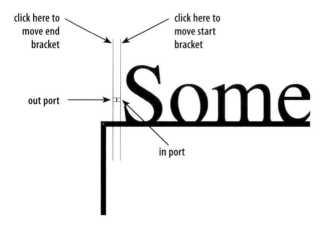

figure | 11–3 |

The in ports and out ports are not handles you can use to adjust the Start and End indicators. Click on the vertical part of the start and end brackets to adjust the location of the text.

5. Select the end bracket. Do not click on its out port; instead click on the upper part of the line (the cursor arrow will show a sideways "t" when you are able to click on the bracket). Slowly drag the end bracket counterclockwise, closer to the end of the text (see Figure 11–4). If you pull the bracket too far the overset symbol will appear. Just bring the bracket to the end of the text.

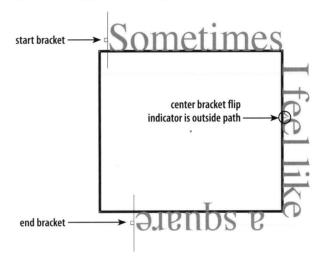

start bracket ⟶

center bracket flip
indicator is outside path ⟶

end bracket ⟶

6. If you look carefully in the center of the text you have typed, you will see a tiny vertical line (see Figure 11–4). This line is the center bracket, and if you click on the line with the Direct Selection tool, you can carefully move your text back and forth around the edge of the rectangle.

7. If you drag the center bracket in, toward the center of the rectangle, your text will flow inside the box. Flip your text inside and outside a few times until it feels comfortable to you (see Figure 11–5).

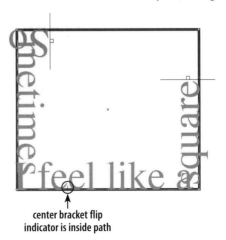

center bracket flip
indicator is inside path

That was easy enough. Try the same technique with a circle as the path object. Be sure to flip the text inside and outside the circle, as in Figure 11–6. When the type is in place, you will want to remove the stroke on the path object.

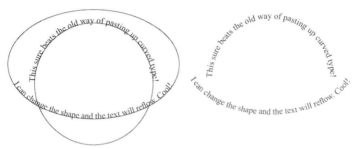

figure | 11–6 |

A stroke is needed only to help you see the path while you are working on the text. Remove the stroke once the text is in place.

Placing Type on an Open Path

Most of the time, you will be creating your own path for type to follow. Type can be placed on paths of any shape. We'll create a few paths using the Pencil tool, the Pen tool, and Bezier curves. You may not use the Pencil tool very often, but you should know it's there. If this is your first time using the Pen tool, note that Chapter 13 will go into detail on using it—you'll just get your toes wet in this chapter.

1. Select the Pencil tool by pressing N or by selecting it from the Toolbox. Draw some squiggles similar to those in Figure 11–7. The Pencil tool makes rough, random-looking paths. (The Pen tool makes smooth, curvy paths.)

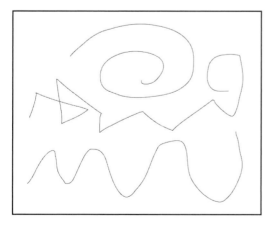

figure | 11–7 |

These paths were made with the Pencil tool.

2. Select the Type on a Path tool and click on one of your paths. (You don't need to select the path first.) Fill the line with text.

You can use placeholder text if you prefer. Fill the remaining lines with text. Now experiment with the position, size and color of your type. The results should look similar to Figure 11–8.

figure | 11–8 |

Type has been placed on the Pencil tool paths.

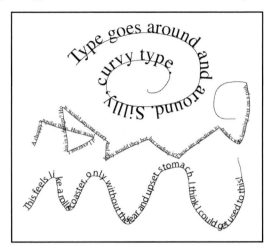

3. Use Command+A (Mac) or Control+A (Windows) to select and delete the text lines created with the Pencil tool. Drag down two horizontal guidelines about 1.5 inches apart. Select the Pen tool by pressing P. Position the cursor by the left margin guide and click once on the bottom guidelines (do not drag). Position the cursor over the top guideline, but over to the right of the first point and click. This will create a diagonal line extending from the bottom to the top guidelines. Next, position the cursor on the bottom guideline, over to the right of the second point and click to create another diagonal line. Continue this pattern across the page to make a zigzag pattern similar to what you see in Figure 11–9.

figure | 11–9 |

Clicking with the Pen tool makes straight line segments.

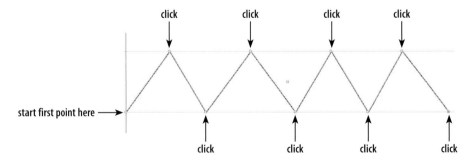

4. Switch to the Direct Selection tool and move the guides out of the way or delete them. Click on an anchor point and drag it. Move it from side to side, then up and down. Continue mov-

ing all the points until your zigzag is a total mess (see Figure 11–10). Now you know how to use the Pen tool to click from point to point, and create paths made of straight line segments. Let's see what else the Pen tool can do. Delete your path.

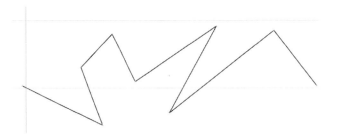

figure | 11–10

Use the Direct Selection tool to move the anchor points of the path.

5. Pull down two horizontal guides about 2 inches apart. You're going to make another path similar to the zigzag, except that you will make it with curved segments. With the Pen tool, click where the lower guideline meets the left margin guide to create the end point of your new path. Here's where the tricky part of creating curved segments comes in. Position the cursor over the top guideline, to the right of the end point, and click without releasing the mouse. This creates a "smooth" corner point. Without releasing the mouse drag horizontally and you will see two handles extend from the corner point. These are called direction lines, as you drag them out a curved line segment will develop. Move the cursor along the guideline to see how changing the length of the direction line affects the shape of the curve. Release the mouse when the curved segment looks similar to the one in Figure 11–11. Move to the lower guideline, click to make the next anchor point and drag the direction line to create another curved line segment. Continue this process until you have waves similar to those in Figure 11–11. Now you know how to use the Pen tool to make curved line segments by clicking and dragging.

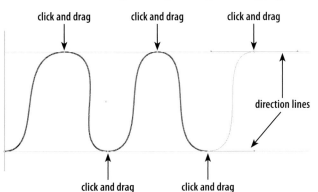

figure | 11–11

Click and drag to make curved line segments.

6. Now, create a bizarre looking path using a combination of clicks (straight line segments) and drags (curved line segments). Your mess should look just as bad as mine in Figure 11–12. To end the path, choose another tool or Command+click or Control+click anywhere on the page. When you're ready to move on, select your line with the Selection tool and delete it.

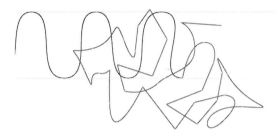

7. Now we're going to make a path in the shape of an arch. If you deleted your two horizontal guidelines, drag down new ones about 2 inches apart. With the Pen tool, position the cursor over the lower guide, click and drag up. A directional line will extend from each side of the starting point. Keep dragging, trying to keep the upper directional line at a 45-degree angle. When the end of the directional line touches the upper guideline, release the mouse (see Figure 11–13A).

8. Now position the Pen tool back on the lower guide, approximately five inches to the right of the first point. Click to set an anchor point and drag the direction line down at approximately 45 degrees. Notice that the upper direction line angles back toward the upper direction line of the first point (see Figure 11–13B). When you release the mouse you should have a nice arch, similar to Figure 11–13C. Use the Text on a Path tool to add text to the arch and experiment with the various options your learned, so far.

figure | 11–13 |

Drag in the direction of the arrows to make this smooth arch.

A.

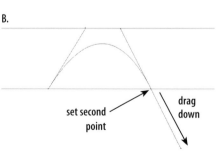

set first point

drag up

B.

set second point

drag down

C.

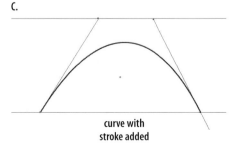

curve with stroke added

You may realize it would be much easier just to draw an ellipse and place the text on its path, rather than using the Pen tool to create the arch shape. And you're right. But very often, you will want to use text paths that don't fit pre-made shapes—like the next one you're going to create next.

1. Delete the arch shaped path and drag down one horizontal guide. With the Pen tool, click on the guideline and drag up and to the right at a 45-degree angle. Release the mouse when the direction handle is about 1-inch long.

2. About 4 inches away, click on the guideline to set another anchor point, again, dragging up and to the right at a 45-degree angle. Release the mouse button when your path looks like Figure 11–14.

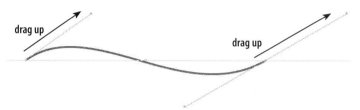

drag up

drag up

figure | 11–14

Using only two anchor points you can create elegant flowing curves.

3. Go ahead, use the Type on a Path tool and and place some text on it. Then flip the type using the center bracket line. If there is a stroke applied to the path, remove it to see only the text (see Figure 11–15).

This is a path shape you'll use often!

And it flips just like the other ones!

figure | 11–15

Use the center bracket to flip and reverse the direction of text placed on a path.

4. Now use the regular Type tool and highlight all the text on the path. Change the color to white. Select the path using the Direct Selection tool. Change the stroke width of the path to be much wider than the point size of your text. Choose Type>Type on Path>Options. When the Type on a Path Options dialog box opens, change the Align and Path fields to Center to the center type vertically on the path (see Figure 11–16). This is a technique you will use often.

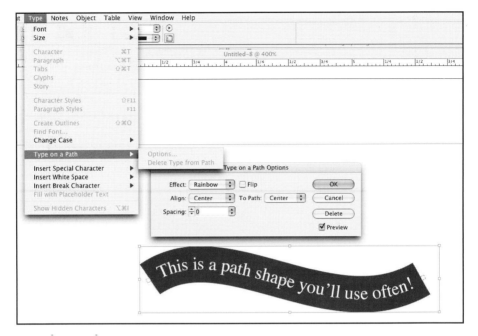

figure | 11—16 |

The stroke width has been increased to a size larger than the point size of the type. The center of the stroke has been aligned with the center of the text.

Creating Shadowed Type

A text frame must be transparent in order for shadows to show on the text. If the frame has a fill, the frame will have a drop shadow, but the text won't. To add a shadow, select the frame with the Direct Selection tool and choose Object>Drop Shadow. In the Drop Shadow dialog box, turn on the Drop Shadow option box and adjust the opacity as desired (75% is usually too dark). See Figure 11–17.

figure | 11–17 |

A filled shape will have a shadow on the shape, not on the type.

Type inside a frame with **no fill** will show shadows.

Type inside a frame with **a fill** will show a shadowed box.

Create Text Outlines

One of the greatest features of InDesign is the ability to convert text to outlines. Once text is converted to outlines, it is no longer text—and you can't correct spelling or apply normal text attributes. Instead, each letter is a tiny piece of artwork—giving you the ability to modify the shape or paste an image into it.

1. Type the phrase Tickle Me! (see Figure 11–18). Use the Selection tool to activate the frame, and press Shift+Command+O (Mac) or Shift+Control+O (Windows) to convert the text into outlines. You can also choose Type>Create Outlines.

2. Now when you look closely at the type you will see a series of anchor points. Even though each letter is now an individual shape, they are still linked together as one object—a compound path.

3. With the outline type selected, choose Object>Compound Paths>Release and the text unit will split apart. Now you can move each letter around with a selection tool. (Notice, however, that the counters in the letter "e" are filled in with black. Select the counters with the Selection tool and fill them with white.)

4. Delete the dots from the exclamation point and the *i*. Draw a small text frame where each of the dots were. Choose a dingbat, like the smiley face shown in Figure 11–18, from the Glyphs palette and place it in the frames. When the size and position of the dingbats looks good, select all the objects and group them. Add a drop shadow to really make the text "pop" off the page.

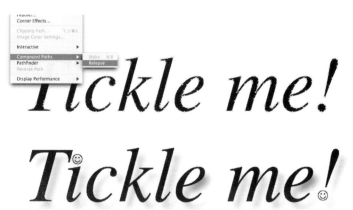

figure | 11–18 |

"Normal" text is first converted to outlines. Then the compound paths are released, allowing you to delete and replace the dots. Adding a drop shadow makes the special treatments stand out.

Creating Shaped Text Frames

By now, you're an old pro at putting text inside a frame. This exercise will teach you how to create a shaped frame using the Pen tool.

1. Delete the images in your document. Select the Pen tool. Click or drag to make an unusual closed shape. When you are ready to close the shape, position the Pen tool cursor close to the path's starting point, you will see a tiny circle appear next to the pen tool icon. This circle indicates that your next click will join the two ends of the path, making a closed shape. Your shape should look very strange, similar to Figure 11–19.

figure | 11–19 |

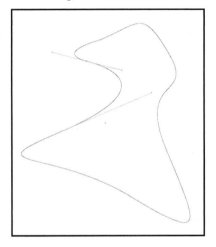

This odd shaped closed path is now ready to become a text frame.

2. Click inside the new shape with the Type tool. You should see a blinking cursor. Fill with placeholder text. Select all the text and change to justified alignment. Adjust the point size and typeface until you have a fairly even fill (see Figure 11–20). Try changing the shape's stroke width to 0 pt. and click the Preview Mode button on the bottom right of the Toolbox.

figure | 11–20 |

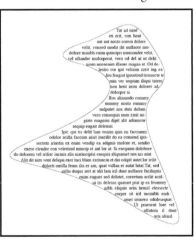

Justified text helps create an irregular shaped text block with defined edges.

BITTER APPLE GAME PRESERVE

The following exercise will introduce some additional text effects. You will be making a two-sided, full-color flyer and a season pass sticker/button design for Bitter Apple Game Preserve. You will use the Gradient tool, create text on a path, convert text to outlines, create inline frames to contain graphics, and apply drop shadows and feathering. Figure 11–21 shows how the finished pieces will look. We will begin with the button.

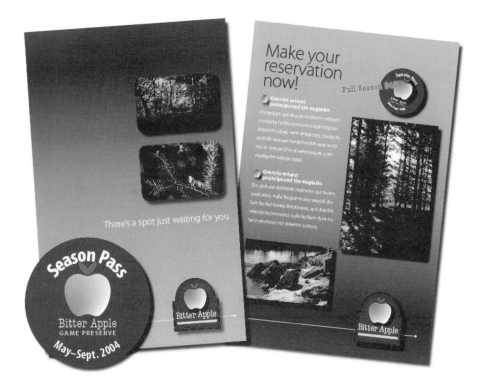

figure | 11–21

Bitter Apple
Game Preserve
design projects

1. Look in the Chapter 11 folder on the CD accompanying this book and open the template, 11 Project Template.indt. The "indt" extension means you are opening an InDesign template. A template is a document that is used as a pattern. A document can be saved as template by choosing Save>Format>InDesign CS template. This template has been prepared with the correct size, bleed, guidelines, and swatches. There are two layers: The bottom layer will hold the background gradient fill and the top layer will hold the images and text. There are three pages in the document. Page 1 is for the front of the brochure; page 2 is for the back of the brochure; page 3 is for the button.

2. Open the library prepared for this project by choosing File>Open and select 11 Bitter Apple.indl from the Chapter 11 folder. The library already has some elements in it and you will be adding additional project elements to it, as they are completed.

3. Open the Pages palette and go to Page 3. Draw a large text frame and when the blinking cursor is visible, open the Glyphs palette. (It doesn't matter which layer this is on.) Look in the Apple Symbols or Symbol typefaces and find an apple. Insert the glyph and enlarge it to 200 points, as shown in Figure 11–22. Switch to the Selection tool and convert it to outlines (Shift+Command+O or Shift+Control+O).

NOTE: If you cannot find an apple shape in the Glyphs palette, there is one stashed on the lower right corner of the pasteboard. You can drag it into your document, enlarge it 2.25 inches high, and continue with Step 4.

figure | 11–22

Find the apple shape in the Glyphs palette. Look in Apple Symbols or Symbol typefaces.

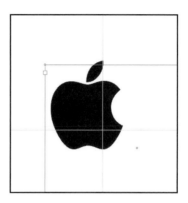

4. Select the apple shape with the Selection tool. Copy it and then use Paste in Place so that it is exactly on top of the original shape.
5. Change the reference point on the Transform palette (in the Control palette) so that it is in the middle. Using the Control palette options menu, choose Flip Horizontal. You now have an apple with two leaves (see Figure 11–23).

figure | 11–23

The apple after flipping the shape.

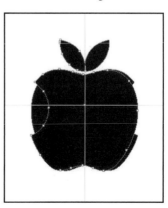

6. Use the Selection tool to adjust the position of the top apple so that the edges line up. Zoom in close to the edge of the apple to be as precise as possible.

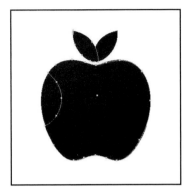

figure | 11–24 |

Lining up the edges of the two apple shapes.

7. With the Selection tool, select both apple shapes. Choose Object>Pathfinder>Add. This command adds the shapes together to make one whole apple shape. With the shape still selected, choose Object>Compound Paths>Release. You have now separated the apple from the leaves.

8. Open the Swatches palette (F5). Select the leaves and fill them with Pantone DS 293-1 C green.

9. Select the apple shape and then apply the Apple Gradient fill from the Swatches palette. This is a radial fill, which means the color blends out from the center like rays of the sun. Use the Gradient tool, found on the Toolbox (press G), to adjust the length and direction of the fill. Click and drag the Gradient tool inside the apple, from edge to edge. Now change the starting location of the gradient by clicking the Gradient tool in another position and drag again. Hold down the Shift key to constrain it to a perfect horizontal or vertical blend. Reverse the direction of the line to reverse the blend. Do this several times until you understand how this tool works. Keep the Gradient tool inside the apple so the whole blend will be in that defined area. When you're finished experimenting, make the final gradient blend red in the top left corner to white in the lower right (see Figure 11–25). Group the apple with the leaves and drag it into the library. Move the apple in your document over to the pasteboard for now.

figure | 11–25 |

The Gradient tool adjusts the direction and length of the gradient. You can also begin or end the gradient outside the shape you are working with.

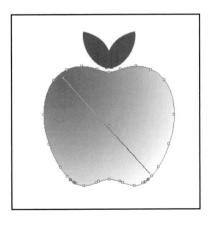

The next step in the button project is to run text around the circle that creates the perimeter of the button. Follow the directions carefully and you'll see the advantage of using layers when placing this type.

1. Still on page 3, hold down Shift+Option (Mac) or Shift+Alt (Windows), draw a 4-inch circle out from the center guides with a stroke and no fill. Be sure you are working on the first layer, Background Gradient.

2. Copy the circle and move up a layer to Text and Photos and use Shift+Option+Command+V (Mac) or Shift+Alt+Control+V (Windows) to Paste in Place.

3. Make a new layer and name it Background Circle. Draw a 4.375-inch circle from the center points and fill it with the blue from the Swatch palette. Lock the position of the circle, Command+L (Mac) or Control+L (Windows). Go to the Layers palette and drag this layer down to the bottom of the stack.

4. Hide the Text and Photos layer, and move down one layer to the Background Gradient layer. Select the Type on Path tool and click on the inner circle. Type **Season Pass** in Myriad Pro Bold Condensed 50 pt. and set the paragraph alignment to centered. Color the text white. Choose Type>Type on Path> Options, and set Align field to Ascender and To Path to Bottom (see Figure 11–26). Remove any stroke or fill on the circle.

5. To center the type at the top of the circle, change the paragraph alignment to centered. This will cause the text to jump to the bottom of the circle. Don't worry. Using the Selection tool, find the center bracket line (it should be at the 6 o'clock position and drag it around your path and release it at the 12 o'clock position. Make sure you are outside of the circle path when you release the mouse button or your type will not stay inside of the path. Now your text is centered at the top of the circle. When you are working with text on a curve you usually need to adjust the tracking. This sample was tracked to -80. Lock the circle by pressing Command+L (Mac) or Control+L (Windows). Hide the layer while we do the next step.

figure | 11–26 |

Choose Type>Type on Path>Options to align the ascenders of the type to the bottom of the path.

6. Turn on the Text and Photos layer. Choose the Type on Path tool and type **May–Sept. 2004** on the inner circle in 30 pt. Myriad Pro Bold Condensed. Color the text white. Use the same methods described in step 4 to position the type inside the circle shape and move it to the bottom center of the sticker (see Figure 11–27). Remove any stroke that might be on the circle and lock the object (Command+L or Control+L).

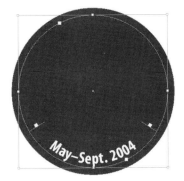

figure | 11–27 |

Position the date at the bottom center of the circle. The other layer has been conveniently hidden, making it easier to work on this circular type.

7. Make all the layers visible and drag the apple in from the pasteboard. Move the apple to the top layer. You will need to resize the apple to fit in the type. To resize the apple, select it with the Selection tool and hold Shift+Command (Mac) or Shift+Control (Windows) as you drag in a corner.

8. Draw a text frame and type **Bitter Apple** in American Typewriter Condensed 32 pt. Type **Game Preserve** in Myriad Bold 16 pt, and change to all caps. If you don't have American Typewriter, choose a similar typeface. Change the color of both lines of type to the yellow in the Swatches palette and center the text. Track the second line. Position and size the text frame and apple inside the circle as shown in Figure 11–28. Your button is almost complete.

9. With the Selection tool, draw a marquee around all your sticker elements. Unlock the position of all the circles: Command+Option+L (Mac) or Control+Alt+L (Windows). Group all the elements. Drag the sticker into your library

figure | 11–28 |

Once the sticker is completed, unlock the position of all the circles, group all the objects, and drag a copy into the library.

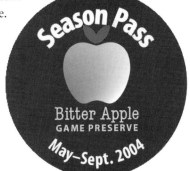

The Bitter Apple Logo

The Bitter Apple logo is the next component to tackle.

1. Go to Page 2. Select the Rectangle tool and click on your page. When the dialog box comes up, enter **1.3** for the width and **.75** for the height. Stroke and fill should be None.

2. Select the Ellipse tool and hold Shift+Option or Shift+Alt to draw a circle out from the center of the rectangle. Make the circle slightly narrower than the rectangle, similar to the example in Figure 11-29. Use the Align palette to align the horizontal centers of the objects and move the circle up so that your two shapes look like Figure 11–29.

figure | 11–29

Use the Align palette
to center the shapes
on each other.

3. Select both shapes and choose Object>Pathfinder>Add. The shapes should blend together as in Figure 11–30. (This is the same technique we used earlier to blend the two apple shapes into one shape.)

figure | 11–30

The shapes have
been added together
to create a precise,
symmetrical frame.

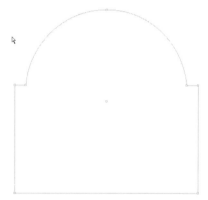

4. Use the Stroke palette to give the shape a 6 pt. Thin-Thick stroke stroked to the center. Make the stroke's color DS 63-1C Red with a blue gap. These colors will be in the Swatches palette. Fill the shape with the blue in the Swatches palette.
5. Use the Selection tool to drag the apple in from the library. Resize it to fit inside the logo as shown in Figure 11–31. Add a drop shadow with 40% opacity using the default shadow offsets.

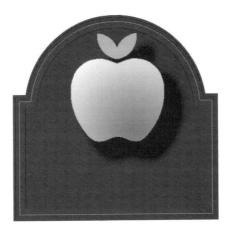

figure | 11–31 |

The apple that was stored earlier in the library has been resized to fit inside the new shape.

6. Draw a text frame below the apple and type Bitter Apple in American Typewriter Condensed, 18 pt., white. Type Game Preserve in Myriad Pro Bold 7 pt. all caps. Add a drop shadow to the outer shape, 40% opacity. The finished logo should look like Figure 11–32. Group the logo and drag it into the library. The logo is now completed. Delete the logo remaining in your document.

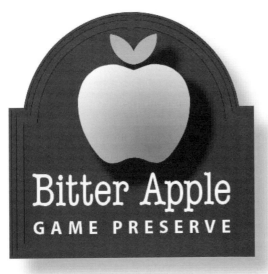

figure | 11–32 |

The finished Bitter Apple logo. The opacity of the shadow has been reduced to 40% for a more natural-looking shadow.

Finishing Up the Flyer

We'll begin with the front of the flyer where we'll drop in a gradient and pull elements in from the library. Figure 11–33 shows the front of the finished flyer for reference.

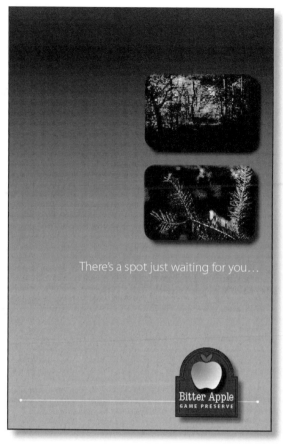

There's a spot just waiting for you...

Bitter Apple
GAME PRESERVE

1. Go to page 1. Make sure you are working on the Background and Gradient layer. Draw a rectangle that fills the page from bleed to bleed. From the Swatches palette, choose the Background Gradient swatch. Use the Gradient tool to place the dark blue on the top and the green on the bottom, holding down the Shift key to constrain it to a vertical blend.

2. Move to the Text and Photos layer. Drag in the photos and headline from the library using the guides for placement. Add an ellipsis to the end of the headline. You make a true ellipsis by pressing Option+; (Mac) or Alt+; (Windows).

3. Draw a 1-point white line on the bottom margin guide. Using the Stroke palette, set the Start and End fields of the rule to Circle Solid.

figure | 11–33 |

The front side of the flyer will use elements from the library.

4. Drag the logo in from the library and position it as shown in Figure 11–33.

The Back of the Flyer

As you finish the back of the flyer you will learn how to add inline frames. Most of the hard work is already done—you'll be pulling most of the elements in from the library. The finished back looks like Figure 11–34.

1. Go to page 2. Make sure you are on the Background Gradient layer. Draw a frame from bleed to bleed and fill it with the Background Gradient swatch. Using the Gradient tool, adjust the color so that the green is on the top and the blue is on the bottom.

2. Move to the Text and Photos layer. Drag in the text block and photos from the library. Place a 1-point white rule on the

bottom margin and use the Stroke palette to add a circle to each end.

3. Go to page 1 and select the logo with the Selection tool. Copy the logo. Now go to page 2 and use Paste in Place. The logo should be in the exact same location as on the cover.

4. The apple at the beginning of each subhead is an inline graphic. It is connected with the text so that it flows just like a word or letter. Pull the apple you created earlier onto the pasteboard of page 2. Select it with the Selection tool. Hold down Shift+Command (Mac) or Shift+Control (Windows) and pull a corner inward until the apple is very small, approximately 0.2 in. (see Figure 11–34).

5. Copy the apple, and then switch to the Type tool and place the cursor in front of the first letter of the first subhead. Paste the apple and add a space. The graphic now sits on the baseline with the type. Even though it is connected to a text line, you can still adjust its vertical position using the Selection tool. Repeat the procedure for the second subhead. Add drop shadows to both apples using the default settings. Enter an Indent to Here before the first word in the first line to create a hanging indent for the apple.

6. Pull the button you made earlier in from the library and place it on the pasteboard of page 2. Select it with the Selection tool and reduce it proportionally by holding down Shift+Command (Mac) or Shift+Control (Windows). Drag it into position at the top of the page. Select it with the Selection tool. In the Control palette, make sure the reference point is in the middle. Now select the Rotate tool, click on the circle, and drag to rotate it as in Figure 11–34.

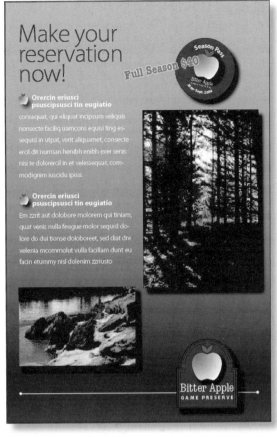

figure 11–34

The back of the Bitter Apple Game Preserve flyer.

7. Use the Selection tool and pull in the Full Season $40 line from the library. Position it on top of the sticker, as shown in Figure 11–34.

8. Proof all your work carefully. The project is done!

SUMMARY

This chapter covered many design techniques that can give text a little more interest. Just like using too many typefaces in one document, you can also overpower your document with special text effects. Knowing how to use these techniques is the first step. Knowing when to use them is the second.

in review

1. How do you know when the Type on Path tool is ready to place text on a path?

2. How does the center bracket work?

3. What is the command for locking the position of an object? For unlocking?

4. What does the Gradient tool do?

5. What is the keystroke for creating a true ellipsis?

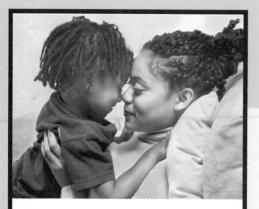

Love cures people…
both the ones who **give** it
and the ones who **receive** it.

℞ Dr. Karl Menninger

charting your course

Some ideas sound good in theory—self-generating electricity, cars that run without an external fuel source, gears that keep turning on their own momentum. But not every great idea works out in reality.

That's what happens to a lot of great design ideas. You spend all kinds of time and creative energy on a document that looks beautiful on your monitor—and when printed on your desktop color printer. Then you take it to your commercial printing company and order 5,000 printed pieces. But, when you pick up your job you also get a bill for hundreds of dollars more than you were quoted. You're told that the additional charges are for something called "pre-press." They explain that it was necessary to take your electronic file—the one you thought was finished—and spend additional time getting it ready to print properly. This chapter will teach you basic production considerations so you can create documents that run smoothly and avoid unexpected budget overruns. This chapter will teach you the essentials of using color properly. For more information on the complex world of color, I recommend *Graphic Communications Today, Fourth Edition,* by William Ryan and Theodore Conover (Thomson Delmar Learning).

 goals

- **Understand the difference between spot and process colors**
- **Become familiar with the Swatches palette**
- **Create and define color, tint, and gradient swatches**
- **Perform document preflight and package operations**
- **Identify printers' marks**
- **Print color separations**

PRODUCTION ESSENTIALS

COLOR BASICS

This chapter will introduce you to the physics and reproduction of color. Color is an important component in any project. If you don't understand how color is created and how a piece will be printed, you will not be able to create a document that uses color correctly. Errors in using color are costly. Of course, color mistakes on garage sale posters printed on your own color ink jet printer aren't going to ruin your life. But making a mistake on a catalog project, where accurate color is critical, will negatively impact your career. We will begin with some theory about the physical characteristics of color.

Color: Transmitted or Reflected Light Waves

Color is created by light waves that are either transmitted or reflected. Your computer monitor transmits light waves to create color. Three primary colors of light—red, green, and blue (RGB)—are combined in different proportions to create the millions of colors on your screen. Colors displayed on a monitor are described by a formula that specifies the level of each component color. The range of levels goes from 0 to 255. For example, the formula R=255, G=55, B=45 would describe a bright red. RGB is additive color. This means that when the levels of RGB are at the maximum, 255, the color you see is white. When all RGB values are at 0, the color is black. When creating documents that will be viewed on a monitor, such as web pages, using colors defined by the RGB system are natural choice.

Ink and toner on paper work differently. They absorb some light waves and reflect the rest. The light waves that are reflected back to our eyes create the illusion of color. Color created by reflected light waves is called subtractive. That means that if all the light is absorbed (subtracted), we see black. The primary colors in subtractive color are cyan, magenta, and yellow (CMY). Again, formulas that specify the amounts of each component color are used to describe subtractive color. The bright red color described in the preceding paragraph would be expressed as C=0, M=80, Y=75. An important difference is that the range of levels is different; from 0–100. It's also appropriate to refer to the levels of component colors as percentages. In theory, when you combine pigments of pure cyan, magenta, and yellow, all the light waves will be absorbed and the object will look black. In reality, pure pigments are impossible to obtain, so 100% cyan, 100% magenta, and 100% yellow blend to create a washed-out black. That's why black ink (referred to as K) is added in the printing process to compensate for the weak black created by the CMY combination. Now we've arrived at what is known as the CMYK color space. But RGB and CMYK aren't the only games in town.

When working with spot or process color, remember that what you see on your screen is probably not what you get from your commercial printer. Unless a color calibration system is in place, every computer monitor will display color a little differently. Use an ink swatch book to select the colors for your document. Even if they don't look just right on the screen, they will print correctly on a printing press.

Printing: Spot or Process?

Commercial printers always work with subtractive color. Defining colors to correctly print on a press is one of the challenges designers face on a daily basis. In commercial printing, color is created by reflected light waves. Therefore, it is not a good idea to put colors in your InDesign file that are defined as RGB (transmitted light waves).

Commercial printers use ink, and they talk in terms of process color or spot color. Spot color ink is like a can of premixed paint. There are about a dozen basic ink colors that can be combined in different proportions, to make thousands of spot color inks. Each spot color is described by a standardized number and a mixing ratio (another formula!). This enables any printer in the world to mix up and match a specific color, as long as they are using the same color/ink system. For instance, one popular color matching system is the Pantone Matching System (or simply PMS). When a printer in Philadelphia puts PMS 347 on his press, it will be exactly the same color as the PMS 347 printed across the ocean in Calcutta. Tints of spot colors can also be used and are described in percentages; 0%–100%. This allows you to use the full strength spot color (100%) or lighter tints to create a variety of color.

Many of your projects will be one-color documents, and yes—black counts as a color. Business forms, reports, books—many of the

figure | 12–1|

A color at 100% is the actual hue. The hue can be tinted in increments, from very dark (95%) to very light (10%). Even though black is the color shown in this example, the same percentage system is used to describe tints for all colors.

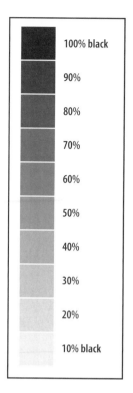

100% black
90%
80%
70%
60%
50%
40%
30%
20%
10% black

materials we read every day are single-color documents, and usually black and white. However, don't underestimate the power of a well-designed single-color document! A blue, for example, can range from a pale 10% shade to a strong 100% navy. And when it is printed on a cream sheet of paper, it can give the impression of a two-color job. For just slightly more than the cost of black ink, you can create an attractive document with just one spot color, incorporating tints and solids, and good design skills.

If your client wants a full-color brochure, but doesn't have a full-color budget, suggest going with a two-color brochure using spot colors. Two spot colors, combined with careful paper selection, can give a project an upscale look without the upscale cost.

Process Color

Process color (also referred to as full-color) is much different from spot color. Full-color posters, magazines, catalogs, artist prints—anything that has the full range of the color spectrum—will be printed using process colors. In process color printing, four basic transparent inks, in different tints, are printed on top of each other to create the illusion of many colors. As discussed earlier, these transparent colors are cyan, magenta, yellow, and black (CMYK). Cyan is greenish-blue and magenta is a violet-red. When you look at a full-color job under a magnifying glass, you will see that the "color" is actually made from a series of tiny dots printed close together. When each of the four inks are printed in the correct location, the dots merge together to give the impression of color. The color could be one hue (like a spot color ink) or the millions of color variations that create a photograph. However, when one ink color is printed slightly off from the others, it makes the finished image looks distorted. This is called "out of register". We have all seen examples of this when Sunday comics aren't printed quite right and have a blurred image.

Digital color printers (used for smaller full-color runs) often use cartridges of cyan, magenta, yellow, and black toner.

Applying Color to Your Document

InDesign has two palettes for assigning color to objects: the Color palette and the Swatches palette (you were introduced to the Swatches palette briefly in Chapter 6). Although you will use the Swatches palette most of the time, let's start by taking a quick look at the Color palette.

1. Make a new document, 8.5 x 11 inches. Open the Color palette (the shortcut key for the Color palette is F6). At the bottom of the palette you will see a bar called the color spectrum. It will contain either a gradient of one single color or a rainbow of colors. If the spectrum contains a single color, click on the palette menu and choose CMYK (see Figure 12–2).

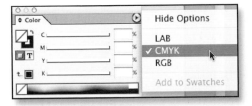

figure | 12–2 |

If the color spectrum shows only shades of one color, choose CMYK from the palette menu.

2. Draw a rectangle and activate the Fill icon on the Toolbox. Move your mouse over to the color spectrum on the Color palette and notice that your cursor turns into the Eyedropper tool. Click the Eyedropper tool on a color that looks good to you. The rectangle instantly fills with the color you have selected. Notice that the Fill icon in the Toolbox has been updated with the same color. Click back and forth along the CMYK spectrum bar and fill your rectangle with different colors (see Figure 12–3).

3. There are four sliders above the CMYK color spectrum. These show the percentages of each of the four process colors. Slide the triangles along each of the individual color bars,

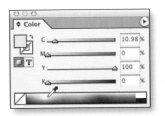

figure | 12–3 |

Every time you select a new color from the CMYK Spectrum bar, the Fill icon in the Toolbox displays the same color.

noticing how the color changes and also how the percentage values in the boxes to the right also change. Fine-tune your color, making it a light shade of the color you want.

4. Click on the None box at the left of the CMYK spectrum (the square with the red diagonal line). The rectangle now has no fill and the Fill icon on the Toolbox also indicates no fill. But you have not lost your color because a new box has appeared in the Color palette: the Last Color used (see Figure 12–4). Click on it and your last color returns. The smaller boxes at the right of the CMYK spectrum are for white or black fills. Remember that assigning white (a color) to the fill or stroke of an object is not the same as applying None (no color at all).

5. Double-click on your rectangle with the Type tool and convert it to a text frame. The Color palette now indicates the color of the text. Type a short sentence and bump up the point size to fill the text frame. Select all the text and change the color of the text in the same way you changed the color of the rectangle. Remember to choose CMYK if your color bar shows a spectrum of only one color.

6. Click on the text frame with one of the selection tools. The two small buttons below the Fill and Text icons in the Color palette (or the Toolbox) will now allow you to choose which color you change; either the text or the frame (see Figure 12–5).

figure | 12–4 |

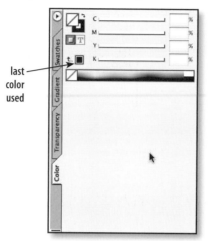

last color used

The Color palette conveniently remembers the last color you used. The None square on the far left end of the color spectrum is not the same as the white square on the far right end.

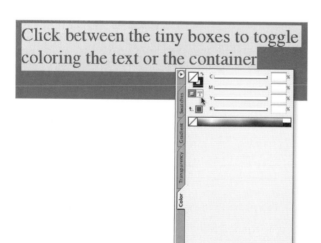

Click between the tiny boxes to toggle coloring the text or the container

figure | 12–5 |

The pointer shows the boxes you use to toggle between applying color to the container or to the text.

7. Open the Color palette options menu again and change the mode from CMYK to RGB (see Figure 12–6). The shades of color do not change, but you are now working in additive color, rather than subtractive color.

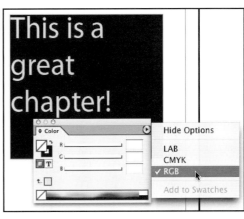

figure | 12–6 |

It is easy to change between single color, CMYK, and RBG color models. Always be aware of what color mode you are working in. CMYK is for commercial printing; RGB is basically for documents that will be viewed on a computer monitor, like web pages.

Now that you have been introduced to the Color palette, a word of caution: avoid using it! The Color palette is handy for applying color in "quick and dirty" documents that you will output yourself on your home laser printer. But if you're working in a production setting—and especially if your file is going out to a service bureau or commercial printer—use the Swatches palette instead.

The Swatches Palette

The Swatches palette can do everything the Color palette does, but with one important difference: you can define each color in your document and assign it a meaningful name. Colors from the Color palette are undefined and unnamed. They may look just as good as Swatch colors, but there's no way to track them throughout your document. For professional purposes, keep the Color palette tucked away. Colors created and stored in the Swatches palette are much easier to manage.

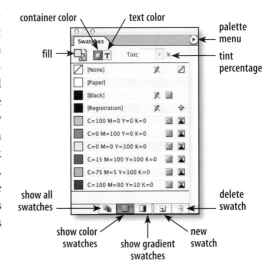

figure | 12–7 |

The keyboard shortcut to open the Swatches palette is F5. As you can see, the palette is set up like all the other InDesign palettes.

Transfer an Undefined Color from the Color Palette to the Swatches Palette

In the following exercise you will learn how to convert an undefined color created in the Color palette into a color swatch.

1. Make sure the Color palette is open and the rectangle is active.
2. Open the Swatches palette (F5). Lengthen the palette by dragging the lower right corner until the scroll bar disappears to make room for additional swatches. Go back to the Color palette and select the color of your active rectangle.
3. Open the Color palette options menu and choose Add to Swatches (see Figure 12–8). The color of your frame is now a swatch in the Swatches palette and has changed from an undefined color to a defined color. Do the same for the color you chose for your text.
4. There are other methods of transferring an undefined color to the Swatches palette. You can select your rectangle and click the New Swatch button at the bottom of the Swatches palette (shown in Figure 12–7). Or you can drag the Fill or Stroke color icon right from the Color palette and drop it into the Swatches palette.

figure | 12–8 |

An undefined color can be easily added to the Swatches palette by selecting Add to Swatches in the Color palette menu. The new swatch is now defined, and is at the bottom of the Swatches palette list.

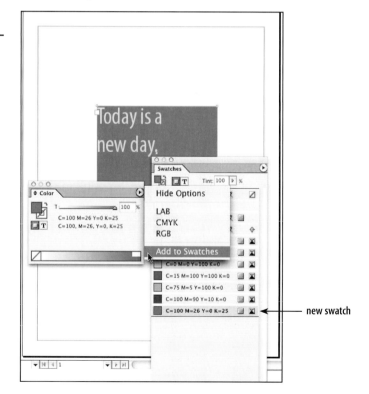

Transfer an Undefined Gradient from the Gradient Palette to the Swatches palette

Generally, it is best to convert undefined colors to defined swatches. The same holds true for undefined gradients. In the last chapter you used gradient fills—undefined gradient fills. Converting an undefined gradient to a gradient swatch is a process similar to the one you just completed for undefined color.

1. Open the Gradient palette and choose Show Options under the palette menu. In the Type field, choose Linear or Radial. A linear gradient changes color along a line, a radial gradient radiates from one color to the next in a circular pattern. You should see a horizontal bar, called a "ramp," extending across the bottom of the Gradient palette. At the top and center of the ramp is a diamond. This diamond is a "stop" that defines the midpoint of the gradient. As you slide the stop toward either end of the ramp, you will see the gradient swatch in the upper left corner change.

2. Open the Color palette and arrange it so that it's next to the Gradient palette. You're going to apply some colors to the gradient.

3. In the Gradient palette you should see two house-shaped icons below the ramp. If you don't see them, click on the ramp and they will appear. These are the color stops. Click on the left color stop and then adjust the color sliders in the Color palette. Notice that the color stop in the Gradient palette changes accordingly.

4. Now, click on the right color stop. Apply a color using the Color palette. Experiment with adjusting the look of your gradient by sliding the mid point and color stops to the left or the right. Watch as the gradient swatch in the upper left corner changes to reflect your color adjustments.

5. You can also apply color to a gradient from the Swatches palette. The process is similar to the one described above, but instead of choosing a color from the Color palette, you press Option (Mac) or Alt (Windows) as you click on a color swatch from the Swatches palette.

6. Now we will define the gradient you have just created. Open the Swatches palette menu and choose New Gradient Swatch. When the New Gradient Swatch dialog box appears, you can name your new gradient swatch in the Swatch Name field.

7. An alternate method is to select the Show Gradient Swatches button at the bottom of the Swatches palette (shown in

Figure 12–7) and then drag the preview from the Gradient palette into the Swatches palette. Double-click the swatch to open the Gradient Options dialog box and rename it.

The icons at the top of the Swatches palette should be familiar to you by now—Fill, Stroke, Container, and Text. There is also a field where you can set the tint of a selected color. The various colors in the list are those available to your document and are labeled with their CMYK values (see Figure 12–7).

Create a Color Swatch from "Scratch"

You can define colors directly from the Swatches palette. But before you can define a color for your document you must know whether you need to create spot or process colors. When you define a color in your document as "spot" it means that the printer will premix the color according to the formula specified by your swatch book and then put the colored ink on the press. A plate on the press picks up the ink and transfers it to the paper. After the color is printed, the press is cleaned, a new plate is put on, and the ink is replaced with the next color needed. A job that uses yellow, blue, green, orange, red, and black will require six premixed colors and six plates—and a significant amount of time for mixing ink and cleaning the press.

Process color works differently. Instead of premixing each individual ink color, only four inks—cyan, magenta, yellow, and black—and four plates are used to create all the other colors that will be printed. The four colors are overlaid in various tints, to create the illusion of many colors. The six-color job we just discussed could be printed by using only four inks and plates and would require much less production time. Orange would be created by percentages of yellow and magenta. Green would be created by percentages of cyan and yellow, and so on. Of course, if your job only has 2 colors—two inks and two plates—using spot colors will be the way to go.

A swatch book should be used at the design stage for selecting and defining either spot or process colors. The swatch book provides the exact color formula needed and shows an accurate sample of how the printed color will look. Basing a color selection on what you see on your computer screen is risky because most monitors do not display color accurately. There are many variables that go into choosing color. Until you have a clear understanding of the printing process, it is a good idea to have an experienced designer check your document files before you send them to the printer. We will now create a new process color swatch.

1. Choose New Color Swatch (see Figure 12–9). A dialog box displaying the four CMYK sliders will open. The color settings in the dialog box will be the last color selected in the Swatches palette.

2. If you know them, type in the percentages of cyan, magenta, yellow and black that define your color. Or slide the color bars until you get the color you want. InDesign will define the color for you in terms of CMYK values, or you can deselect the Name with Color Value option box and assign it a name of your own choosing.

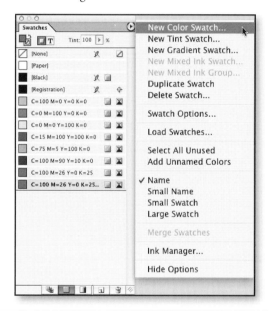

figure | 12–9

Look through the options in the palette menu and notice the checkmark beside the word Name. This means that the colors in the Swatches palette are being displayed by their names. If you select Small Swatch, the colors will be displayed in tiny swatches. Switch back and forth between these views to find which works best for you.

NOTE: It's better to name a color by its CMYK values because that's a language everyone understands. Even though a color may look exactly like what you saw when your cat was car sick, naming a color Sick Kitty conjures up a very different color in each person's mind.

Make a New Gradient Swatch from "Scratch"

When you select New Gradient Swatch from the Swatches palette menu, you are making a defined gradient.

1. Choose New Gradient Swatch from the palette menu.

2. Click on the Starting color stop icon at the left end of the gradient ramp. The Stop Color field becomes active, allowing you

to select CMYK from the list and then adjust the sliders in the CMYK mode. You can also select Swatches from the Stop Color field list and then choose a color from your swatches.

3. Click the Ending color stop icon at the right side of the gradient ramp and assign it a different color.

4. Drag one of the Stop icons to the middle of the gradient ramp. Click below the ramp where the original color stop was, and a new stop will appear. Give this new stop a third color.

5. Slide the diamond shaped midpoint stops at the top of the gradient ramp, to adjust the span of each color between color stops.

6. Click OK to add this swatch to the Swatches palette.

7. The Show Gradient Swatches button at the bottom of the palette toggles the display of all the defined gradients in the document. If you have a gradient swatch selected and click the New Swatch button, the gradient swatch will be duplicated. If you select the Trashcan icon, the gradient swatch will be deleted.

Make a Color Tint Swatch

If you were designing a single-color document using many shades of blue, you would want to first create the solid blue swatch and then make tint variations from it.

1. Create a new swatch —Color Type: Spot, Color Mode: Pantone solid coated. Scroll down the list and select a Pantone blue that you like. Press Return.

2. With the new blue swatch selected, open the Swatches palette menu and choose New Tint Swatch. In the New Tint Swatch dialog box, drag the Tint slider to 10% and click Add. You can type numerical values into the Tint field, but you have to press the Tab key before the Add button becomes active again.

3. Repeat this process, creating tint swatches from 20% to 90% blue, in 10 percent increments. Your Swatches palette should look like Figure 12–10. Notice that the percentage of each tint is displayed to the right.

figure | 12–10

Tint swatches display the percentage to the right of the color name.

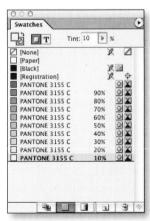

4. If the tint isn't exactly what you want, you can double-click on the tint swatch in the palette list, when the Swatch Options dialog box opens move the sliders and other options as desired. You can also give the swatch a new name.

Changing the CMYK values of a tint swatch also changes the values of the original color the swatch is based on. Be sure that when you are in the Swatch Options dialog box, you don't change CMYK values—unless you also want the original color swatch to change, too.

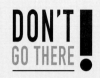

Adding Swatches from Other Documents

You can pull color swatches from other InDesign documents into a document you are working on. The following method allows you to pick and choose which colors you bring into your document.

1. Open the Swatches palette menu and choose New Color Swatch. In the New Color Swatch dialog box pick Other Library at the bottom of the Color Mode list (see Figure 12–11).
2. Navigate to the document you want to borrow color from, and click Open.
3. Select a color you want from the list of available colors in the document and click Add to transfer them to your Swatches palette. When you are done adding colors, click OK.

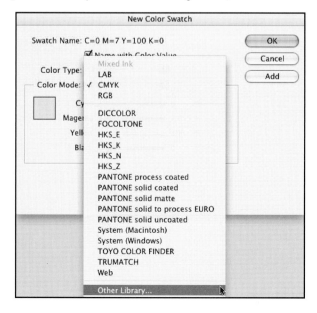

figure | 12–11

At the bottom of the Color Mode field menu, choose Other Library. Find the existing document and choose the colors you want to bring into your new document.

Loading Swatches

You can also add swatches from another document by using the Load Swatches option and then selecting the file. This method will load all the colors from the second document rather than letting you pick and choose the ones you want (see Figure 12–12).

figure | 12–12 |

The Load Swatches command is the one to use when you want all the colors from an existing document to come into the document you are working on.

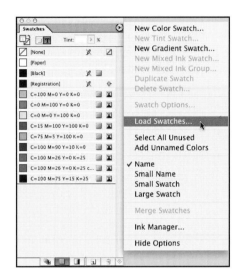

Standard Swatch Libraries

Although it stimulates your creative juices to create your own colors from the color spectrum ramp and those cool little CMYK bars, the safest thing to do is choose colors from standard swatch libraries—like Pantone or Trumatch. You find the standard swatch libraries in the Swatch Options dialog box. First open the Swatch palette menu and choose New Color Swatch (or Swatch Options if you have a swatch selected). When the New Color Swatch (or Swatch Options) dialog box opens, choose Color Mode. Each of the names in the center section of the list corresponds to a specific color swatch system (see Figure 12–13).

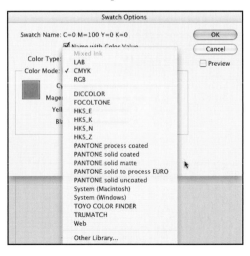

figure | 12–13 |

Each of the names in the center section (Diccolor, Pantone, TruMatch, and so on) corresponds to a specific manufacturer's color swatch system. Be sure to choose a system that your printer uses.

Using a swatch book to choose colors assures that you are speaking the same language as your printer—as long as you use the same swatch book he uses!

Creating a 2-color layout

Let's say you're designing a small flyer for a large bank. The bank wants the piece to look good, but doesn't want to spend the money on four colors. You suggest going with two colors on coated ivory paper. The finished product will look like Figure 12–14.

Gibraltar Metropolitan Bank

How We Protect Your Information

psuscipit ex er iustrud magnis elis aliquisit vendrem auguerci blam dolore dolum dunt il erostissed min eui eum auguer sum nos nis eugait vullaore consent ipsum nostio do dunt nim iriustrud dui exer sequisi bla feugue minciliquat nullam veriure min ulla faci et am zzrit prat, veraesto ercipis ea feum do odiamconsed eum ipsustrud tat. Ut lutpat.

Our Security Procedures

Bore molor sim ipis dolent wisit accumsan ut veril et dolor ad modo diatuer susto diamcon sequat ullut am eugiametue ting etum del dionsecte duipis nostrud eros ex estio consequamet in velessendre facipis adit iriusto dipsum ing exerit eummy nulla feu feuisci tie magnibh eu facillaore dolorem del exerci eu facing ea aliquat dio ex eugiam nim acidui tinim ing ent acidunt lore dolore vel eu facing euisi.

What Information We Disclose

tet ea commodolore feuismolore commodiat ad eugait velit lamet, quisit adipit iuscil ero od dolortincin henibh et praesse quipsumsan hent dui blaore feum ilis nulla ad tionsed exero consequisi.

• Re tionsed dolorperos am inibh eugiam nos at, quis euguerit nummy nos ex estin hendipis acidunt am
• volorero od et, quis amet la feugiate magnibh enisse consequat.
• Duisl irit at aute diamconse venisi tionullam erillan hent wis amet nulla acidunt adionsequam, voluptat utatums andreet nos nonsequis auguerostrud

endiam zzriustin velesequisl irilisim ex elisLiquis autet prat. Velit esed mincidunt laore venibh eratet quisisisis autate mod eu facillaor ad eugueros et prate vullaor sit quisl il dolortion el eugiat, volenim vel ute tinibh eugait velendrer sit vero consequat lorper sed tie con ulputet velis eugait ipit ipit vulpute diate tatum dolore con ullut

Gibraltar Metropolitan Bank
123 Center City Suites
Yorkton, Virginia 09876
121-233-4567   www.gibraltarmetro.com

figure | 12–14

This is a two-color project called a "bill stuffer," just like the ones that come in your credit card statements.

1. Make a new document 22p x 8.5 inches, .25 margins, and .125 full bleed.

2. Delete all swatches that may be in the Swatches palette. (You will not be able to delete None, Paper, Black, or Registration.)

3. Choose New Color Swatch in the palette menu. In the New Color Swatch dialog box, choose Pantone solid coated in the Color Mode list. Scroll down the list of available colors, select 202C and click Add. Without closing the dialog box, scroll down to 876C (or type 876 in the Pantone field), select this color and click OK. You have selected two standard Pantone colors to use in your document (if you had a Pantone Color Swatch book you'd see that 876 is an eye-catching metallic gold).

4. Draw a text frame from margin to margin and place the 12-Gibraltar Bank.txt text file. You will find the file in the Chapter 12>Artwork/Resources folder on the CD accompanying this book.

5. Open the Paragraph Styles palette and choose Load All Styles. Find the 12 Gibraltar Style Sheets file in the same folder as the text file.

6. Select all the text and assign the Body Copy paragraph style.

7. Apply the Headline style to the first line of type.

8. Apply the Sub Head style to the lines "How we Protect…", "Our Security…", and "What Information…".

9. Apply the Body Copy-Bulleted style to the three bulleted paragraphs. Remember to use the Indent to Here character to hang the bullet. Mac users will use Command+\ and Windows users, Control+\ .

10. Apply the Footer style to the bottom four lines, making sure there is a soft return at the end of each line. Place a flush right tab between the phone number and web site (Shift+Tab). Your document should look like Figure 12–15.

11. Draw a rectangle that bleeds from the top, left, and right sides. Include just the first section of placeholder text in the rectangle (refer to Figure 12–14). Fill the rectangle with 876C and send it to the back.

12. Make a similar rectangle at the bottom of the document, bleeding it off the right, left, and bottom edges. The rectangular shape should enclose the name, address, and web information. Fill it with 876C and send it to the back. Deselect everything. We've now used our two colors: 876C for the background rectangles and 202C for the type.

figure | 12–15 |

Gibraltar Metropolitan Bank

How We Protect Your Information

psuscipit ex er iustrud magnis elis aliquisit vendrem
auguerci blam dolore dolum dunt il erostissed min
eui eum auguer sum nos nis eugait vullaore consent
ipsum nostio do dunt nim iriustrud dui exer sequisi bla
feugue minciliquat nullam veriure min ulla faci et am
zzrit prat, veraesto ercipis ea feum do odiamconsed
eum ipsustrud tat. Ut lutpat.

Our Security Procedures

Bore molor sim ipis dolent wisit accumsan ut veril et
dolor ad modo diatuer susto diamcon sequat ullut am
eugiametue ting etum del dionsecte duipis nostrud
eros ex estio consequamet in velessendre facipis adit
iriusto dipsum ing exerit eummy nulla feu feuisci tie
magnibh eu facillaore dolorem del exerci eu facing ea
aliquat dio ex eugiam nim acidui tinim ing ent acidunt
lore dolore vel eu facing euisi.

What Information We Disclose

tet ea commodolore feuismolore commodiat ad
eugait velit lamet, quisit adipit iuscil ero od dolortincin
henibh et praesse quipsumsan hent dui blaore feum
ilis nulla ad tionsed exero consequisi.

- Re tionsed dolorperos am inibh eugiam nos at, quis
  euguerit nummy nos ex estin hendipis acidunt am

- volorero od et, quis amet la feugiate magnibh enisse
  consequat.

- Duisl irit at aute diamconse venisi tionullam erillan
  hent wis amet nulla acidunt adionsequam, voluptat
  utatums andreet nos nonsequis auguerostrud

endiam zzriustin velesequisl irilisim ex elisLiquis autet
prat. Velit esed mincidunt laore venibh eratet quisisisis
autate mod eu facillaor ad eugueros et prate vullaor
sit quisl il dolortion el eugiat, volenim vel ute tinibh
eugait velendrer sit vero consequat lorper sed tie con
ulputet velis eugait ipit ipit vulpute diate tatum dolore
con ullut

Gibraltar Metropolitan Bank
123 Center City Suites
Yorkton, Virginia 09876
121-233-4567   www.gibraltarmetro.com

13. Since the document will be printed on ivory paper, let's add a color to our paper and see what it will look like when it is printed. Double-click the [Paper] color in the Swatches palette. In the Swatch Options dialog box, give the paper a light ivory color: 5% Cyan, 10% Magenta, 36% Yellow, 0.39% Black. Press Return. Save your document, and let's try printing color separations.

Color Separations

One of the most common problems printers have when designers bring in "finished" documents is in creating color separations. Every color in your document needs its own plate and printing unit on the press. A two-color document will need two plates and two printing units; a four-color document will need four plates and four printing units, and so on. (Tints based on an original spot color do not require an additional plate.)

In smaller print shops, a two-color document will sometimes be run on a single-color press. One plate and color are run first, and then the paper is run through again with the second plate and second color. If the printer has a two-color press, he can use the same procedure for a four-color job: Two colors are laid down on the first pass; the next two colors on the second pass.

You may think you are bringing a two-color document to your printer, but when he runs separations, he gets four, five, six, or more colors. Why? It could be that what looks like a single color on your monitor is actually a blend of CMYK or RGB values. It could be that you didn't notice a hairline stroke on a text frame. It could be that a hidden character is assigned a color you can't even see on your monitor. There can be any number of reasons why there are more colors in your document than it appears. The following exercise uses features in the Print dialog box to identify how many colors are really in your document.

1. Go to the Print dialog box. On the Setup page, in the Page Position field, choose Centered (see Figure 12–16).
2. On the Marks and Bleed page, select Crop Marks, Bleed Marks, Registration Marks, and Page Information. Be sure that Use Document Bleed Settings is selected (see Figure 12–17).
3. On the Output page, select Separations in the Color field (see Figure 12–18).

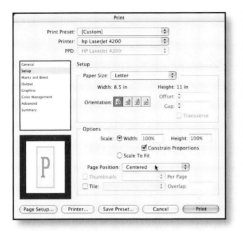

Choosing setup options in the Print dialog box.

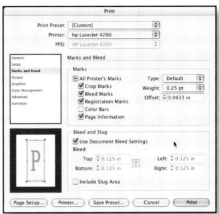

Choosing settings for marks and bleeds.

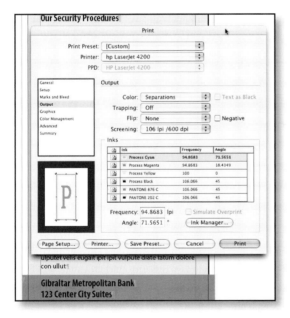

The Output pane offers choices for color separations.

4. Click Print. You should get two sheets from the printer, one labeled Pantone 202C and the other labeled 876C.

5. Go back to your document and deliberately confuse things. Make hidden characters visible and select a single hard return character. Color it black and run separations again. You will get a third sheet labeled Black, although you won't see any text or element. InDesign "saw" a hidden character with a third color

(black) that nobody else saw. Since we're printing separations, it printed a black plate—just for that one invisible character.

6. Make a new process swatch: C=0, M=100, Y=61, K=43 (the equivalent values of PMS 202C). Call it Process Red or something like that. Select all your text and change it to Process Red. The color of your text looks exactly the same, but now when you print you get four separations: Magenta, Yellow, Black, and 897C. (Cyan didn't print because its value was zero. Also notice how the Black plate is screened back to 43%.)

It is a good idea to print out a sample set of separations on your laser printer before sending the project to the commercial printer. Printing sample separations is an effective way of catching color mistakes before they end up costing you money. Knowing a few color basics and always paying attention to how color is defined and used in your document will help avoid production pitfalls and increase your chances of being the next one in line for that promotion.

Remember the colors you assigned to the bank flyer paper stock? Those colors did not print with your color separations. They are "for your eyes only" to give you an approximate feel for how your final document will look. Modify the paper color in your Swatches palette as close as possible to the real paper, but remember that your monitor will not give you a 100% match. Also keep in mind that a single PMS color may look different when printed on different color papers.

Printers' Marks

You will also want to be familiar with the marks your printer uses for printing and finishing your document. Since all printers' marks are outside the copy area of the document, the paper size will always have to be larger than your finished document size in order to use them.

- Crop Marks (sometimes called trim marks) are placed just outside the four corners of your document and tell the cutter where to cut the paper to its finished size. If a document is printed on oversized paper, the cutter will trim away the excess according to the crop marks. You can adjust the weight and placement of crop marks using the Weight and Offset fields, on the right side of the Marks area in the Print dialog box.

- Manual Crop Marks. If more than one copy of your document will be printed on a single sheet (two up, three up, and so on) or if the front and back of your document will be printed in a single pass (work and turn, work and tumble—types of imposition), you may want to manually draw your own crop marks. Make your manual crop marks short and thin—about a quarter of an inch long and hairline width—and maybe an eighth of an inch away from the edge of the finished piece. Make sure the corners don't touch (see Figure 12–19). Before you take your document to final production, it's a good idea to print it from your laser printer and with a pencil, connect the crop marks you created. This is a way to double-check the accuracy of your marks to make sure that you're not cutting off something you want to keep.

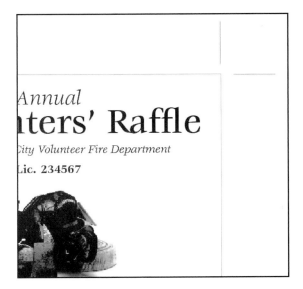

figure | 12–19

In this Exploring on Your Own project from Chapter 7 crop marks were manually drawn around the entire document. Notice that the lines are quite thin and the corners do not meet.

- Bleed Marks sit in the corners of your document just outside the crop marks, and set the limits of your printed bleed (see Figure 12–20). You will usually use the settings you entered when your document was first set up, but you can also enter new settings in the Bleed and Slug area of the Print dialog box. Even if the bleed in your electronic file extends beyond the settings in the Bleed and Slug area, it will print only out to the bleed marks.

- Registration Marks are the "bull's-eyes" along the sides of your document (see Figure 12–20). Your printer uses these marks to straighten and center your document and to align multiple colors. All your hard work and great design ideas will go down the drain if your job is printed out of register.

- Color Bars are used in production to be sure that ink coverage is running right—not too light and not too heavy. They appear at the top of a document (see Figure 12–20).

- Page Information will give you the title of the document, the date and time printed, and separation color (see Figure 12–20). Very handy stuff.

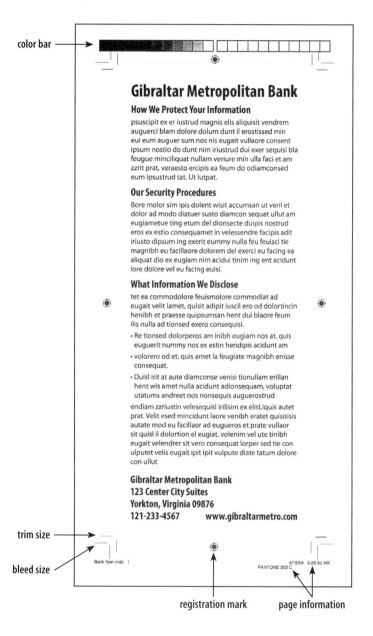

color bar

Gibraltar Metropolitan Bank

How We Protect Your Information

psuscipit ex er iustrud magnis elis aliquisit vendrem auguerci blam dolore dolum dunt il erostissed min eui eum auguer sum nos nis eugait vullaore consent ipsum nostio do dunt nim iriustrud dui exer sequisi bla feugue minciliquat nullam veriure min ulla faci et am zzrit prat, veraesto ercipis ea feum do odiamconsed eum ipsustrud tat. Ut lutpat.

Our Security Procedures

Bore molor sim ipis dolent wisit accumsan ut veril et dolor ad modo diatuer susto diamcon sequat ullut am eugiametue ting etum del dionsecte duipis nostrud eros ex estio consequamet in velessendre facipis adit iriusto dipsum ing exerit eummy nulla feu feuisci tie magnibh eu facillaore dolorem del exerci eu facing ea aliquat dio ex eugiam nim acidui tinim ing ent acidunt lore dolore vel eu facing euisi.

What Information We Disclose

tet ea commodolore feuismolore commodiat ad eugait velit lamet, quisit adipit iuscil ero od dolortincin henibh et praesse quipsumsan hent dui blaore feum ilis nulla ad tionsed exero consequisi.

- Re tionsed dolorperos am inibh eugiam nos at, quis euguerit nummy nos ex estin hendipis acidunt am

- volorero od et, quis amet la feugiate magnibh enisse consequat.

- Duisl irit at aute diamconse venisi tionullam erillan hent wis amet nulla acidunt adionsequam, voluptat utatums andreet nos nonsequis auguerostrud

endiam zzriustin velesequisl irilisim ex elisLiquis autet prat. Velit esed mincidunt laore venibh eratet quisisisis autate mod eu facillaor ad eugueros et prate vullaor sit quisl il dolortion el eugiat, volenim vel ute tinibh eugait velendrer sit vero consequat lorper sed tie con ulputet velis eugait ipit ipit vulpute diate tatum dolore con ullut

Gibraltar Metropolitan Bank
123 Center City Suites
Yorkton, Virginia 09876
121-233-4567   www.gibraltarmetro.com

trim size

bleed size

Bank flyer.indd   1

4/15/04   9:26:30 AM
PANTONE 202 C

registration mark   page information

Collecting and Packaging

Once you have your document ready to go to press, you need to collect all the electronic elements of your file—all fonts and graphics—and bundle them up for transporting to your service bureau or printer.

Preflight the Document

Choose File>Preflight to access the Preflight dialog box. The Summary page appears first, telling you how many fonts, colors, and graphics are included, and other document information. If an electronic element is missing or needs your attention, there will be a yellow caution icon in front of it.

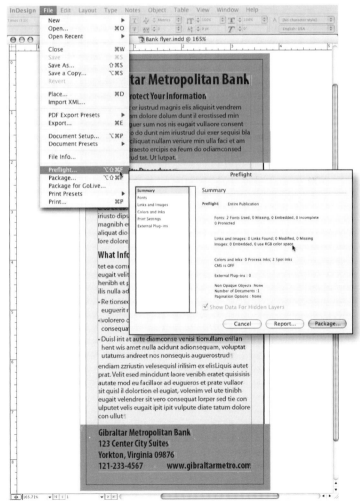

figure | 12–21 |

When you look at the Summary pane of the Preflight dialog box, always check for yellow caution triangles that indicate a problem you need to fix.

Let's say your colleague created a document on her computer and the day before it goes to press she goes on vacation. It comes to you to finish up and everything looks good until you see a caution icon in front of Fonts. Click on the Fonts page (below Summary in the list on the left of the Preflight dialog box), and it will display the names of all fonts used in the document and their status. If a font is missing you have the option to replace it (not a good idea in this case). What you will usually do is track down the font and add it to those available on your computer.

Use a similar process for Links and Images. A link is the path from your InDesign document to the location of the original graphics file you placed in the frames. If the original file has been moved since the file was created, InDesign needs help finding the new path to the image. Click on a missing image and click Relink. InDesign will lead you through the navigation necessary to find the source file. Again, if the original graphic is not on your computer you will have to find the CD it came from and pop it into your machine. Preflight will also tell you if there are problem RGB images that need to be converted to CMYK. For that you will have to open the image in Photoshop and change the color mode.

Package the Document

When all your electronic elements are in order, click the Package button in the Preflight dialog box. Fill in necessary information in the Printing Instructions dialog box and click Continue. Name your package folder, check the appropriate options and save it.

figure | 12–22

The Package command creates an organized folder that contains necessary fonts, images, and instructions for printing your file.

Printing Instructions

Filename: Gibraltar Metropolitan Bank

Contact: Designer Name Here

Company: ABC Advertising

Address: 1225 Capital Drive

Smith

Washington

Phone: 123 334 5678   Fax: 123 334 5677

Email: dname@aol.com

Instructions: Print 5000, shrink wrap in groups of 100

Ship to Gibraltar Metro Bank, 2202 Captial Drive, Smith, WA

Send bill to Lane Johnson, Gibraltar Metro Bank

Continue

Cancel

SUMMARY

The world of color is technical and complex, but essential to understand when creating effective communications. You have taken the first steps to finding your way through the color maze, and you will learn much more with experience. You have learned the basics of packaging a document so that others in the production process will have clear directions and all the electronic elements they need.

in review

1. Explain the difference between RGB and CMYK color. What does it mean that one of them is additive and one is subtractive?

2. When would you use spot color? When would you use process color? When might you use both?

3. What is the difference between the Color palette and the Swatches palette and why should you prefer to use one instead of the other?

4. Why is it best to use standard Pantone or Trumatch colors rather than create your own?

5. True or false: When you're finished with a project, a good way to check how many colors you actually have in your document is to print color separations.

6. When might you make your own crop marks rather than select the Crop Marks option in the Print dialog box?

7. Why is it important to preflight and package your document before sending it off to the service bureau or printer?

↗ EXPLORING ON YOUR OWN

Three projects accompany this chapter on the *Exploring InDesign* CD. You can find the projects and specifications in the Chapter 12 folder. The copy is courtesy of Freedom Consumer Credit Counseling, www.freedomccc.org.

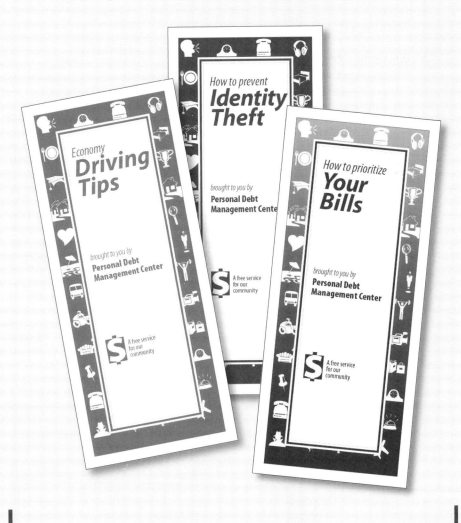

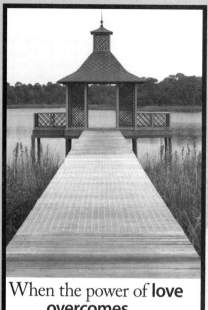

When the power of **love**
overcomes
the love of power
the world will know peace.

Jimi Hendrix

13

charting your course

Twenty years ago if you wanted to buy a comfortable family car, you more than likely bought a four-door sedan. If you wanted to haul cargo you bought a pick-up truck or full-size van. Both did a good job for their particular purposes.

Then someone asked the perfect question: Why not combine the two? And the mini-van was born! It was the perfect way for the whole family to go to Grandma's, and just the right vehicle for picking up a few sheets of 4′ × 8′ drywall for that weekend project in the utility room. The mini-van changed the course of the U.S. auto industry and has proven to be one of the most successful innovations in American transportation.

InDesign has combined the digital page capability of an electronic publishing program and the creative artistry of a drawing program into the most successful innovation in graphics software today. The extraordinary page layout features of InDesign are the reason this program is taking the world by storm. But with the addition of many drawing features similar to those you'll find in Adobe Illustrator, you now have a tool that—like the mini-van—is changing the face of an entire industry.

If you have already worked with Adobe Illustrator, much of this chapter will be a review of what you already know. Have fun combining your drawing skills with the good typography and digital page layout principles you have been learning in *Exploring InDesign*.

 goals

- **Review basic drawing tools**
- **Master the mighty Pen tool**
- **Create and modify open, closed, and compound paths**
- **Integrate drawn elements with text**

GRAPHICS TOOLS

You already know how to use the Rectangle, Ellipse, and Polygon tools to create two-dimensional shapes and the Line tool for—well—lines. You know that the Shift key will constrain shapes to perfect squares or circles, and lines to increments of 45 degrees. You know that if you hold down the Option or Alt key while you drag, you will draw a shape from its center instead of a corner.

In the following exercise you learn to make a shape by specifying dimensions numerically in a dialog box.

1. Make an 8.5 × 11 document (with the ruler set to inches) and select either the Rectangle or Ellipse tool (but not the Polygon tool). Put the cursor where you want the upper left corner of the shape positioned and click (do not drag).
2. The dialog box for creating the Rectangle or Ellipse will appear. Enter Width and Height dimensions in the Options fields and click OK.
3. Do this a few times to make several different-sized shapes. If you hold down the Option key (Mac) or Alt key (Windows) when you click on your document, the shape will be centered on that point.
4. Use the Direct Selection tool and drag one of the points of a shape. You can distort the shape any way you want it. Click and drag on a line segment and move it around without moving the rest of the shape. Select different combinations of points and line segments by dragging a marquee or Shift+clicking. See what kinds of weird shapes you can make.

figure | 13–1 |

Pen tool options in the Toolbox. Notice how to access them with keyboard shortcuts.

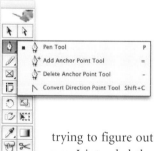

The Mighty Pen Tool

One of the most versatile tools in the InDesign arsenal is the Pen tool. For some it can also be a difficult one to master. I sat in my first Illustrator class for hours, trying to figure out why my shapes never ended up the way I intended them to look. But once I mastered the Pen tool it became one of my favorite tools.

Making a Closed Path

Rectangle, Ellipse, and Polygon tools make closed paths—their paths are unbroken. If you were to break a line segment or anchor point on the path, they would become open shapes. Paths and are made up of a series of line segments which can be either curved or straight. These line segments are connected by anchor points, which can be either corners or smooth. With the Pen tool you can create both open and closed paths.

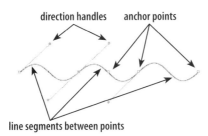

direction handles   anchor points

line segments between points

figure 13–2

Parts of a path.

1. Delete the shapes you made in your document and select the Pen tool. (As with every tool, always use the keyboard short-cut—in this case press P.) Set the Stroke color to black, the Width to 1 pt., with no fill. Place your cursor about two inches in and two inches down in your document (so that X = 2 and Y = 2). Notice that the Pen icon has a little "x" by it. This means that the path you are about to draw begins a new shape. Hold Shift and drag horizontally to the right about an inch. As you drag, two direction handles appear: one following the cursor and the other extending 180 degrees in the opposite direction (see Figure 13–3). These direction handles are like a teeter-totter, pivoting on your anchor point. The direction handles are not part of the actual line segment you are drawing; they only point you in the direction the path will be going when you begin your next stroke. So far, you have only established an initial anchor point for the first segment of your shape.

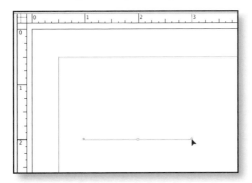

figure 13–3

Direction handles appear when you drag with the Pen tool.

Direction handles for drawing tools are like hidden characters when you are working with text. They are not part of your shape and do not print, but they determine much of what your path will look like. Direction handles and anchor points—like hidden characters—give you a critical advantage: They allow you to see your document as the computer sees it.

2. When you release the mouse, the little x next to the Pen icon has disappeared. This means that the next stroke of your pen will be "step 2" in creating your path. Place the cursor so that coordinate X = 4 and Y = 1. Again, click, hold down Shift and drag horizontally for about an inch. Your path should look like Figure 13–4. You now have two anchor points and the first curved line segment of your shape.

figure | **13–4** |

Two anchor points have been established.

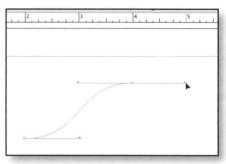

3. Place your cursor at these coordinates: X = 6; Y = 2. Click, hold down Shift and drag for the direction handle for about an inch. You now have a path that looks like a bell curve (see Figure 13–5).

figure | **13–5** |

The path takes the shape of a bell curve.

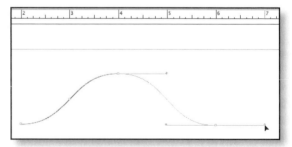

Holding the Shift key while you drag with the Pen tool will constrain your direction handles to increments of 45 degrees, just as it does with the Line tool. Press Shift after you begin to drag. Holding Shift continuously may send your path in unexpected directions.

NOTE: Maybe someday you'll be in the middle of drawing a shape and you get distracted doing something else. When you get back to your path, the little x has reappeared next to your Pen icon. (You don't want this because it means you will begin a new path instead of continuing on the same one you were working on.) To get rid of the little x, place your cursor over the last anchor point you made and the x will change to a little slash. Click and you are now ready to continue with the next line segment of your path.

4. Activate the Fill icon in the Toolbox and apply a black fill color. Notice that you can fill a path that is not closed. An imaginary straight line, from the starting anchor point to the ending anchor point, is used as the boundary for the fill. Deactivate the fill before you continue, by applying None.

5. Place your cursor so that X = 4 and Y = 3. This time instead of dragging, simply click. You have established a new anchor point, but notice how the path is sharply curved at the previous point (see Figure 13–6). The direction handle—extending further to the right—told this new line segment to continue on to the right, but your new anchor point told it to go the opposite direction: down and to the left. Choose Undo.

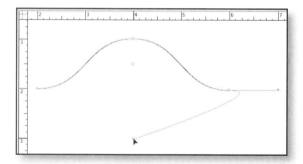

figure | 13–6 |

A new anchor point changes the direction of the path.

6. This time hold down the Option (Mac) or Alt (Windows) key and your Pen tool will turn into the Convert Direction Point tool (see Figure 13–7). Click on the right end of the last direction handle you made and drag it down so that X=5 and Y=2.5 and release the mouse button (see Figure 13–8).

7. Release the Option or Alt key and the Pen tool is active again. Place your cursor at approximately X = 4, Y = 3 and click. Your new path now has a crisp corner at the previous anchor point (see Figure 13–9). Your converted direction handle told the path to go down and to the left, and your new point also told the path to go down and to the left.

figure | 13–7

Holding the Option or Alt key will change the Pen tool to the Convert Direction Point tool. Use the Convert Direction Point tool to move just one of the two direction handles that extend from a selected point.

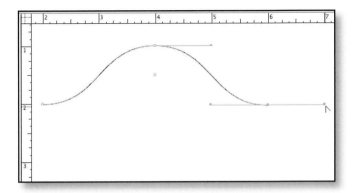

figure | 13–8

Drag the direction handle down and to the left as shown.

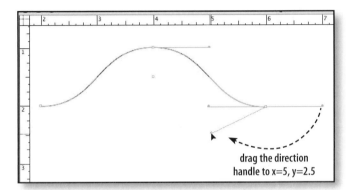

drag the direction handle to x=5, y=2.5

figure | 13–9

A corner has been created at the previous anchor point.

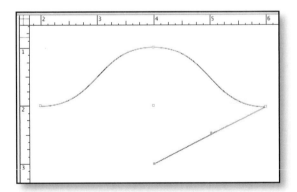

8. Move the Pen tool to the first anchor point you made for your path. (Always check to see that there are no little x's or slashes next to your Pen tool cursor.) When you get close to the starting anchor point, a small circle should appear next to the Pen tool cursor. This means that your path will be closed with your next click. Go ahead and click to close your path. It should look something like Figure 13–10. Now, activate the Fill icon on the

Toolbox and apply a fill to your path. Practice applying different colors to the fill, as well as applying None.

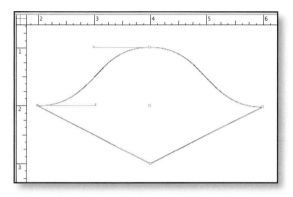

figure | 13–10 |

Closing the
path completes
your shape.

Making an Open Path

You made your first open path in Chapter 11 working with text on
a path. Let's review and practice another open path.

1. Delete your bell curve. Place the Pen tool (now with the little
   "x" next to it—beginning a new path) at X = 0.5, Y = 2. Click
   and drag up and to the right until X = 2 and Y = 0.5 (see
   Figure 13–11). Release the mouse button.
2. Now place your Pen tool cursor at X = 4 and Y = 2, click and
   drag a new line segment down and to the right until X = 5 and
   Y = 3 (see Figure 13–12). Release the mouse button.
3. Finally, place your tool cursor at X = 7, Y = 2. Drag up to X = 8,
   Y = 0.5 and release the mouse button (see Figure 13–13).

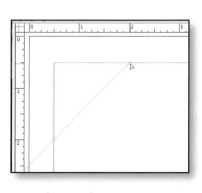

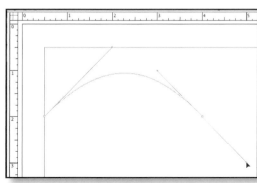

figure | 13–11 |

figure | 13–12 |

Drag up and to the right.

Drag a new line down and to the right.

figure | **13–13**

Drag the tool up
and to the right.

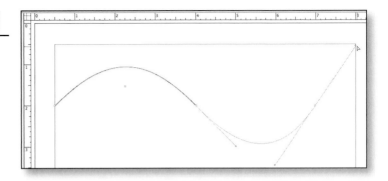

4. Deselect all. (Be sure you have a stroke width set for your line or it will disappear!) Your path looks like a wave of the ocean, similar to the wave in Figure 13–14. This line is an open path because the last anchor point is not connected to the point of origin. Toggle the Fill icon on and off. Again, the open path is filled along an imaginary line that connects the starting and ending anchor points. The effect is not exactly what you might have expected.

figure | **13–14**

The resulting
path looks like an
ocean wave.

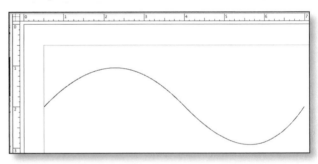

5. With the Direct Selection tool, click anywhere on the top curve (you can switch to the Direct Selection tool while still using the Pen tool by holding down Command [Mac] or Control [Windows]). You have selected the first of the two line segments in your "wave" and you can see the direction handles indicating the direction each segment is going (see Figure 13–15).

figure | **13–15**

New direction
handles appear.

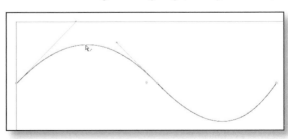

6. Click on the direction handle extending up from the middle anchor point and move it back and forth. Your wave changes pitch. Notice how both direction handles move simultaneously (see Figure 13–16).

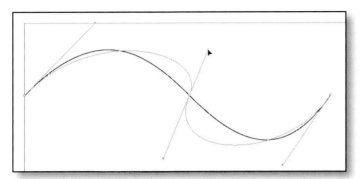

figure | 13–16 |

Moving both direction handles with the Direct Selection tool.

7. Select the Convert Direction Point tool by pressing Shift+C. Again, when you move the end of the top direction handle, it changes the shape of the wave, but only the selected direction handle moves (see Figure 13–17). You have just changed a smooth anchor point into a corner anchor point.

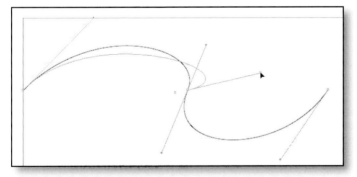

figure | 13–17 |

Moving one direction handle with the Convert Direction Point tool.

8. Go back to the Direct Selection tool by pressing A. Click on the middle anchor point to select it. This time instead of moving the direction handles, move the point itself to the left (see Figure 13–18). The curve of your wave changes dramatically as you move the middle anchor point between the start and end anchor points. Move the center anchor point of your wave left and right, up and down. If you want to make your wave longer or shorter, select one of the end anchor points and move it in or out.

figure | 13-18 |

Moving the middle
anchor point
with the Direct
Selection tool.

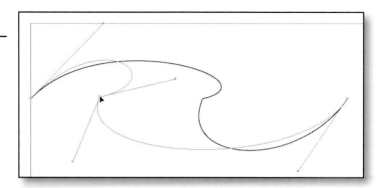

If an anchor point is hollow it is not selected, and an anchor point
that is filled in is selected. In Figure 13–19, you will see one more
small box to the left of the path. This point is not an anchor point,
and you do not draw it. This box indicates the center of your path's
bounding box. It functions just like the center point of a frame or
circle: you can click and drag it with a selection tool to move the
entire path.

figure | 13-19 |

An anchor point that
is selected is "filled
in" and its direction
handles extend in
both directions.
Anchor points not
selected are hollow.

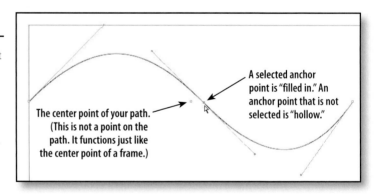

The center point of your path.
(This is not a point on the
path. It functions just like
the center point of a frame.)

A selected anchor
point is "filled in." An
anchor point that is not
selected is "hollow."

Adding and Deleting Anchor Points

You will sometimes finish a path you thought was perfect, only
to discover that you need an extra anchor point here or there, or
maybe there are too many points in one area. No problem! Adding
and deleting points in InDesign is just a click away.

1. Get your wave back to its original shape or (if it's beyond repair)
   delete it and make a new one, repeating steps 1 through 3 in the
   previous exercise.
2. Let's say your wave is not wavy enough. Press = to activate
   the Add Anchor Point tool. The Add Anchor Point tool has

a small "+" by the Pen tool cursor (see Figure 13–20). Click in two or three places on each segment of your wave. (Notice that direction handles extend out from each new point, and the new points all remain selected.) Deselect all and press A to switch to the Direct Selection tool.

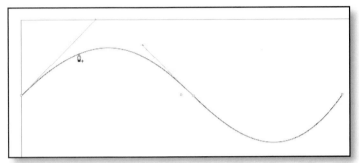

figure | 13–20

The Add Anchor Point tool about to add a point to a path.

3. Click on the line and you will see all the anchor points—hollow (deselected). Drag each of the new anchor points up or down to make a series of shorter waves, similar to Figure 13–21. Then adjust the length and angles of the direction handles to get a relatively smooth wave.

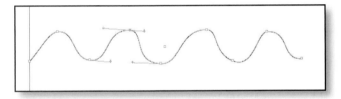

figure | 13–21

Drag the new anchor points up and down to make shorter waves.

Sometimes you will want to delete one or more points from a path. Press the – key to activate the Delete Anchor Point tool. As you click on the anchor points you want to delete they will disappear.

Smooth Points and Corner Points

Smooth points are made by dragging, after you place an anchor point. Smooth points have direction handles. Corner points are made by a one click of your mouse. Corner points do not have direction handles.

1. Delete everything in your document and press P for the Pen tool. Make a circle by dragging four successive curve points: one at the top, the right side, bottom, and left side. Click on the starting anchor point to close the circle. See Figures 13–22

to 13–26. (This last point is a little tricky. You will need to drag the Pen tool to the left to create a reasonable looking curve.) Don't worry if your circle is a little lopsided.

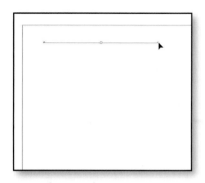

figure | 13–22 |

Click with the Pen tool, hold Shift and drag to make the first part of the circle.

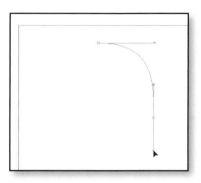

figure | 13–23 |

Click with the Pen tool, and Shift+drag to make the second part of the circle.

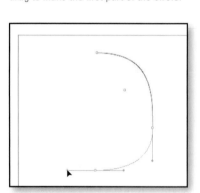

figure | 13–24 |

Click with the Pen tool, and Shift+drag to make third part of circle.

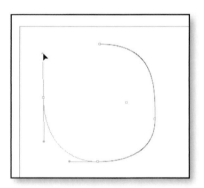

figure | 13–25 |

Click and Shift+drag to make the fourth part of the circle.

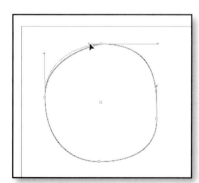

figure | 13–26 |

Click and Shift+drag to complete the shape.

When using the Pen tool, use as few anchor points as possible. The fewer the points, the smoother your path will be. Too many anchor points will make what should be a graciously curved line look jagged and choppy. Practice making circles with only four anchor points.

2. Hold down the Option or Alt key to switch to the Convert Direction Point tool and click on one of your smooth anchor points. It becomes a corner point. Click the Convert Direction Point tool on the other three points (see Figure 13–27). Your circle has become a rectangle.

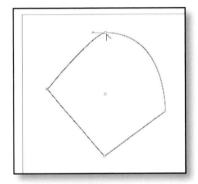

figure | 13–27

The Convert Direction Point tool changes smooth points to corner points.

3. With the Option or Alt key still held down, drag with the Convert Direction Point tool on one of the corner points of your newly created rectangle. The corner point will change into a curve point with direction handles (see Figure 13–28). Be careful! Dragging in the same direction as the original point will restore the curve of the circle, but dragging the opposite way will twist your curved line segment into a pretzel. Don't worry, though. If your line segment is twisting in the wrong direction, just do a 180-degree turn and drag the handle in the opposite direction.

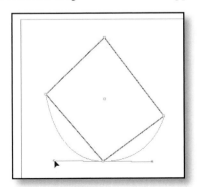

figure | 13–28

Now you have a corner point with direction handles.

The Scissors Tool

The Scissors tool does just what you might expect—it will cut a line segment into two parts. Do you still have the circle from the last exercise? Use it for the following exercise.

1. Press C to get the Scissors tool (or select it from the Toolbox). The cursor will look like a set of crosshairs and when it moves over your path, the point in the middle of the crosshairs becomes a small circle (see Figure 13–29). With the crosshairs directly over the path, click the mouse. A new point appears on the line segment. Although it looks like one point, there are actually two new points—one on top of the other.

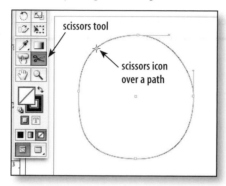

scissors tool

scissors icon over a path

figure | 13–29

The Scissors tool about to take a snip.

2. Press A for the Direct Selection tool and drag the new point away from the center of the circle. You have just cut one of the line segments, and the closed path is now an open path (see Figure 13–30).

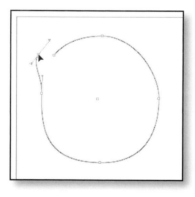

figure | 13–30

Your closed path is now an open path.

Joining Paths

Sometimes you will have two paths and need to combine them into one. Here's how to do it.

1. With the Pen tool, begin a new path at X = .5 and Y = 2. Hold down Shift and drag the direction handle horizontally to the right until X = 2. Next place your cursor at X = 3.5 and Y = 0.5, click, hold down Shift and drag horizontally until X = 5.5. After you release the mouse button, press the Option or Alt key to switch to the Convert Direction Point tool. Click and drag the end of the direction handle that extends to the left, of the last anchor point. Release the mouse button when X = 3 and Y = 0.875. Release the Option or Alt key and click the Pen tool at X = 4 and Y = 2, hold down Shift and drag horizontally until X = 6. When you release the mouse button, your path should look like Figure 13–31.

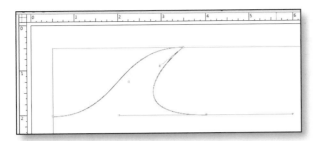

figure | 13–31

Drawing a wave is as easy as placing three anchor points.

2. Let's say this is the perfect shape for a cresting wave you need for a project, but you need two of them exactly the same. Duplicate it using the Option+drag or Alt+drag method (switch to the Selection tool, first) and place the new wave to the right of the original as in Figure 13–32.

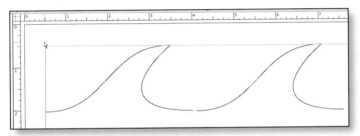

figure | 13–32

The new wave next to the original.

3. To join these two waves into one, switch to the Pen tool and select the last anchor point of the first path. The little "x" by the Pen tool cursor will turn into a slash when you get near the point. (It's often a good idea to zoom in closely when editing anchor points.)

4. Place the tool cursor over the first point of the second wave and a small square with two little line segments will appear next to the Pen tool cursor (see Figure 13-33). Click and your two paths will be joined into one. However, you now have an unwanted line segment connecting the two points.

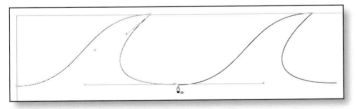

figure | 13–33

The Pen tool is about to join two separate paths into one.

5. Undo to get two separate paths again and, before you connect them a second time, retract the left direction handle of the first

point you selected with the Convert Direction Point tool. Drag that direction handle all the way back until it nearly touches the anchor point. Now join the two paths into one.

figure | 13–34 |

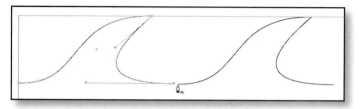

The Pen tool is about
to join two paths
with the direction
handle retracted
on the first path.

Compound Paths

You will love compound paths when it comes to making logos, transparent areas inside of shapes, and creative picture and text frames. Begin the next exercise with a new document.

1. Draw two circles, one larger than the other, using the Ellipse tool. Select all and use the Align buttons on the Control palette to center them horizontally and vertically. Fill them both with black. Your document should look similar to Figure 13–35.

figure | 13–35 |

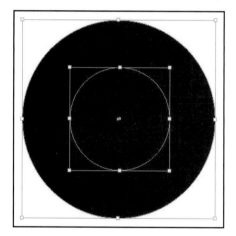

2. Press Command+8 (Mac) or Control+8 (Windows), or choose Object>Compound Paths>Make. Now you have a donut!
3. Make a larger oval with a gradient fill and send it to the back. Move your donut around and you will see that your donut has a real donut hole! (See Figure 13–36.)
4. If you change your mind and don't want the compound path, select your donut and choose Object>Compound Paths>Release.

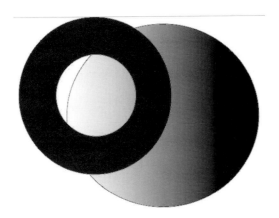

figure | 13–36 |

Move your donut around to see the donut hole.

5. Delete everything and start over. This time draw two rectangles, one above the other with the smaller one on top. Put them close together, but do not have them touch or overlap. Select them both and choose Object>Compound Paths>Make. Although it may appear that nothing has occurred, notice that a bounding box now surrounds both rectangles. This means that the two are now part of one path (see Figure 13–37).

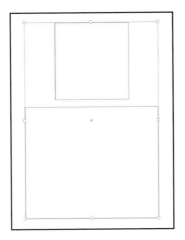

figure | 13–37 |

Draw two rectangles independent of each other, but part of the same path.

6. Press Command+D or Control+D and place an image large enough to fill both rectangles. Drag the image around inside the rectangles using the Direct Selection tool.

7. Next you will change the shape of your small rectangle to a trapezoid. Deselect everything, and click on a bottom corner point with the Direct Selection tool. Hold down Shift and drag it out so that it's above the corresponding upper corner of the large rectangle. Do the same for the other bottom corner (see Figure 13–38).

figure | 13–38 |

Using the Direct
Selection tool, hold
down Shift and
drag each corner
point out to create a
trapezoid.

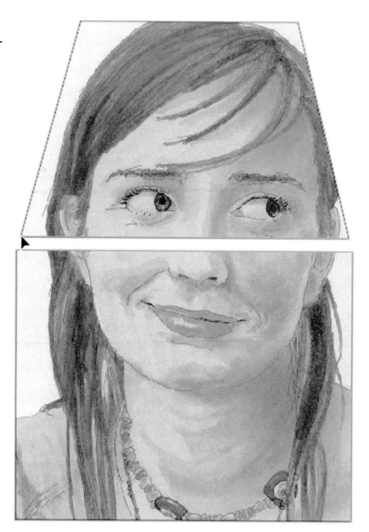

8. Delete the picture from the compound path and click in the
   path with the Type tool. Fill with placeholder text. Your compound path now works like linked text frames.

So far, you have made compound paths using basic shape tools:
the Rectangle tool and the Ellipse tool. Practice making compound
paths with shapes you create, using the Pen tool.

SUMMARY

After completing the exercises in this chapter, you can see why there's no way any other page layout program can compete with InDesign. Combining the best of both worlds, InDesign gives you advanced page layout and drawing capabilities, right at your fingertips. And once you master the versatile Pen tool, your creative energy knows no bounds. Use compound paths to make your readers sit up and take notice of your message and images. And when you are done with this book, there's much… MUCH more to explore!

in review

1. What effect does holding down the Shift key have when drawing shapes and lines?

2. When working with a shape or path, how do you tell the difference between a point that is selected and a point that is not selected?

3. What is the keyboard shortcut for accessing the Convert Direction Point tool when you are using the Pen tool?

4. What is the difference between a smooth point and a corner point?

5. You have made a path with the Pen tool, but it looks jagged and you think you might have too many points on it. How do you smooth it out?

6. What is the difference between an open path and a closed path?

7. Describe the process for joining two open paths.

8. Describe the process for making compound paths.

notes

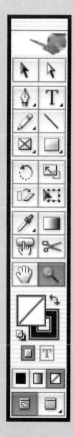

index